Han Sŏrya and North Korean Literature

Han Sŏrya
and
North Korean Literature

The Failure of Socialist Realism
in the DPRK

Brian Myers

East Asia Program
Cornell University
Ithaca, New York 14853

The *Cornell East Asia Series* publishes manuscripts on a wide variety of scholarly topics pertaining to East Asia. Manuscripts are published on the basis of camera-ready copy provided by the volume author or editor.

Inquiries should be addressed to Editorial Board, Cornell East Asia Series, East Asia Program, Cornell University, 140 Uris Hall, Ithaca, New York 14853.

ISSN 1050-2955
ISBN 0-939657-84-8 cloth
ISBN 0-939657-69-4 paper

FOR KO MYŎNGHŬI

Contents

Acknowledgments

This book consists of a slightly amended version of a doctoral dissertation presented to the Eberhard-Karls-Universität-Tübingen in October 1992, and a translation of a North Korean novella completed in the following months. In preparing this study I was greatly aided in many ways by my *Doktorvater*, Professor Dieter Eikemeier of the Department of Korean Studies in Tübingen, whose devotion to familiarizing himself with North Korean literature made his advice and criticism especially invaluable. I am also indebted to Assistant Professors Jörg Trappmann and Peter Paek for taking time out from their own work to answer my questions about Korean literature and history. In addition, I would like to thank a pair of European scholars (who, I understand, would rather remain anonymous) for assisting me in my search for material despite their ideological opposition to my views on North Korean culture.

I am also grateful to Dr. Key P. Yang of the Library of Congress for his patient help, and to Professor Dae-Sook Suh of Hawaii for answering a query of mine about North Korean history. Both Professor David McCann and Professor W. Skillend were kind enough to point out errors I had made in the original text. For their assistance and encouragement during my stay in Germany I would especially like to thank Nina Berger, Rainer Deschler, Markus Maurer, Martin Müller, Sabine Schwarzl, and Hisa Trappmann.

A diagram from Hans Günther's book, *Die Verstaatlichung der Literatur* is adapted for use in this study with the kind permission of Professor Günther himself.

I should like to make clear that I received no financial assistance from North or South Korean sources, nor, for that matter, from any institution outside the peninsula. Such costs as were incurred during my research fell entirely on my family, and it is to them that I owe my greatest thanks. Responsibility for errors in the book is mine.

Brian Myers
Aztec, New Mexico
November 12, 1993

Introduction

Though little remembered today, Han Sŏrya (1900-1970?) was without a doubt one of the most important writers of prose fiction in Korean history. As chairman of the DPRK's Federation of Literature and Art (hereafter KFLA) from 1948 to 1962, Han played a decisive role in all major events and policy developments on the Pyongyang literary scene, while devising in his own writings the iconography of a personality cult which has since come to dominate every facet of life in North Korea. No Korean writer has in his lifetime enjoyed an official stature such as that accorded Han Sŏrya at the height of his fame.

There is nothing extraordinary in the fact that Han enjoyed such success with a writing style which the Western reader will likely find unpolished at best. North Korean writers have always been taught to see their mission in the consistent production of accessible propaganda, not in the creation of timeless literary works. What *is* remarkable about Han's literature is its thorough incompatibility with socialist realism—the very doctrine which he, as head of the KFLA, was sworn to implement on the fledgling republic's cultural scene. The following study is an attempt to chronicle Han's chairmanship, and to assign responsibility for its central paradox to the patrimonial functioning of the North Korean cultural apparatus.

The term patrimonialism (literally "inheritance from ancestors") has come to be used at the "broadest level of generalization" to refer to "any type of government that originated from a royal household,"[1] but I use it here in accordance with the specific model presented by sociologist Norman Jacobs in *The Korean Road to Modernization and Development*.[2] Based on

---

[1] *The International Encyclopaedia of Sociology*, ed. Michael Mann (New York, 1984), s.v. "patrimonialism."

[2] Norman Jacobs, *The Korean Road to Modernization and Development* (Urbana/Chicago, 1985).

the work of Max Weber and other predecessors, as well as on his own study, Jacobs describes Korean society as a patrimonial one in which

> the right to authority is determined primarily by moral-intellectual considerations, monopolized by a self-asserted elite, and validated by the dissemination of moral service (termed prebends) in the society through political means by that elite. This may be contrasted with a right to authority determined by superior pragmatic ability.[3]

Jacobs further explains that in Korea's patrimonial bureaucracy (in contrast to China's) devotion to ideology has rarely been able to overcome parochial loyalties. Korean bureaucratic allegiance, in other words, is to superiors, not to an organization or a task.[4] Though Jacobs focuses on South Korea in his study, I shall be making use of his patrimonial model to help explain how it was possible for Han to head the North Korean cultural apparatus while in his own writing flouting the aesthetic to which that apparatus was ostensibly committed.[5]

The term socialist realism is used here as it was professed in the DPRK during the 1940s and 1950s, namely, in the "orthodox" sense of the official aesthetic doctrine developed under Stalin in the USSR. There it was defined as the "artistic method whose central principle is the accurate, historically concrete presentation of reality in its revolutionary development, and whose main task is the communist education of the masses."[6] Even in its strictest interpretation, of course, socialist realism was not aimed at producing a uniform literature in its various spheres of influence. Indeed, one of its central principles, that of *popular spirit*, demanded that literature speak to the masses in the national language and forms they understand. Though I will mention aspects of Han's literature which can be regarded as typically Korean, therefore (such as his emphasis on the chastity of his

---

[3] Ibid., 1-2.

[4] Ibid., 18-19.

[5] Needless to say, Jacobs also describes historical, economic, legal, and other aspects of the Korean patrimonial social order, but such matters do not bear directly on this paper. I am no sociologist, and have no intention of dealing with anything but the DPRK's cultural apparatus, or of presenting this apparatus as a microcosm of North Korean government in general.

[6] Quoted in *Sowjetsystem und demokratische Gesellschaft: Eine vergleichende Enzyklopädie*, ed. C.D. Kernig (Freiburg, 1972), s.v. "sozialistischer Realismus." As we shall see, neither the various unofficial theories of socialist realism espoused in the thirties by Lukács and others nor the theoretical debate which took place after the Soviets' Twentieth Party Congress played a significant role in the DPRK's metaliterary discourse.

heroines), I have no intention of dwelling on them, let alone of claiming that they suffice to disqualify the author as a socialist realist. Rather, I will focus on those elements of his writing—some peculiar to his style, some rooted in the colonial era's proletarian literary tradition—which are clearly at odds with the doctrine's basic postulates. Finally, I plan to go so far as to show that Han's *very worldview is fundamentally incompatible with the ideology a socialist realist literature is by definition obliged to reflect.*

The greatest problem encountered while preparing this dissertation involved access to primary materials. Financial considerations restricted research to a year and a half in the US and Germany. Requests for book-related assistance were mailed to relevant institutions in both Koreas but were never answered. Fortunately most materials needed could be found in the Library of Congress in Washington, D.C., the Harvard-Yenching Library, the Humboldt University Library (in what was once East Berlin), and the personal libraries of European scholars. Unfortunately the Soviet occupation period is sorely underrepresented in all these collections, and few literary journals and newspapers are available from the years before the Korean War truce. The oldest issue of the literary monthly *Chosŏn munhak* I could find, for example, is from January 1954, though it seems to have begun appearing long before that. Particularly lamentable is the fact that no library contains a complete set of *Han Sŏrya sŏnjip* (Selected Works of Han Sŏrya, 1960-62). Since all libraries have the same few volumes, it looks as if Han's purge prevented the North Koreans from sending the rest. All of his better known works, however, could be located in other editions.

Like my fellow scholars in Seoul, I have for the most part relied on modern South Korean editions of Han's colonial fiction. It is possible that these contain the odd textual deviation from the original, but having checked the same publishers' editions of North Korean novels, I do not believe any such deviations would be significant enough to have any bearing on this study, which is in any case only marginally concerned with Han's fiction before 1945. I have been somewhat warier in using the North Korean *Hyŏndae Chosŏn munhak sŏnjip* (Anthology of Modern Korean Literature, 1958-60), referring to it primarily for colonial writings that bear no sign of willful alteration by Pyongyang's official mythmakers, such as the articles in which Han laments his lack of talent.

Of invaluable help in preparing this study have been the memoirs of Hyŏn Su, O Yŏngjin, Yi Ch'ŏlchu, and Yi Hanggu, all intellectuals who defected from North Korea at different times.[7] Taken together, these writings offer a continuous record of the literary scene above the 38th parallel between 1945 and the early 1960s: Hyŏn and O both describe the KFLA's early years under Soviet occupation, Yi Ch'ŏlchu covers the Korean War and its aftermath, and Yi Hanggu deals with the period from the start of the Ch'ŏllima era in 1958 to Han's purge in 1962-63. These firsthand reports are surprisingly evenhanded. Though all four men make no secret of their loathing for Kim Il Sung and communism, they display a great deal of sympathy for the colleagues they left behind, including Han Sŏrya and other high-ranking conformists. Their versions of events are also corroborated to a reassuring degree by official North Korean publications. One only wishes the defectors had not been so averse to dating events, nor concentrated so exclusively on factional struggles at the expense of policy developments and literary issues.

In the West (particularly in the US), the study of Korean literature has generally been characterized by a strong advocatorial tendency, usually expressed in terms of a desire to help Korean culture attain the international recognition it deserves. Scholars have thus tended to concentrate on the handful of colonial and South Korean writers whose work is considered likely to appeal to Western readers. South Korean grant providers caught up in their country's growing preoccupation with the Nobel Prize have understandably done nothing to discourage this tendency.[8] At the same time, a fear of offending South Korean authorities appears to have caused at least some scholars to steer clear of controversial themes.[9] One need only look at leading scholar Peter H. Lee's recent anthology of Korean literature to gauge the effect of this general climate on the study of the DPRK's literature.[10] Mr Lee sees no reason to include in his book anything written north of the 38th parallel in the past half-century—nor even to justify the omission to his readers.

---

[7] O Yŏngjin, *Hanaŭi chŭngŏn: Chakkaŭi sugi* (Seoul, 1952); Hyŏn Su, *Chŏkch'i yungnyŏn Pukhanŭi mundan* (Seoul, 1952); Yi Ch'ŏlchu, *Pugŭi yesurin* (Seoul, 1966); Yi Hanggu, "Pukhanŭi chakka taeyŏlsogesŏ," in *Pukhan*, 118 (1 1974): 240-253.

[8] A good indication of this preoccupation is given by the chairman of the Daewoo conglomerate who, when asked to name the two main goals facing his country, named the reunification of North and South, and the bestowal of a Nobel Prize on a Korean. Mun Pyŏngmun, *Chaebŏl: Nalgaerŭl tarara* (Seoul, 1992), 325.

[9] An established Western scholar once told me, without the slightest embarrassment, that he had deliberately omitted relevant Pyongyang-published titles from a bibliography he had compiled, in order not to complicate its sale in South Korea.

[10] See *Modern Korean Literature: An Anthology* (Honolulu, 1990).

While American studies of Chinese communist fiction alone could fill a small library, the sum total of all published Western research on North Korean literature consists, as far as I can see, of two articles published fifteen years apart in the Hawaii-based journal *Korean Studies*. The first, "Engineers of the Soul: North Korean Literature Today" (1977), is a general introduction to its subject in which Marshall Pihl convincingly argues that the DPRK's fiction should be seen in the context of the peninsula's didactic cultural tradition.[11] (In keeping with the title of his article, Pihl mentions Han Sŏrya only in passing.)[12] The other study, my own "Mother Russia: Soviet Characters in North Korean Fiction" (1992), is a short survey of Soviet-Korean friendship stories, among them Han Sŏrya's *Nammae* (Brother and Sister, 1949).[13]

Ironically, the most important single contribution to Western knowledge of DPRK literary history remains that made by Robert Scalapino and Chong-sik Lee in their two-volume classic *Communism in Korea* over twenty years ago.[14] Though the book says little about North Korean literature *per se*, it does provide much useful information about the DPRK's intellectual scene, including what I consider the most reliable account of Han Sŏrya's purge.

As for scholarship in the East Bloc, a few North Korean anthologies were published in the 1950s, at least one of which, *Korea erzählt* (GDR), contains a translation of Han Sŏrya's short story *Ŏlgul* (The Face, 1948).[15] Han also wrote a few articles on Korean culture which were translated for Soviet publications like *Ogonek*.[16] Yet even at the height of his career he received only a fraction of the attention devoted by Soviet Koreanologists to his contemporary Yi Kiyŏng (1896-1984), whose literature was somewhat easier to reconcile with socialist realist principles. Norbert Adami's bibliography of Russian Koreanology lists only one study of Han Sŏrya's

[11] *Korean Studies* 1 (1977): 63-110.

[12] Ibid., 72, 76.

[13] *Korean Studies* 16 (1992): 82-93. See 86-89.

[14] Robert Scalapino and Chong-sik Lee, *Communism in Korea* (Berkeley, 1972).

[15] Translated into German as *Der Freund*, in *Korea erzählt: Ein Einblick in die koreanische Literatur*, ed. J. Herzfeldt (Berlin, GDR, 1954), 84-92.

[16] Khan Ser ia (Han Sŏrya), "Geroicheskie budni Korei," *Ogonek* (April 1953): 5-6; idem, "Radostnoe chuvstvo: Ob uspekhakh sotsialisticheskogo stroitel'stva v KNDR," *Inostrannaia literatura*, January 1959, 164-166.

work, and even this deals only with his colonial-era fiction.[17] After the DPRK's cultural revolution in the mid-1960s, the study of North Korean literature in Eastern Europe dropped off dramatically. The few who continued publishing on the subject throughout the 1970s and 1980s felt compelled to respect the taboo which the North Koreans imposed on Han's name after his purge.[18] Equally diplomatic were the compilers of the Soviet *Bibliografiia Korei: 1917-1970*, who omitted everything ever published by and on the author in the USSR.[19] East Germany's Helga Picht was an exception of sorts, acknowledging Han's role in the colonial proletarian movement in her 1984 book *Asien: Wege zu Marx und Lenin*.[20]

In South Korea writers who went north (or simply stayed there) after liberation or during the Korean War were made the subject of considerable if unsystematic stigmatization. Like all these so-called *wŏlbuk chakka* (lit., "writers gone north") Han Sŏrya was ignored by many reference works, while others wrote his name with a blank circle in place of the second character.[21] After 1948 none of his writings was published or republished in the South, and he was never permitted to become the object of sustained scholarly attention. The few entries on him in encyclopediae and reference works are carelessly written. As if it were not bad enough that the DPRK's paranoid secretiveness prevents us from learning when (or even if) Han died, three South Korean reference works offer three conflicting years of birth for the author, all of which appear to be incorrect (1898, 1899 and 1902).[22]

In the relatively free atmosphere that reigned during the last months of the Chun Doo Hwan regime in 1987, Han's novel *T'ap* (Pagoda, 1940)

---

[17] D. Usatov, "Obraz rabochego v rannem tvorchestvo Khan Ser ia," in *Koreiskaia literatura* (Moscow, 1959), 117-144; Norbert Adami, *Die russische Koreaforschung: Bibliographie 1682-1976* (Wiesbaden, 1978), 44-50.

[18] See for example V.I. Ivanova, "Sovetskaia literatura v Koree (1945-1955)," *Problemy Dal'nego Vostoka*, 3 (11 1974): 187-193; Reta Rentner, "Koreanische Literatur: Literaturhistorischer Abriß," in *Lexikon ostasiatischer Literaturen*, ed. Jürgen Berndt (Leipzig, 1985), 81-93.

[19] *Bibliografiia Korei: 1917-1970* (Moscow, 1981).

[20] *Asien: Wege zu Marx und Lenin* (Berlin, GDR, 1984), 114-115.

[21] See for example Paek Ch'ŏl's *Sinmunhak sajosa*, 4th ed. (Seoul, 1980), 332, 430, 584.

[22] *Pukhan taesajŏn* (Seoul, 1974), *Pukhan inmyŏng sajŏn* (Seoul, 1983), *Han'guk munhak taesajŏn* (Seoul, 1973), s.v. "Han Sŏrya."

was allowed to be republished,[23] as were selected works by other *wŏlbuk chakka*. Only in July 1988, however, several months after Roh Tae Woo's assumption of the presidency, were all major restrictions finally lifted on the dissemination of books by *wŏlbuk chakka* and other North Korean authors. In 1989, in the course of the minor "DPRK boom" that followed, *Hwanghon* (Dusk, 1936) and *Ch'ŏngch'un'gi* (Prime of Youth, 1937) were republished as the first two volumes of a collection of Han's novels.[24] *Sŏlbongsan* (Mt Sŏlbong, 1958) was also published for the first time in the South.[25] A three-volume collection of his colonial short stories appeared in the same year.[26] This was followed in 1990 by a selection of stories from before and after the liberation.[27] Alas, Han's work was not exempted from the dramatic decline of public interest in North Korean fiction which followed hard on the initial *succès de curiosité*, and plans to put out more of his novels were apparently shelved.

On the other hand, scholarly interest in North Korean literature, and in *wŏlbuk chakka* in particular, has continued unabated up to this writing. While not quite as popular an object of study as, say, Yi Kiyŏng or Yim Hwa (Im Hwa, 1908-?), Han Sŏrya has come in for his fair share of attention. This published scholarship should be used cautiously. Let us take Kim Yunsik's *Han'guk hyŏndae hyŏnsilchuŭi sosŏl yŏn'gu* (Studies in Korea's Modern Realistic Prose, 1990), which contains, with minor alterations, most of the prominent scholar's many articles on Han.[28] Though

---

[23] *T'ap*, vol. 5 of *Sülgi sosŏlsŏn* (Seoul, 1987). Song Hosuk's claim that the ban on Han Sŏrya's work was enforced longer than that on most other writers is difficult to accept for this very reason. Cf. "Tanp'yŏn sosŏl chungsimŭro pon Han Sŏryaŭi munhak segye," in *Kwihyang: Han Sŏrya chakp'umjip* (Seoul, 1990), 399.

[24] *Hwanghon*, *Ch'ŏngch'un'gi*, vols. 1 and 2 respectively of *Han Sŏrya sŏnjip*, ed. Kim Ch'ŏl (Seoul, 1989), which is not to be confused with the Pyongyang collection of the same name. The abbrevation *HSYS* refers in this paper to the latter only.

[25] *Sŏlbongsan*, vol. 12 of *Tonggwangminjok munhak chŏnjip*, ed. Im Hŏnyong (Seoul, 1989).

[26] *Han Sŏrya tanp'yŏn sŏnjip*, ed. Kim Woegon, 3 vols. (Seoul, 1989).

[27] *Kwihyang: Han Sŏrya chakp'umjip*, ed. Song Hosuk (Seoul, 1990).

[28] *Han'guk hyŏndae hyŏnsilchuŭi sosŏl yŏn'gu* (Seoul, 1990). Kim's articles on Han include: "Han Sŏryaron: Kwihyang mot'ip'ŭwa chŏnhyangŭi yulli kamgak," *Hyŏndae munhak* 416 (8 1989): 354-375; "Han Sŏryaron: *Kwadogi* esŏ *Sŏlbongsan* kkaji," in two parts, *Tongsŏ munhak* 194 (9 1990): 162-189; 195 (10 1990): 196-215; "Pukhan munhagŭi segaji chikchŏpsŏng: Han Sŏryaŭi *Hyŏllo Moja Sŭngnyangi* punsŏk," *Yesulgwa pip'yŏng* 21 (9 1990): 179-204; "Inyŏmŭi hyŏngsikkwa kyŏnghŏmŭi hyŏngsik: Han Sŏrya/Yi Kiyŏngŭi ch'angjakpŏmnon pip'an," *Yesulgwa pip'yŏng* 23 (3 1991): 81-106.

Dr Kim offers much useful information, especially on the KAPF era, his dates are often off by a few years. He claims Han's novel *Ryŏksa* (History) appeared in 1951, for example, though the official North Korean literary history states it was written in 1953.[29] The scholar also dates Han's trilogy *Taedonggang* (Taedong River) to 1951, when only the first volume was completed in that year.[30] One even finds 1951 given as the year of *Mt Sŏlbong*, a novel which Han did not express his intention of writing until 1957.[31] To be sure, the absence of a national bibliography of the DPRK makes it difficult to ascertain when a work was first published, but one cannot help suspecting the Seoul National University professor simply took these dates from the mistake-ridden flyleaves of recent South Korean editions of Han's works.[32] Another leading scholar of North Korean literature, Kwŏn Yŏngmin, gives two different birthdays and birthyears for Han Sŏrya in the same book.[33]

The foreigner with only limited access to primary materials is thus faced with certain difficulties, such as: Which of the four years (and counting) of Han's birth is to be accepted? In this case the date consistently given by the North Koreans themselves—3 August 1900—was taken. More problematic are diverging versions of Han Sŏrya's whereabouts before the DPRK's inauguration in 1948, particularly when the scholars in question fail to name their sources. Was Han a founding member of KAPF, as Kim Yunsik claims, or was he in Manchuria at the time, as is stated by Kwŏn Yŏngmin?[34] Is Kim Sŭnghwan correct in claiming Han first entered the liberated capital in December 1945, or had he been in Seoul throughout the autumn, as Yi Kibong asserts?[35] I have done my best to resolve these questions, but my conclusions are far from confident, and I have tried

---

[29] Kim Yunsik, *Han'guk hyŏndae hyŏnsilchuŭi*, 269; *Choson munhak t'ongsa* (Pyongyang, 1959), 2:240.

[30] *Han'guk hyŏndae hyŏnsilchuŭi*, 286.

[31] Ibid., 212, 286, 298; see Han Chungmo, *Han Sŏryaŭi ch'angjak yŏn'gu* (Pyongyang, 1959), 393.

[32] See for example the flyleaf of *Kwihyang: Han Sŏrya chakp'umjip* (Seoul, 1990).

[33] Kwŏn gives Han's birthday as 30 August 1900 on page 44 of his *Wŏlbuk munin yŏn'gu* (Seoul, 1989), and as 3 August 1901 on page 397. Both dates appear to be incorrect.

[34] Kim Yunsik, *Han'guk hyŏndae hyŏnsilchuŭi*, 51; Kwŏn Yŏngmin, *Wŏlbuk munin yŏn'gu*, 44, 397.

[35] Kim Sŭnghwan, "Haebang konggganŭi Pukhan munhak: munhwajŏk minju kiji kŏnsŏllonŭl chungsimŭro," *Han'guk hakpo* 17 (Summer 1991): 206; Yi Kibong, *Pugŭi munhakkwa yesurin* (Seoul, 1986), 31.

1
Han and Korea's Proletarian Culture Movement

The concept of the social and ethical mission of literature achieved currency in Korea long before the spread of Marxist aesthetic theories in the colonial era. Even before the rise of Neo-Confucianism in the latter 1300s, literature had come to be viewed on the peninsula as a medium for the propagation of virtue and the maintenance of a public order as close as possible to the ideal state of Chinese antiquity.[1] For centuries Korean bureaucrats, like their counterparts in the Middle Kingdom, endeavored to curtail the influence of literature deemed immoral or subversive.[2] Yet as the works of Hŏ Kyun (1569-1618), Pak Chiwŏn (1737-1805) and other Yi Dynasty authors attest, the written word was no mere propaganda tool of established power, for just as Confucianism sanctioned rebellion against tyrannical rule, so did it sanction the use of literature to expose social injustice or warn the king against the abuse of his position.[3]

For all the modernist rhetoric of their creators, the didactic *sinsosŏl* (lit., "new novels") of the early 1900s represented the continuing fulfilment of the Confucian aesthetic.[4] So too did the hugely popular novels of Yi Kwangsu (1892-1950?), who aimed his pen at the institution of arranged marriage and other perceived obstacles to progress. The Korean reading

---

[1] Cho Tongil, *Han'guk munhak sasangsa siron* (Seoul, 1978), 169.

[2] Hans-Jürgen Zaborowski, "Die klassische Erzählliteratur Koreas," in *Ostasiatische Literaturen*, ed. Günther Debon (Wiesbaden, 1984), 250; cf. Raymond Dawson, *Confucius* (New York, 1981), 24.

[3] Marshall R. Pihl, "Engineers of the Human Soul: North Korean Literature Today," *Korean Studies* 1 (1977): 63-68. For a Marxist interpretation of Korea's literary history with emphasis on the tradition of social engagement, see Reta Rentner, "Koreanische Literatur: literaturhistorischer Abriß," in *Lexikon ostasiatischer Literaturen*, ed. Jürgen Berndt (Leipzig, 1985), 81-93.

[4] Pihl, "Engineers of the Human Soul," 67.

15

public's predilection for a didactic, stridently moralizing (and thus sentimental) style also characterized its reception of European literature, as can be seen by the early popularity of Maksim Gorky's writings even among those unsympathetic to Marxism,[5] or in the fact that the most beloved of Tolstoy's novels on the peninsula was (and remains) the preachy *Resurrection*, a work widely disdained by Western critics and readers alike.[6]

The limited success of the theory of *l'art pour l'art*, which arrived on the peninsula around 1914, was thus largely due to the fact that it constituted a radical break with tradition, whereas the aestheticists of western Europe and Japan had merely taken a long-established consensus in favor of the autonomy of art to an extreme. The theory's decline in Korea in the early 1920s was of course expedited by political and socioeconomic developments. The spread of newspapers and publishing houses led to a rise in the genre of the novel, which, being a "dialogized representation of an ideologically freighted discourse, is of all verbal genres the one least susceptible to aestheticism as such." (Bakhtin)[7] More importantly, the failure of the 1919 uprising against Japanese rule caused readers to turn increasingly to literature for the articulation of their concerns. One did not have to be a Marxist to realize that a "pure art" under such conditions amounted to tacit approval of oppression—as Yi Kwangsu made clear in an attack on the aestheticists in the magazine *Ch'angjo* in 1921.[8]

Yi's call for an "art for *life's* sake" was echoed two years later by three disillusioned members of the aestheticist movement's own *Paekcho* faction, namely Kim Kijin (1903-1985), Pak Chonghwa (1901-1981) and Pak Yŏnghŭi (1901-?), who had been introduced to the left-wing literary theories of Henri Barbusse by Japanese interlocutors.[9] The three rejected *l'art pour l'art* for much the same reasons as Yi Kwangsu, but instead of his brand of enlightening realism they demanded a literature more

---

[5] See Yi Songwŏn, "Han'guk munhagŭi Maksim Gorŭk'i suyong," *Kugŏ kungmunhak* 88 (12 1982): 171; Helga Picht, *Asien: Wege zu Marx und Lenin* (Berlin, GDR, 1984), 136.

[6] According to Chŏn Yŏngt'ae, many Koreans even today lament the absence in their literature of a "masterpiece like Tolstoy's *Resurrection*." See "Iyagi pulgamjŭnge kŏllin chakkadŭl," *Tongsŏ munhak* 170 (9 1988): 68-72. The novel's heroine Katyusha is a household name in Korea, invoked in everything from pop music (Kim Puja's "Kach'yusya") to poetry (No Ch'ŏnmyŏng's *Hwangmach'a*, in *Mogajiga kirŏsŏ sŭlp'ŭn sasŭmŭn: No Ch'ŏnmyŏng siwa saengae*, ed. Sin Kyŏngnim [Seoul, 1984], 15).

[7] "Discourse in the Novel," in *The Dialogic Imagination: Four Essays by M. M. Bakhtin*, ed. M. Holmquist (Austin, Texas, 1981), 333.

[8] "Munsawa suyang," *Ch'angjo* 8 (1 1921): 9-18.

[9] Kim Ujŏng, *Han'guk hyŏndae sosŏlsa* (Seoul, 1968), 198-199.

In November 1926 Han's *"P'ŭro yesurŭi sŏnŏn"* (Manifesto of Proletarian Art) appeared in the newspaper *Tonga ilbo*.[24] Far from evincing a higher ideological standard than his New Tendency predecessors, Han actually expanded the term proletariat to include right-minded people of wealth and privilege, thus creating an even more amorphous category than the old "unpropertied class":

> The real proletariat cannot understand art, so proletarian art is unnecessary," some say....The mistake of such people is to regard narrowly the difference between the bourgeoisie and the proletariat as the difference between those possessing and those lacking material goods, as the difference between rich and poor. *If a person understands the proletariat and belongs to it ideologically and class-consciously, then he is a magnificent proletarian, no matter how well off he may be materially, i.e., economically.* By the same token, needless to say, the poorest person is a bourgeois, or at least a tool of the bourgeoisie, if he consciously admires and follows them.[25] (emphasis mine)

A contemporary Soviet intellectual aspiring to write proletarian literature had to acquire a proletarian *orientation* through constant contact with the masses, and then use this orientation in his literature to enlighten them in return.[26] His Korean counterpart, according to Han, could become a proletarian—and a "magnificent" one at that—through a mere act of will, and then simply write for fellow intellectuals who had done the same! Though KAPF's members may not have agreed in theory with this facile equation of "proletarian" with "anti-bourgeois," they seemed comfortable with it in practice, at least during the group's first two years.

During this period Han joined comrade Pak Yŏnghŭi in engaging non-Marxist writers in serially published debates of extraordinary acerbity. The moribund theory of *l'art pour l'art* played little role in these *nonjaeng* (as the debates were called), despite later North Korean claims. Outsiders did, however, question the compatibility of art and ideological *control*; Kim Tongin (1900-1951) and Yi Kwangsu, for example, pleaded for a politically autonomous literature transcending class barriers, while the anarchist Kim

---

[24] "P'ŭro yesurŭi sŏnŏn," *Tonga ilbo*, 6 November 1926.

[25] Ibid.

[26] See Edward J. Brown, 62-63.

Hwasan espoused the creative freedom of the individual artist.[27] Han Sŏrya's published responses to such views are marked by the same limited understanding of Marxism as the 1926 manifesto—stock phrases like "quantitative change becomes qualitative change" are invoked like mantras—as well as by a flair for invective. In one article he attacked Kim Hwasan for "wrapping individualist anarchism and spasmodic Dadaism in a...socialist cloth" in the hopes of dividing the proletarian movement.[28]

Yet KAPF was already divided from within. On the one hand were moderate members like Kim Kijin, who lamented the low artistic quality of the group's literature. On the other were the more numerous militant elements, among them Pak Yŏnghŭi and Han himself, who denied that the formal aspect of art had any value as an independent criterion. This issue was at first suppressed, however, in order to present a unified front to outsiders.[29]

The "proletarian" fiction that appeared from August 1925 to 1927 bore little relation to the exclusivist zeal and orthodox posturing of the nonjaeng. Ch'oe Sŏhae, KAPF's only genuine proletarian of note, was touted as the group's premier "ideological" writer, but his stories remained (as Kim Kijin lamented) in the naive hunger-and-arson style of the New Tendency.[30] The only difference was that now his benevolently naive farmer-heroes, as in Hongyŏm (Red Flame, 1926), escaped punishment for their spontaneous rampages; this may have been Ch'oe's understanding of "revolutionary optimism."[31] Cho Myŏnghŭi's short story Naktonggang (Naktong River, 1927), a lyrical attempt to interweave the history of the Korean labor struggle with the love between two activists, was of higher literary quality, but equally removed from the professed ideal of a revolutionary fiction.[32]

Dissatisfied with the group's general aimlessness and the poor quality of its literature, militants in KAPF's Tokyo branch began pushing in 1927 for its transformation from a small gathering of artistically inclined intellectuals into a mass organization with an openly revolutionary character.

---

[27] Cho Tongil, Han'guk munhak t'ongsa, 2nd ed. (Seoul, 1989), 5:229-230.

[28] "Musan munyegaŭi ipchangesŏ Kim Hwasan'gunŭi hŏgu munyeronŭi kwannyŏmjŏk tangwironŭl pakham," in 9 parts, Tonga ilbo, 15-27 April 1927. The quotation is from part 4 (20 April).

[29] An Mak, 115.

[30] Kim Ujŏng, 209, 213, 205.

[31] See Hongyŏm, in Ch'oe Sŏhae sŏnjip (Pyongyang, 1963), 1:166-193.

[32] Naktonggang: Cho Myŏnghŭi sŏnjip (Seoul, 1988), 148-160; An Mak, 116.

The implementation of this "shift to the left" ushered in what is commonly regarded as KAPF's second developmental stage. Now as never before the need to reach a truly proletarian and dispossessed audience was recognised, which led in turn to a revival of the old debate over form and content. Kim Kijin, as form-oriented as ever, pleaded for a literature moderate enough to satisfy the censors and aesthetically appealing enough to attract a wide readership. Tokyo-based militant Yim Hwa, however, who enjoyed broader support, responded by charging Kim with accomodationism.[33]

Han, who by now had apparently returned from Manchuria and formally joined KAPF,[34] took the militants' side in this debate as in all others. Yet he was far from pleased to see his position as chief Marxist ideologue usurped by Yi Pungman, the leader of the Tokyo branch and a prominent member of the Korean Communist Party. In a magazine article in February 1928 Han scolded Yi for dismissing KAPF's literature as "nauseating."[35] Yi responded with a withering attack on Han for trying to "monopolize" the movement's theoretical discussion, "though in reality he doesn't understand the first thing about dialectics."[36] According to KAPF member Paek Ch'ŏl (1908-1985), Yim Hwa also looked down on Han as something of a bumpkin and an embarrassment.[37]

In contrast to later North Korean myth, KAPF was anything but a bastion of cultural nationalism—as its Esperanto acronym alone should indicate. Though opposed to colonial rule, the group's spokesmen preferred to envisage national liberation in the context of the liberation of the world proletariat, and took constant care to stress their brotherhood with the Japanese working class. Han Sŏrya and many other members thus wrote Japanese-language works in the 1920s and early 1930s, well before it became virtually compulsory to do so, and occasionally submitted their stories to leftist magazines in Tokyo.[38] Far from championing the national heritage, KAPF spokesmen categorically dismissed pre-colonial Korean

---

[33] An Mak, 120.

[34] See Kwŏn Yŏngmin, *Wŏlbuk munin yŏn'gu*, 397.

[35] "Munye undongŭi silch'ŏnjŏk kŭn'gŏ," in *HCMS*, 8:79-102.

[36] Quoted by Kim Yunsik in "Han Sŏryaron: *Kwadogi esŏ Sŏlbongsan kkaji*," 1:168.

[37] *Munhak chasŏjŏn* (Seoul, 1975), 424-425.

[38] Kim Yunsik, "Han Sŏryaron: *Kwadogi esŏ Sŏlbongsan kkaji*," 1:187; note also that the immediate stimulus to form KAPF in 1925 had been a visit to Seoul by Japanese leftist Inoue Nakanishi. See Dae-Sook Suh, *The Korean Communist Movement 1914-1948* (Princeton, 1967), 134.

literature as "feudal," and reserved their harshest scorn for those who spoke of searching for "a Korean spirit" in literature.[39]

This did not stop progressive intellectuals outside the movement from asking whether the Korean underclass would not be better served by a literature more nationalist in tone. From his Chinese exile the famous writer Sin Ch'aeho (1880-1936) vehemently rejected all talk of brotherhood with the Japanese proletariat (pointing out that it comprised the backbone of the occupying army) and demanded a patriotic-revolutionary "people's literature."[40] After the establishment in 1927 of the *Sin'ganhoe* (New Korea Society), a broad coalition of nationalist and communist political groups, this call was taken up by Yang Chudong (1903-1977) and others.[41] While supporting the New Korea Society itself, KAPF remained opposed to any alliance of proletarian and nationalist literature.[42]

During this second phase in KAPF's roughly ten-year history members were called upon to adhere to the so-called dialectical realist method then being propagated by the Russian Association of Proletarian Writers (known by its Russian acronym RAPP). According to this method the writer was to depict, with a "Tolstoyan" realism, the dialectical conflict both in society and the individual psyche. A profound understanding of both dialectical materialism and the life of the proletariat was considered a prerequisite for such a style.[43] Determined to move beyond the ideological crudities of the past, many in KAPF now decided to postpone the creation of further literary works in order to gain first a thorough grounding in Marxist social and literary theory. Han Chaedŏk, who joined the group's Tokyo branch while a student, remembers:

> We read whatever we could get our hands on, starting with Marx and Engels, and moving on to Lenin, Stalin, Bukharin and Lunacharskii. Like today's South Korean students preparing for the state examinations, we tied towels around our heads and shouted while we studied, spurred on by "reading clubs" and "study circles."[44]

---

[39] Cho Tongil, *Han'guk munhak t'ongsa*, 5:226, 230.

[40] Ibid., 5:230.

[41] Ibid., 5:232-233.

[42] See for example Han Sŏrya, "Munye undongŭi silch'ŏnjŏk kŭn'gŏ," in *HCMS*, 8:95.

[43] Edward J. Brown, 77-82.

[44] Han Chaedŏk, *Kim Ilsŏnggwa pukkoeŭi silsang* (Seoul, 1969), 20.

Yet there is little to substantiate the conventional assertion that 1927's "shift to the left" succeeded in bringing forth a truly revolutionary literature radically different from what the group had hitherto produced,[45] nor does it seem that the group's writers, most of whom were of landowner stock, made much effort to seek sustained contact with the masses. Han Sŏrya's experience was probably not atypical: after an admittedly halfhearted attempt to find work at a mine, he contented himself with viewing a workers' dormitory, which he later made the subject of a short sketch.[46] Many such sketches were written in this period, though they did little more than offer a glimpse into the life of the working class.[47]

To be sure, the hunger-and-arson stories were finally replaced by a literature that stressed collective action, but the New Tendency's pastoralism and—for all KAPF's internationalist rhetoric—ethnocentricity remained very much alive. The crude country mouse/city mouse antinomy of Yi Kiyŏng's short story *Wŏnbo* (1928), for example, which tells of a benevolently naive farmer's disastrous excursion to decadent Seoul, can hardly be regarded as an ideological advance over Ch'oe Sŏhae's fiction.[48] Nor can Han Sŏrya's *Kwadogi* (Transition Period, 1929), a short story rather inexplicably praised by Yim Hwa.[49] After a catastrophic stay in Manchuria, Han's farmer-hero Ch'angsŏn returns to Korea to find a factory where his village used to be.[50] Befuddled by the noise and smoke, he reminisces about the good old days, which are presented in a flashback as a carefree time of lovers' repartee and tree-shaded afternoon naps. Han sees no reason to dwell on the crushing poverty that made Ch'angsŏn leave home in the first place, and shares the hero's negative perspective when describing the workers at the new factory:

> Strange people—he could not tell whether they were Chinese, Korean or Japanese—walked around busily in navy-blue factory uniforms and high, dark brown galoshes. Chinese walked past in long sleeves, their waists tied in, chattering loudly among each other. The only people he thought were Koreans were a group

---

[45] Cf. An Mak, 122; Kim Ujŏng, 204.

[46] Han Sŏrya, "Saenghwarŭi kyohun," in *HSYS*, 14:332; idem., *Hapsuksoŭi pam*, in *HSYT*, 1:100-109.

[47] See also Song Yŏng, *Kippŭn nal chŏnyŏk*, in *HCMS*, 5:90-91.

[48] V.I. Ivanova takes a somewhat more positive view; see "Sovetskaia voenno-patrioticheskaia literatura v Koree," 126-127.

[49] Yim Hwa, *Munhagŭi nolli* (Seoul, 1940), 561.

[50] *Kwadogi*, in *KHSYC*, 7-23.

with short hair and high boots that did not suit them, speaking in
a southern dialect. None of the friends of old, with their topknots
and long pipes, could be seen.[51]

Industrial labor is thus seen as involving the sacrifice of national and
individual identity, symbolized respectively by the cutting of the traditional
topknot and the wearing of an ill-fitting uniform. Yet the indigent hero has
no choice but to become a worker himself:

From the next day, Ch'angsŏn became an unfamiliar person, who
cut his topknot, donned leggings, and kneaded concrete with a
shovel.[52]

Note the mindset reflected by the word "unfamiliar" (*saengso han*); not for
nothing was it changed in a 1955 Russian translation to read "new."[53] A true
proletarian writer, of course, would have made the farmer's transformation
into a politically conscious worker-hero the theme of the story, but Han,
who later admitted that he "agonized considerably" whenever forced to
depict industrial workers, simply ended the story here.[54] A desultory attempt
to rectify matters was made in *Ssirŭm* (Wrestling Match, 1929), which,
though purportedly a sequel, presented an already "developed" activist-hero
(with a different name) engaged in the traditional rural custom of outdoor
wrestling.[55]

In the spring of 1930 Yim Hwa and other young militants returned
from Tokyo and took over control of KAPF entirely, demanding the
"Bolshevization" of the proletarian art movement.[56] This term was never
clearly defined, but it was generally agreed that KAPF needed to perceive
itself as an arm of the party, and to produce a more openly agitatory
literature in response to the crisis of world capitalism in general and the
spread of labor unrest in Korean factories and villages in particular. In
accordance with theoretical trends that had emerged in the Soviet Union
during the Five Year Plan, writers began to move away from the dialectical
materialist method towards an easier-to-read and less consciously literary

---

[51] Ibid., 9.

[52] Ibid., 23.

[53] In Russian the sentence translates as: "From now on he too was like a new man—a concrete worker." See *Perelom (Kwadogi)*, in *Khan Ser ia: Sbornik rasskazov* (Pyongyang, 1957), 23.

[54] Han Sŏrya, "Saenghwarŭi kyohun," 331.

[55] *Ssirŭm*, in *KHSYC*, 24-44.

[56] Scalapino and Lee, 1:122.

style.[57] A typical product of the time was Song Yŏng's *Ŭlmiltae* (1931), a one-page story of a woman who climbs on a factory roof to inspire her striking comrades. It was disseminated to factories with instructions to display it in a prominent place.[58]

Meanwhile the group's moderates urged caution, warning that KAPF was on a collision course with the colonial authorities. They were proved right in February 1931, when police raided KAPF offices and individual homes, arresting roughly seventy members on the pretext of possessing copies of *Musanja*, a KAPF publication printed in Japan but banned in Korea. Kim Namch'ŏn (1911-?) and two other members were sentenced to longer terms of imprisonment, but the rest were released on suspended sentences after gruelling interrogations.[59] Morale was shaken further by a petty feud with KAPF's Kaesŏng branch, whose leaders finally seceded from the group, and by Stalin's abolition of the mother organization RAPP in 1932.[60] As KAPF projects ground to a standstill, disillusioned and intimidated members began to defect. Pak Yŏnghŭi left in 1932, later renouncing the cause with the famous words, "What we gained was ideology, what we lost was art," a statement taken at face value by conservative scholars as confirmation of the mutual exclusivity of art and politics.[61] Literary historian Cho Tongil is right to point out, however, that KAPF never evinced a real understanding of Marxist ideology, "nor did it have any art worth losing in the first place."[62]

Those who stayed in the movement busied themselves by trying to understand just what was meant by the new term socialist realism (1932-34), which had found its way into the Korean literary discussion by 1933. As in the USSR itself, it was at first widely misinterpreted as a simple call for higher formal quality and a reduction of open tendentiousness.[63] Happily enough, this fallacy resulted in KAPF's first bestseller, Yi Kiyŏng's

---

[57] An Mak, 127.

[58] *Ŭlmiltae*, in *HCMS*, 10:90-91.

[59] Changboh Chee, "Korea Artiste Proletarienne Federation: A Case of Literature as A Political Movement," in *Korea under Japanese Colonial Rule*, ed. Andrew C. Nahm (Ann Arbor, 1973), 245.

[60] See An Mak, 131; Brown, 208-209.

[61] See Kim Ujŏng, 206, and Peter H. Lee, *Korean Literature: Topics and Themes* (Tucson, 1956), 105.

[62] *Han'guk munhak t'ongsa*, 5:235.

[63] See for example Yi Kiyŏng's 1934 article, "Ch'angjak pangbŏp munjee kwanhayŏ," in *HCMS*, 8:257-267.

Kohyang (Home Town, 1933-34), which combines an insightful depiction of a colonial Korean village with the romance of yet another progressive-student-back-from-Japan.

In spring 1934, however, months before the new theory took on sharper contours at the Soviet Writers' Congress, Japanese colonial authorities launched their most extensive raid yet on KAPF and its theater group *Sin'gŏnsŏl* (New Construction). More than eighty members and associates were arrested.[64] On 5 May 1935 Kim Namch'ŏn, Yim Hwa and Kim Kijin finally succumbed to pressure and presented KAPF's dissolution notice to police.[65] Han Sŏrya was furious, especially when Yim, the man most responsible for charting KAPF's confrontational course in the first place, was released from custody after pleading illness:

> "Slipped away like a rat," [Han] complained, "this is what Seoul people are like, I tell you,"...and he would curse Yim, saying "Traitor!" and "Crafty womanish bastard!"[66]

At the trial in June 1935 Han and twenty-two others, including Yi Kiyŏng, were convicted of subversive activity. The fact that newspaper reports of the trial make almost no mention of Han indicates he was still a rather obscure figure on the national scene.[67] In the winter of 1935/1936, after having spent over a year in jail, Han was released, and returned to the Hamgyŏng area.[68]

Hardly had he been released from prison when he published in serial form a work as leftist as any of his earlier literature. *Hwanghon* (Dusk, 1936), his first long novel, tells of a young woman who vacillates emotionally between a student and a labor activist before finally joining the latter in his struggle against the rationalization of their workplace.[69] Han certainly deserves credit for having had the courage to produce such a work in 1936. But though it was later touted in the DPRK as a pioneering work of Korean socialist realism, nothing in *Dusk* suggests even a superficial understanding of the new doctrine. Far from being an inspiratory *positive heroine*, Han's Ryŏsuk is the usual pathetic country girl in the big city, prone to hysterical outbursts and incapable of independent thought. Her

---

[64] Changboh Chee, 245.

[65] Pihl, 73.

[66] Paek Ch'ŏl, *Munhak chasŏjŏn*, 425.

[67] Kim Yunsik, "Han Sŏryaron: Kwihyang mot'ip'ŭ," 362.

[68] Cho Tongil, *Han'guk munhak t'ongsa*, 5:235.

[69] *Hwanghon*, vol. 1 of *Han Sŏrya sŏnjip*, ed. Kim Ch'ŏl (Seoul, 1989). The novel appeared from February to October 1936 in the newspaper *Chosŏn ilbo*.

"truly Korean" *sobak ham* remains unsullied throughout; she joins the labor struggle not because she has attained political consciousness, but because she finds the activist a more reliable romantic partner. The fact that the activist receives only a fraction of the space devoted to the student was later attributed in the DPRK to censorship, but it was more likely the result of Han's lifelong reluctance to deal with the true proletariat.

Korean literary histories meant for foreign consumption often claim that when Japanese colonial authorities clamped down on cultural expression in the late 1930s, most men of letters "broke their writing brushes and went into hiding."[70] In fact, virtually all established writers wrote steadily on, adjusting their literature to the demands of the age. Leftist writers showed no more fortitude than their bourgeois and nationalist rivals. By 1940 *all* KAPF veterans had renounced the revolutionary cause, either in their literary work or in formal declarations to their probation officers.[71]

Han was no exception, though his apostasy or *chŏnhyang* took the form of a steep decline in the tendentiousness of his literature and not an explicit, Pak Yŏnghŭi-style renunciation of communism. The serially published novels *Ch'ŏngch'un'gi* (Prime of Youth, 1937) and *Maŭmŭi hyangch'on* (Paradise of the Heart, 1939) are love stories as harmlessly banal as their titles suggest.[72] In *Inyŏng* (Quagmire, 1939) Han approvingly described a former political prisoner's decision to let his probation officer make him a productive member of colonial society.[73] From August 1940 to February 1941 the pro-Japanese newspaper *Maeil sinbo* serialized Han's *T'ap* (Pagoda), an autobiographical novel about the trivial vicissitudes in the life of a provincial boy who moves to Seoul.[74] Though written in the Korean language, it portrays Japanese soldiers as handsome, sophisticated and childloving, and Korean villagers as backward figures of fun. During the Pacific War, Han, together with numerous KAPF veterans, joined the *Kokumin sōryoku Chōsen remmei* (Korean League for Concerted National Power) and the *Chōsen bunjin Bokokkai* (Patriotic League of Korean Writers), both of which were devoted to supporting the Japanese war effort and the goal of *Nai-Sen ittai* (Japan and Korea as one body), which called

---

[70] Kim Donguk (Kim Tonguk), *History of Korean Literature* (Tokyo, 1980), 251; see also Changboh Chee, 246.

[71] Kim Yunsik, "Han Sŏryaron: Kwihyang mot'ip'ŭ," 363.

[72] *Ch'ŏngch'un'gi*, vol. 2 of *Han Sŏrya sŏnjip*, ed. Kim Ch'ŏl (Seoul, 1989); *Maŭmŭi hyangch'on* later published as *Ch'ohyang* (Pyongyang, 1958).

[73] *Inyŏng* published as *Chinch'ang* in *KHSYC*, 155-179.

[74] *T'ap*, vol. 5 of *Sŭlgi sosŏlsŏn* (Seoul, 1987).

for the extirpation of Korean culture as a separate and distinct entity.[75] In contrast to former "proletarians" Pak Yŏnghŭi, Yu Chino (1906-1987) and Paek Ch'ŏl, however, who rivalled Yi Kwangsu in their vocal support of Japanese militarism,[76] Han kept quite a low profile during the Pacific War, contenting himself with turning out innocuous Japanese-language romances. *Chi* (Blood, 1942), for example, dealt with the failed relationship between a married Korean artist and a young Japanese woman.[77]

Han's will may not have been completely broken, for in summer of 1943 he was apparently jailed for passing on to friends the contents of Syngman Rhee's patriotic radio broadcasts from Hawaii.[78] After being released on probation in May 1944 he retired to his home town of Hamhŭng on the northeast coast, where, according to his own account, he wrote a sequel to *Pagoda*. He later claimed to have been in the middle of a third volume when the Japanese surrendered in August 1945.[79]

As Han himself lamented, his work was marked by an extraordinary discrepancy between intention and realization.[80] Even taking official and self-imposed censorship into account, it is difficult to understand how so many empty romances and dull psychological studies of intellectuals could have been written by a man who felt that art must be a weapon of the revolutionary vanguard.[81] It is equally hard to reconcile Han's professed intention of reproducing cinematic techniques in literature[82] with his

---

[75] "Han Sŏryaron: *Kwadogi esŏ Sŏlbongsan* kkaji," 1:187.

[76] Im Chongguk, *Ch'inil munhangnon* (Seoul, 1966), 253-282.

[77] *Chi*, in *Kungmin munhak/Kokumin bungaku* 1 (1 1942): 167-190.

[78] Song Hosuk, "Tanp'yŏn sosŏrŭl chungsimŭro pon Han Sŏryaŭi munhak segye," 401. Song does not say where she found this information, but her version of Han's life is more accurate than most, and it is indeed strange that the usually prolific Han produced nothing from late 1943 to the liberation. North Korean sources also maintained that he was imprisoned for "anti-Japanese activities" in 1943, but never said just what those activities were; Song's version would certainly explain their reticence.

[79] Han Sŏrya, "Haebang chŏnhu," in *HSYS*, 14:182.

[80] "Saenghwal kamjŏngŭi chaehyŏn chŏndal: 1932 nyŏn mundan chŏnmang," in *HCMS*, 9:97. This phenomenon is of course hardly uncommon in literature; Rene Wellek and Austin Warren point to Zola, who "sincerely believed in his scientific theory of the experimental novel, but actually produced highly melodramatic and symbolic novels." *Theory of Literature*, 3rd ed. (New York, 1956), 137.

[81] Han Sŏrya, "P'ŭro yesurŭi sŏnŏn," *Tonga ilbo*, 6 November 1926.

[82] "Naŭi in'gan suŏp, chakka suŏp," in *HSYS*, 14:103.

uniquely "phlegmatic"[83] and tautological style:

> She found no way out of her situation but to sever her ties to
> Kyŏngjae. For his sake as well as for her own....Of course, it
> would be difficult to separate after they had come such a long
> way together, but there was no alternative; they could only live
> together if she were to "sacrifice" herself. So there was nothing
> to do but part. The separation would mean a new beginning for
> both (Ryŏsun and Kyŏngjae), a new beginning which could
> eventually end in a truer union. When she closed her eyes and
> blocked out the past, this way opened itself before her. It was
> only right to set off on this way, for all she was doing now was
> floundering in a morass....Of course it was true that she was also
> leaving Kyŏngjae to rescue him and his family from bankruptcy.
> But even more than this, the decision to leave Kyŏngjae had
> crystallized out of the desire to save Kyŏngjae and herself from
> the morass they had fallen into. But in any case, it would be
> difficult to leave Kyŏngjae. [*Dusk*, 1936][84]

> "Mr Pak! I want to live sincerely. Seeing the way you and those
> around you have treated me, I have learned the need to live
> sincerely. The more insincere you are, the more sincerely will I
> live." T'aeho calmed his pounding heart. Then he continued: "Do
> you want to teach me to be as insincere as you? Well, I refuse
> to be. What are you here for, Mr Pak? To demand insincerity
> from me? To teach me insincerity? Whatever it is, I'll have none
> of it." [*Prime of Youth*, 1937][85]

There is a certain condescension, perhaps the subconscious condescension
of a landowner's son writing for the masses, in the many repetitions,
especially of proper names (not to mention the almost insultingly
superfluous brackets in the first quotation). The same underestimation of the
reader characterizes all levels of Han's work. Little effort is made to depict
the visual world or to describe character development convincingly. Stilted
dialogues and verbose psychological descriptions are linked together through
outrageous coincidences and contrived situations. We shall have cause to
return to these characteristics when discussing Han's North Korean
literature.

---

[83] Kim Tongni, ed., *Han'guk munhak taesajŏn* (Seoul, 1973), s.v. "Han Sŏrya."

[84] *Hwanghon*, 238-239.

[85] *Ch'ŏngch'un'gi*, 364.

Han harbored, as we have indicated, few illusions about his writing, referring to it as "hack work" (literally *t'ajak* or "threshing"),[86] and acknowledging "with shame" in 1939 that he had produced nothing of worth in his career.[87] Such comments were too frequent and bitter to permit one to interpret them as false modesty. In the article "*Chakka chŭk tokcha*" (The Writer as Reader) he begged forgiveness for his latest failure:

> As had been the case with the novel *Dusk*, I was very confident when preparing to write *Prime of Youth*, thinking "This will be the one!" But now that it's finished, I must concede that it too has come to nothing....This time there has been almost no response from readers to the novel, except that friends have told me it should have been written "a little more interestingly." I am told also that the style does not flow, and that for a novel called *Prime of Youth* it lacks passion....In the end intention is one thing, and the result another. The important thing is to have talent.[88]

Han nonetheless refused to revise his extreme disregard for form, preferring to see his main problem in an inability to harmonize the ideological and emotional elements of his stories[89]—a peculiar diagnosis, in view of the low level of explicit political content even in his KAPF fiction. With more justification, he acknowledged his lack of imagination, his tendency to psychologize, his difficulty in depicting character development, and his ignorance of the life of the common people.[90] Yet despite public indifference to his work, Han refused to give up writing, convinced that perseverance would someday result in a sudden breakthrough to excellence. Explaining this belief in 1936 in an open letter to Yi Kiyŏng (whom he seems to have admired greatly), Han referred to Engels' illustration of how a "quantitative"

---

[86] "Saenghwal kamjŏngŭi chaehyŏn chŏndal: 1932 nyŏn mundan chŏnmang," in *HCMS*, 9:97.

[87] "Changjinho kihaeng," in *HCMS*, 9:141-142.

[88] "Chakka chŭk tokcha," in *HCMS*, 9:107-108. Han also laments his lack of talent in "Chihasirŭi sugi," in *HCMS*, 9:111.

[89] See "Kamgakkwa sasangŭi t'ongil," in *HCMS*, 9:82-84.

[90] See "Sasilgwa kongsang: naŭi ch'angjak suŏp," in *HCMS*, 9:155-156; "Saenghwal kamjŏngŭi chaehyŏn chŏndal," 97; idem, "Chihasirŭi sugi," 111; idem, "Ŏmŏni," in *HCMS*, 9:128.

increase in temperature can result in a "qualitative" transformation of water to steam.[91]

The water, in Han's case, would never boil; he was already a middle-aged man when he wrote these words and his most accomplished work (such as it was) lay behind him. Yet he would soon become one of the most influential and celebrated novelists in his country's history. His role in the early development of North Korean literature is the subject of the following chapters.

---

[91] "Kohyange torawasŏ," in *HCMS*, 8:154.

Japanese interrogators with an analysis of KAPF so detailed that it still represents the prime source of information on the movement.[22] Critic An Hamgwang (1910-?), once a prominent member of the pro-Japanese Patriotic Society of Korean Writers,[23] was made chairman of the Writers' Union.[24] As for Han Sŏrya, his other duties prevented him from playing a major role in the organization at first. He was, however, appointed to the central committees of the NKFLA and the Writers' Union, and entrusted with the task of editing the NKFLA organ *Munhwa chŏnsŏn*.[25]

Although the breakup of Ch'oe Myŏngik's Art and Culture Association took place under pressure, it would be wrong to portray it as a totalitarian *Gleichschaltung* of dissident elements. No attempt was made to exclude anyone from the new organization, and members of all ideological leanings were soon meeting daily at NKFLA headquarters for informal chats.[26] (The contrast to the polarized atmosphere in contemporary Seoul is striking.)[27] Even Ch'oe himself soon came to terms with the new dispensation. The ease with which the intellectuals allowed themselves to be "unified" resulted in part from the adaptability they had acquired in the colonial era, but also from their ignorance of party cultural policy. Even many left-wingers seem to have reckoned with little more than a vague social mission in keeping with Korea's traditional aesthetic.

[22] Scalapino and Lee, 1:120, 2:884.

[23] Cho Tongil, *Han'guk munhak t'ongsa*, 5:497; Im Chongguk, 153, 156.

[24] NKFLA affairs in Pyongyang itself were taken over by the already mentioned Han Chaedŏk, a former pro-Japanese journalist of some notoriety. Kim Saryang, who had been virtually run out of Seoul for his Japanese-language prolificacy, was named chief of NKFLA affairs for P'yŏngnam. See Im Chongguk, 109-216; Kim Yunsik, "Haebanghu nambukhanŭi munhwa undong," in *Haebang kongganŭi munhak undonggwa munhagŭi hyŏnsirinsik*, 12-13. For all appointments see Yi Kibong, 32; Hyŏn, 12. The fallacy that the higher echelons of North Korean officialdom were virtually free of former collaborators has been reinforced by historian Bruce Cumings, who seems to consider a colonial prison record a sufficient indicator of a consistent revolutionary or patriot (see *The Origins of the Korean War* [Princeton, 1981], 395). This fallacy in turn causes scholars to presume that writers Yim Hwa and Kim Namch'ŏn were purged in 1952-53 as punishment for their colonial collaboration—as if that had somehow set them apart from their colleagues.

[25] Kim Yunsik, "Haebang kongganŭi nambuk munhak chojik pigyo," 134.

[26] Hyŏn, 22.

[27] Cf. Kim Song, "Mundanŭi chwauik taegyŏlgwa 'Paengmin munhak': 1945 nyŏn," *Pukhan* 164 (8 1985): 59-60.

There was thus widespread bewilderment in early March 1946, a few weeks before the NKFLA's official founding ceremony, when the order came down for writers to prepare works on the recent land reform:

> We had never dreamed it would come to this. How was one to write a novel or poem on land reform?....All put their heads to one side, finally concluding it was an impossible task.[28]

Not surprisingly it was an outsider, the Soviet-Korean Red Army officer Cho Kich'ŏn (1913-1951), who produced the first major work on the subject. His epic poem *Ttang* (Land) was elevated to model status soon after appearing in the Red Army-licensed newspaper *Chosŏn sinmun*. Cho was then presented to the curious Pyongyang literati at a party-sponsored soirée, where he gave a talk on Soviet literature. Hyŏn was there:

> Of course those present knew very little about Soviet literature. At the most one had heard of Gorky, Ehrenburg, Sholokhov and Fadeev, or knew that Mayakovsky was a futurist poet. Those who had always been interested in Soviet literature could pride themselves on also knowing the names of the poet Tikhonov, or of Ostrovskii, the author of *How the Steel was Tempered*. But during Cho's talk we learned numerous names of unfamiliar writers and the titles of some of their works [these are given in a long list-BM]....Everything he said was new and interesting, and he seemed like a visitor from a strange and mysterious land.[29]

Hyŏn is exaggerating a little here; many in Cho's audience undoubtedly knew more than just the *names* of Gorky, Ehrenburg and Fadeev.[30] Yet he is probably correct in assuming that even the KAPF veterans knew little about the new generation of Soviet writers, or, for that matter, about socialist realism itself. As we have seen, they had been unable to stay abreast of Soviet literary developments arising after 1932—and socialist realism had only taken on coherent form in the USSR in 1934, when most KAPF members were either in prison or frantically trying to distance themselves from the cause.

The difference between socialist realism and the older Soviet theories familiar to the KAPF veterans is best explained by contrasting the various

---

[28] Hyŏn, 25.

[29] Ibid., 50-51.

[30] See V.I. Ivanova, "Sovetskaia literatura v Koree: 1945-1955," *Problemy Dal'nego vostoka*, 3 (11 1974): 187, for an account of the popularity of these writers in colonial Korea.

provide was the literature of KAPF, which he claimed had led the masses' triumphant resistance against Japanese cultural imperialism.[53] There was undoubtedly more than a little self-aggrandizement in this outrageous distortion of history. The entire regime, however, also needed to exaggerate KAPF's importance, in order to present the implementation of socialist realism as the culmination of a proud indigenous tradition, instead of the political *oktrois* it really was.

For all his recognition of KAPF's achievements, Han went on to find Korean literature lagging behind that of the "great Soviet Union." Like Kim Il Sung, he saw the cure for this backwardness in the assimilation of Soviet culture. With effort, he promised, Korea could even produce a Gorky someday.[54] One cannot help but feel sorry for Han's fellow intellectuals; hardly had they been liberated, and again they were being told to emulate the "advanced" culture of an occupying power! Only too aware of the unpleasant associations he risked evoking, Han took pains to explain that *this* time, everything was different:

> The fact that we are now talking of cultural intercourse has nothing at all to do with diplomatic or political considerations that might be connected with the stationing of Soviet troops above the 38th parallel. We have raised this topic because we recognise the leading international role of the superior Soviet culture, which continues to flourish on the basis of a rich tradition.[55]

And later:

> If one reflects on the barbarity of the Japanese marauders, who sought to destroy the Korean nation, culture, language and script, one cannot fail to see a world of difference between their cultural policy and that of the internationalist Soviet Union.[56]

---

[52](...continued)
produced it. (Goethe's humanism makes him a "people's writer," etc.) See Boris Groys, *Gesamtkunstwerk Stalin* (Munich/Vienna, 1988), 53-55.

[53] "Kukche munhwaŭi kyoryue taehayŏ," 78.

[54] Ibid., 71.

[55] Ibid., 78-79.

[56] Ibid., 81.

Han might have sounded less defensive had the Red Army not incurred widespread ill will in Korea with its depredations.[57] Just how serious Han considered this problem can be seen by his inclusion in the same issue of *Munhwa chŏnsŏn* of the short story *Moja* (The Hat, 1946). In it a Ukrainian soldier tries to forget the Nazis' murder of his family by carousing drunkenly in a Korean town, until he espies in a street urchin the promise of the future socialist paradise—and gives up his antisocial ways. Han was of course calling for understanding of the occupying troops, but the unflattering depiction of the soldier is said to have caused the Soviet Military Administration to lodge a protest.[58]

Kim Il Sung stood by Han, even ushering him into the Central Committee of the Workers' Party of North Korea at its founding congress on 28 August 1946, though his decision to assign him to the post of Director of Education for the North Korean People's Committee in 1947[59] may have been aimed at keeping him out of the cultural sector until the fuss died down. Others in the NKFLA appear to have been intimidated by the negative reaction to this first work on life in the Soviet zone—and one written by an experienced and high-ranking "proletarian" writer no less—for despite pressure from Kim Ch'angman, who exhorted them to emulate their prolific Chinese colleagues, they continued to avoid topical themes.[60]

By winter 1946/1947 the impatient authorities saw no choice but to confront the same "harmful tendencies" of creative abstention and "insufficient ideology" that functionary Andrei Zhdanov was then crusading against in the USSR. Like Zhdanov in Leningrad, Kim Ch'angman found a pretext for a press offensive in the eastern port of Wŏnsan, where a lyrical-romantic anthology entitled *Ŭnghyang* (Fragrant Scent) had appeared in December 1946.[61] Ku Sang, a contributor to the volume, promptly fled south, where he looked back on the incident decades later:

---

[57] See Scalapino and Lee, 1:315, 348.

[58] Hyŏn, 42. The version in Han's collected works (1960) shows the character positively from the start; an allusion to occasional indiscretions is confined to one sentence. See *Moja*, in *HSYS*, 8:32-64, 55. Since the anti-Soviet Hyŏn praises the 1946 original as "realistic," it is safe to assume it focused on the time before the soldier's reformation.

[59] See Dae-Sook Suh, *Korean Communism 1945-1980* (Honolulu, 1981), 317; Han Sŏrya's "Uri sŭsŭng Kim Ilsŏng changgun," in *STP*, 184-191, deals with this period in his life.

[60] Hyŏn, 31.

[61] Han's later claim that Kim Il Sung himself alerted the cultural world to the problem ("Kim Ilsŏng changgun'gwa munhak yesul," in *HSYS*, 14:20) is impossible to take seriously.

Among the contributors were Chŏng Ryul, the Soviet-Korean Red Army officer, and party members...who were proud of the anthology, but soon a lightning bolt from Pyongyang descended on us....In early January 1947 a resolution of the executive committee of the North Korean Federation of Literature and Art appeared on the front page of a North Korean newspaper, accusing the anthology *Fragrant Scent* of insufficient ideology and ordering a comprehensive investigation of North Korea's regional art unions. It was all so self-important; one could hardly believe a few poems could cause such a fuss.[62]

Two other anthologies consisting of older material were criticised on similar grounds.[63] Apart from being ordered to perform self-criticism, however, none of those involved appears to have been punished. (Chŏng Ryul, in fact, became vice-chairman of the Writers' Union shortly thereafter.)[64] Stricter measures proved unnecessary; the vehemence of the official rhetoric alone sufficed to effect a dramatic change in the cultural climate. There is no record of anyone voicing even token dissent. The intellectuals' uniform docility—perhaps the legacy of Japanese oppression—left the regime confident in its ability to rectify future problems on the cultural front without resorting to Soviet or Chinese style purges.

The call for a partisan literature was amplified throughout 1947, as the party began to dispatch thematic tasks with increasing frequency and peremptoriness. A Central Committee resolution in May sharply criticised remaining signs of "political indifference and insufficient ideology" and demanded the elimination of all so-called "superfluous figures" (the bourgeois antipodes to socialist realism's "positive heroes") in literary works. Again and again the writers' "aloofness from the people" was singled out for criticism.[65]

In January 1948 the NKFLA underwent organizational changes. The "tens of thousands of friends of the arts" recruited after liberation were summarily divested of their membership. Only writers and artists "in a

---

[62] "Sijip *Ŭnghyang* p'irhwa sakkŏn chŏnmalgi," in *Ku Sang munhak sŏnjip* (Seoul, 1975), 404. For the full text of this resolution see "Sijip *Ŭnghyang* e kwanhan kyŏlchŏngsŏ," in *Han'guk hyŏndae hyŏnsilchuŭi pip'yŏng sŏnjip: Wŏnbon*, ed. Kim Yunsik (Seoul, 1989), 398-401.

[63] Han Hyo, "Uri munhagŭi 10 nyŏn," *CM*, June 1955, 142.

[64] Hyŏn, 35.

[65] Han Hyo, "Uri munhagŭi 10 nyŏn," 1:142.

narrow sense" were now eligible to join.[66] It was at this time that Han Sŏrya, who had gained a reputation as "a more political brain,"[67] replaced Yi Kiyŏng as chairman. It was a post he would occupy for fifteen years. Han got off to a running start in his new post, using his highly placed connections to solve the NKFLA's chronic financial problems and to secure a publishing house of its own.[68] The long-demanded campaign of immersion in the masses also began in earnest. Several writers were sent to industrial zones and farming villages to seek out themes and establish cultural workshops.[69] Notwithstanding Han's initial successes, Kim Il Sung's bestowal of the NKFLA's top post on a writer of little literary stature, who had apparently produced nothing in the way of fiction since 1946, must have indicated to the organization's members that an intellectual's advancement in the DPRK would depend more on patronal approval than on job performance.

Several months later, in September 1948, the Democratic People's Republic of Korea was inaugurated. The Soviet Union began withdrawing its troops from the peninsula at roughly the same time. The NKFLA was now subject to both the party's department of propaganda and agitation and the State's Ministry of Culture and Propaganda. This duplication of authority, a characteristic of communist regimes,[70] existed in name only; much to the annoyance of its largely Soviet-Korean staff the Ministry was in effect limited to the role of conduit for the party's cultural directives.[71]

Like Han's appointment to the post of NKFLA chairman, the creation of the Propaganda Ministry appears to have exacerbated a problem whose consequences would resonate well into the 1960s: the factionalization of the cultural scene. In retrospect this can be seen as an inevitable consequence of transplanting Soviet forms of cultural organization into Korean soil. As with its counterpart in the USSR, membership in the NKFLA provided the sole basis for professional advancement and material security for those active in the arts.[72] This does not mean that every member was

---

[66] *CCY 1949*, 141.

[67] Hyŏn, 20.

[68] Ibid., 21. The NKFLA had been running a brewery to help cover its operating costs.

[69] *CCY 1950*, 352.

[70] See Hannah Arendt. *The Origins of Totalitarianism*, rev. ed. (San Diego, 1973), 395.

[71] See Hyŏn, 17.

[72] Cf. Wolfgang Kasack, *Dictionary of Russian Literature since 1917* (New York, 1988), 466.

automatically guaranteed a living on which to support a family; most were paid only for manuscripts accepted for publication. The Propaganda Ministry, however, which directly controlled the nation's theaters, would confer upon select dramatists, scenario writers, composers and lyricists the special status of *ch'angjak wiwŏn* (literally "creative delegate"). In return for agreeing to create works on Ministry-prescribed themes, these writers would be granted a regular salary in addition to manuscript royalties. Some are said to have earned more than Kim Il Sung himself.[73] For a while other members, among them Han Sŏrya, received "endowments," which were drawn from a fund made up of publishing and theater profits.[74] A similar system functioned reasonably well in the USSR. In the DPRK, however, as anyone familiar with Korea's patrimonial tradition can imagine,[75] the cultural apparatus tended not to confer offices and other career benefits on the basis of performance or superior ability, but as rewards for personal allegiance to superiors.

Another important difference between the Soviet and DPRK systems consisted in the preferential treatment accorded high-ranking North Korean writers by official censors and critics. The work of less prominent writers could be subjected to as many as thirty "criticism meetings" under the auspices of a Writers' Union committee before being submitted to the Publications Bureau for administrative censorship. Higher ranking writers, on the other hand, needed expect only one "criticism session,"[76] and we will see that this was a mere formality in the case of the Federation chairman. Soviet censors and critics, in contrast, were just as strict if not stricter on high-ranking writers. Soviet Writers' Union chairman Aleksandr Fadeev, for example, is said to have been driven to alcoholic despair by repeated demands that he rewrite his novel *The Young Guard*.[77]

The NKFLA's members reacted to this traditionally Korean style of administration in equally traditional fashion,[78] namely by coalescing on the basis of personal or regional loyalties around certain high-ranking or well-connected colleagues, in order to help them maintain and increase their power and influence in the organization—for only then could these

---

[73] Hyŏn, 111-120; Yi Ch'ŏlchu, *Pugŭi yesurin* (Seoul, 1966), 50.

[74] Hyŏn, 121-127.

[75] See Norman Jacobs, *The Korean Road to Modernization and Development*, 14-41.

[76] Scalapino and Lee, 2:895.

[77] See John and Carrol Garrard, 64.

[78] See Chong-sik Lee, *The Politics of Korean Nationalism* (Berkeley, 1963), 14.

colleagues bestow privileges on them in return. The largest faction thus formed was the so-called KAPF group, which consisted mainly of the KAPF veterans who had joined the Proletarian Art Federation in Seoul in 1945—Han Sŏrya, Yi Kiyŏng, Pak Seyŏng (1907-?), etc—as well as some intellectuals of northern Korean origin, such as Namgung Man (1915-?) and Hong Sunch'ŏl.[79] Though Yi Kiyŏng had been NKFLA chairman, it is likely that Han Sŏrya led this faction from the start, on the basis of his special relationship with Kim Il Sung.

Another, smaller group was the so-called Soviet-Korean faction. Led by NKFLA vice-chairman Cho Kich'ŏn and made up of Korean and Soviet-Korean employees of the Red Army-licensed newspaper *Chosŏn sinmun*—Chŏng Ryul, Min Pyŏnggyun (1914-?), etc—they were affiliated to the Soviet-Koreans who dominated the Propaganda Ministry and edited the party organ *Rodong sinmun*.[80] These in turn owed allegiance to Hŏ Kai, a former Soviet occupation official who became the party secretary, then vice-premier of the North.[81] Aware of the numerical inferiority of their allies in the NKFLA, the Soviet-Koreans tried whenever possible to place unaffiliated new arrivals in their patrimonial debt. When writer Yi T'aejun (1904-?) had arrived in Pyongyang in 1947, for example, he had been greeted by the Soviet-Koreans with effusive lectures and newspaper tributes in his honor, and was soon awarded the NKFLA's second vice-chairman post. The fact that Yi had spent the colonial era espousing aestheticism seemed not to matter.[82]

The last group, the so-called *Namnodangp'a* or South Korean Workers' Party (SKWP) faction,[83] was led by Yim Hwa and made up of members of his Center for the Construction of Korean Literature. After trying to stage-manage leftist literary activities in Seoul from the town of Haeju, just north of the 38th parallel, they finally followed Korean Communist Party leader Pak Hŏnyŏng (1900-?) to Pyongyang in 1947. There Yim's longstanding enmity with Han Sŏrya and his lack of a powerful

---

[79] Hyŏn, 76.

[80] Ibid., 75.

[81] Dae-Sook Suh, *Kim Il Sung*, 83, 353.

[82] Hyŏn, 96.

[83] The Workers' Party of South Korea was founded in Seoul in November 1946, as the result of a coalition of the Korean Communist Party, the New Democratic Party, and the People's Party. See Dae-Sook Suh, *Kim Il Sung*, 74.

patron (as foreign minister, Pak had no influence on cultural matters) propelled the SKWP group into a loose alliance with the Soviet-Koreans.[84]

The early effects of the factionalization of the literary scene can be seen in the abuse of the so-called Festival Prize. Established in 1947, it was no doubt intended, like the Soviet Stalin Prize, to expedite the canonization process by providing budding socialist realists with officially approved "model" works to emulate. Eyebrows had been raised in its first year when Cho Kich'ŏn, presiding over the panel of judges, received first prize in the epic poem category, and then bestowed the prize for short poem on factional ally Min Pyŏnggyun, but it was hard to deny that Cho's work at least (the famous epic poem *Paektusan/Mt Paektu*, 1947) was deserving of the honor. A decisive blow to the Festival Prize's efficacy as a canonizing instrument was dealt in 1948, however, when word leaked out that Cho and Min were to receive the top awards *again*, and this time for works that had aroused widespread derision:

> The literary scene's interest in the Arts Festival began to drop off. As if waiting for Cho's *Uriŭi kil* [*Our Road*] and Min's *Punnoŭi sŏ* [*Epistle of Rage*] to receive the prizes, writers did not submit ambitious works, or even works with which they were satisfied. All that was left was the struggle over second prize between new writers eager to emerge on the scene. They now fell over themselves to pay Cho Kich'ŏn their respects.[85]

The official yearbook confirms that Cho and Min did indeed receive the prizes in their categories in 1948. (Cho went on to win the next year for a third time.)[86]

None of this is surprising when one remembers that in a patrimonial organization loyalty to superiors and factional allies supersedes loyalty to an ideology or task—the ideology and task being in this case socialist realism and its implementation. But it was Cho's factional rival Han Sŏrya who benefited the most from this. Though much of his time was taken up by official duties, which included attending annual World Peace Conferences (where he met Picasso and the Archbishop of Canterbury),[87] he managed to maintain a prodigious output of short stories from 1948 to the outbreak of

---

[84] Ibid., 76.

[85] Ibid., 68.

[86] *CCY 1949*, 142.

[87] Han tells of his peregrinations in "A. Pajeyebŭe taehan hoesang: kŭŭi sŏgŏrŭl ch'umo hamyŏnsŏ," in *HSYS*, 14:129-150.

the Korean War, mainly by writing in great haste; one of his longest short stories was written in a week (see below). Apart from a lack of formal polish, these works evinced a profound neglect of socialist realist principles. That they were allowed to appear at all supports Hyŏn's assertion that KAPF-faction member and Writers' Union chairman An Hamgwang, who decided which works were published, automatically approved everything Han submitted.[88] An would have been able to instruct those in charge of the obligatory criticism sessions to do the same.

An also praised Han's work profusely, thus initiating a blatant double standard that would run through North Korean criticism until Han's purge in 1962. One example must suffice here. In 1949 Han completed *Nammae* (Brother and Sister). Though its many nostalgic flashbacks flouted Soviet macrostructural guidelines, and its pathetic protagonist was the very antithesis of a *positive hero*, this story of a sick worker in a Soviet-run hospital was approved for publication by An and soon touted as a model realization of the internationalist theme (see below). Soon after, Kim Saryang (1914-1950), who was affiliated to the Soviet-Koreans, produced *Kayagŭm* (The Kaya Harp), another tale of a sick worker in a Soviet hospital. This work, however, came under immediate fire from both An and fellow KAPF-faction member Han Hyo, who complained that the choice of an inactive protagonist violated the postulate of *typicality*—and this although Kim's hero, in contrast to Han's, puts his time in hospital to good use by writing propaganda.[89]

Such a double standard would have been impossible to maintain had critics explained socialist realism in an accessible form. This they neglected to do. Judging from Hyŏn's accounts and the literary magazines of the 1950s, critics of all factions concentrated largely on *typicality*, the doctrine's vaguest and most flexible postulate, while disregarding more straightforward concepts like *subjectness*. This was no accident; socialist realism was the cultural "law" of the DPRK, and Korean authorities have traditionally been averse to explaining laws to their subjects, for fear of losing the right to enforce them according to the patrimonial needs of the moment.[90] The NKFLA's members reacted by treating the new doctrine as something to be not so much observed as appeased or circumvented—through factional allegiance to a powerful patron and slavish conformity to *actually existing* literary conventions.

---

[88] Hyŏn, 81.

[89] Ibid., 84-85, 88.

[90] See Norman Jacobs, 43-44.

On the surface, none of this seemed to be hindering the development of North Korean literature. Production of new works rose steadily throughout 1948. To boost it even further the NKFLA in March 1949 adopted a "Two Year Plan for Literature," which obliged writers to produce a certain number of works per quarter. It was later reported that 172 prose works had been published between August 1948 and September 1949 alone.[91] The problem of creative abstinence, in other words, had been solved (though a few *refuseniks* remained until the Korean War). In general, writers could also be seen to have acquired *party spirit* in that they no longer sought refuge in historical themes. According to literary histories, the vast majority of the prose works of the period 1948-1950 were short stories dealing, in a laudatory fashion of course, with the three themes of land reform, industrial development, and Soviet-Korean friendship.[92] The personality cult still played a far lesser role in prose fiction than in poetry, where panegyrics to Kim were already common.[93] Writers also evinced *popular spirit* by writing in a much simpler, more accessible style than they had used during the colonial era.

Yet socialist realism cannot be said to have been implemented. For one thing, the critics' neglect of the doctrine's macrostructural postulates resulted in the virtual absence of the genre best suited to fulfilling them: the novel. Nor did the many short stories written by NKFLA members in these years reflect the Marxist-Leninist discourse in a meaningful way. Instead of depicting the dialectical struggle between the old and the new, writers tended to localize the forces of reaction in South Korea or the colonial era, while presenting the nascent DPRK as an already classless *Gemeinschaft* that had returned to the ideals of a mythologized pre-colonial past. One finds little trace of either social, domestic, or generational conflict in these works. The once privileged class has absconded (apart from the occasional buffoon), women have returned to the traditional ideal of submissive chastity, and youths again show proper respect for their elders. Party cadres, the ubiquitous heroes of Soviet and Chinese fiction, are seldom seen, their agitatory and organizational skills obviated by virtually unanimous support for Kim Il Sung. This support is presented as self-explanatory, as if it were

---

[91] *CCY 1950*, 352-353.

[92] Han Hyo, "Uri munhagŭi 10 nyŏn," 1:147ff.; *Chosŏn munhak t'ongsa* (Pyongyang, 1959), 2:168-169.

[93] Apart from Han Sŏrya, most writers apparently regarded the glorification of a living leader in epic form as too strange and difficult a task, particularly in view of the paucity of information about his past.

an ethnic reflex and not the product of ideological conviction. Accordingly, it is "truly Korean" virtues, not political categories, that are embodied by the young heroes and heroines—praiseworthy but unremarkable workers and peasants far removed from the concept of the *positive hero*. In a New Tendency-style travesty of socialist realism's "master plot," the development of these protagonists often proceeds in the direction not of political consciousness, but of greater spontaneity, presented of course as "truly Korean" naivete or *sobak ham.*

This was in other words a literature which, for all its affirmation of a revolutionary regime and its policies, remained marked by tendencies incompatible with both socialist realism and the Marxist-Leninist discourse itself: the ethnocentric pastoralism, anti-urbanism and anti-industrialism which had become part of the country's "cultural matrix" (Im Hŏnyŏng) during the colonial era. Ironically enough, these tendencies were nowhere quite as clearly expressed as in the writings of the man most responsible for implementing socialist realism: NKFLA chairman Han Sŏrya.

b)   Han Sŏrya's Fiction

T'an'gaengch'on (Mining Settlement, 1946)
In summer 1946 Han responded to Kim's call for writers to "immerse themselves in the masses" by spending a day in the industrial zone of Sadong.[94] Characteristically, he did not seek contact with workers, choosing instead to join students of the local engineering school on a class excursion to an adjacent mine.[95] As he prepared to go underground he was overcome with "extreme terror," but a portrait of Kim Il Sung by the shaft entrance gave him courage, and he was soon absorbed in jotting down notes of the sights and sounds around him. Witnessing the students' rapturous expressions as a rock wall was dynamited, he felt he finally understood their enthusiasm for the occupation they had chosen.[96] This experience formed the

---

[94] Han Sŏrya, "Saenghwarŭi kyohun," in *HSYS*, 14:330-334. Critic Han Chungmo was embarrassed enough by the brevity of this visit to claim that his idol had spent "a few days" in Sadong (*Han Sŏryaŭi ch'angjak yŏn'gu*, 232), but the latter's account indicates that no more than a day was involved.

[95] "Saenghwarŭi kyohun," 330.

[96] Ibid., 334.

basis of the short story *T'an'gaengch'on* (Mining Settlement, 1946), the plot
of which is as follows:

A young man named Chaesu begins a course of study at an engineering
school in newly liberated Korea. Though of peasant background, he has the
bourgeois notion that academic work is nobler than the physical variety. He is
therefore disappointed to learn that no special uniforms are issued to students,
and that half of all instruction takes place outside the classroom.

On the first day of school he joins his classmates on a guided tour of a
coal mine. Though terrified at first, he draws courage from the Kim Il Sung
portrait at the shaft entrance. Soon he is listening attentively as his teacher
explains the various sights and tells of the country's new Stakhanovite heroes.
Yet for all the excitement his thoughts keep returning to the trauma inflicted on
his father, a poor tenant farmer, by the Japanese colonizers.

On the next day in the mine Chaesu wields a drill for the first time. As
he does so, it occurs to him that by serving Korean industrial construction he is
avenging his father's tormentors and restoring honor to the fatherland. Fortified
by this thought, he is able to adjust to the mine within a few days.[97]

Mining Settlement reflects Han's ignorance of the fundamental
difference between the anti-literary Soviet trends in fashion during the
KAPF era and the newer doctrine of socialist realism. A journalistic and
factographical tone reminiscent of the Soviets' First Five-Year Plan (1928-
1932) runs through the story from the very first paragraph:

It was decided that from the third day after the beginning of term
the students of the Technical School of Mining Engineering
would enter the mine every day at twelve and come out at four.
In other words they would spend the morning studying and the
afternoon engaged in the actual mining of coal.[98]

The new student Chaesu is then introduced to the reader with the
information that before his arrival he had harbored "typical student"
fantasies of a school like a "royal palace"—a clear indication that he will be
transformed, like so many Five-Year Plan heroes, into a revolutionary
worker. Chaesu's main reason for joining the school, one is told, is his
enthusiasm for the Soviet slogan "Technology is the key to everything!"[99]
The same message is paraphrased soon after by the school's director.[100]

---

[97] *T'an'gaengch'on: chihaesŏ ssaunŭn saramdŭl*, in *HSYS* 8:65-109.

[98] Ibid., 65.

[99] Ibid., 65.

[100] Ibid., 67.

Han's apparent unawareness that this slogan had been changed in 1935 to "Cadres are the key to everything" is particularly striking, as it is in the context of the Soviets' ideological shift from positivism to voluntarism that the formulation of socialist realism, with its emphasis on larger-than-life heroes, must be seen.[101]

Han's outdated concept of literature comes into its own when the students leave the institute and go underground for the first time. The mine and its various curiosities—the water dripping from the ceiling, the wind blowing through the shaft—are described and explained in the dry expository prose of RAPP factory correspondence. Even one unfamiliar with the circumstances surrounding the story's conception cannot but receive the impression that the entire description of the mine (which occupies over a third of the narrative) has been lifted *verbatim* from the notes of a tour made by the author himself. The teacher's elementary commentary seems aimed more at a visiting functionary than at engineering students:

> Then, while he pointed to one area after the other with his finger, he said, "*Excavation* means the digging out of coal, *shaft repair* means the repair of the tunnels; *hollowing out* or *digging through* means the explosion and boring of rocks encountered during excavations; *ventilation shafts* are the tunnels that bring in fresh air; the *network* is what the coal cars move around on; the *pumps* pump water out of the shafts; *autoroads* are what the trucks move on; *coal transport assistance* relates to the help while loading the coal. Since each of these sectors is adequately manned, they are always in operation."[102]

In light of such speeches it is hardly surprising that the students "wanted quickly to meet the miners."[103] The reader versed in socialist realism is even more impatient, anticipating as he does a confrontation between the students' effete self-importance and the workers' true revolutionary spirit that will throw an ironic light on the superficiality of the preceding narrative. But the meeting proves to be nothing of the sort:

> The first [workers] they met had been busy repairing the shaft. They were now taking a rest on a pile of wood they had chopped into little pieces.

---

[101] See Katerina Clark, "Utopian Anthropology as a Context for Stalinist Literature," in *Stalinism. Essays in Historical Interpretation*, ed. R.C. Tucker (New York, 1977), 184.

[102] *T'an'gaengch'on*, 73-74.

[103] Ibid., 78.

"Keep up the good work, comrades," said the professor.
"Keep up the good work," echoed the students. In that
moment they felt an unprecedented surge of emotion; the workers
no longer seemed like strangers. Sŏngch'un, who had worked for
a long time in this mine making briquets, lingered behind to talk
with the workers about something, before he too said "Keep
working, comrades," and ran to catch up with his classmates.

Kim Il Sung could hardly have found better evidence of the Korean
intellectual's "aloofness from the masses" than this passage; though the
students are from lower-middle and lower class backgrounds themselves,
Han sees no reason why they would not feel the same "unprecedented surge
of emotion" that he apparently felt at being able to greet real workers in the
flesh. In keeping with the "technology-is-the-key" message, of course, is that
the contents of Sŏngch'un's conversation with the workers are omitted,
unlike the teacher's talk of pumps and ventilation shafts.

Later the boys run into the miners again at the cafeteria: "Keep up
the good work," they say again, this time with a "sincere" nod.[104] Then,
satisfied that they have at last "come closer to the dark, sweltering mine,"
they run off to take a bath, of which the reader is assured that the water was
"very hot."[105]

It will be remembered that Han's reluctance to deal with the
industrial proletariat was particularly extreme. For all their faults Yi
Pungmyŏng's *Rodong ilga* (A Working Household, 1947) and Hwang Kŏn's
T'anmaek (Coal Seam, 1949), the two other famous industrialization stories
of the period, evince a genuine familiarity with the workplace.[106] On the
other hand, Han's avoidance of a potentially fascinating confrontation
between the students and workers is characteristic of a widespread North
Korean aversion to depicting the sort of dialectic conflict—"the struggle of
the old in the new"—prescribed by Soviet theorists. In its place one most
often finds a simple *temporal contrast*, effected by a flashback or other
excursion, which juxtaposes the paradisical present with the hellish colonial
past. This technique is of course in violation of socialist realism's demand
for a linear, fast-moving plot devoid of non-narrative interruptions.[107]

---

[104] Ibid., 88.

[105] Ibid., 91-93.

[106] Yi Pungmyŏng, *Rodongŭi ilga*, in *Kaesŏn* (Pyongyang, 1956), 56-86; Hwang Kŏn,
T'anmaek, in *Mokch'ukki* (Pyongyang, 1959), 5-82.

[107] In his novel *Ttang (Earth)* Yi Kiyŏng uses this technique with particularly dizzying
frequency. See *Ttang*, 3rd ed. (Pyongyang, 1960).

In *Mining Settlement*, therefore, the happy scene of the students' bath is followed by the description of how Chaesu's father lost his sight performing slave labor for the Japanese, and how Chaesu himself was conscripted into the imperial army.[108] This is not the usual biographism by which an author provides quick insight into his hero by referring to a background that has "predestined" his development. (On the contrary, the boy's military experience is hard to reconcile with his homesickness and naivete.) It seems instead that his past, with the drastic turnabout in family fortune after the liberation—the land reform miraculously coincides with the recovery of the old man's eyesight—is meant to symbolize the entire country's journey from colonial dark to revolutionary light, and thus to compensate for the absence of a dialectic in the central narrative itself.

As so often in other works, however, this technique only renders the storyline more "private," by making Chaesu's eagerness to serve socialist construction appear motivated less by ideological conviction (though he does display an instinctive affection for Kim Il Sung), than by a personal vendetta against his father's tormentors. This is clear in the climactic scene when he tries out a drill for the first time:

> The sweat still poured off him like rain. But Chaesu was somehow happy, as happy as if he was ramming and twisting the mighty drill into the evil Japs' hearts. He had the feeling he was avenging his father's enemies. If only his father and his wife were here now, nothing could stop him from showing them this sweet revenge.[109]

Such thoughts can no more be interpreted as expressing the attainment of revolutionary consciousness than a few minutes experimenting with a drill can be regarded as an introduction to genuine labor. ("Conviction," a Soviet critic once wrote, "does not follow from [a] feeling of enthusiasm for work."[110]) Han nonetheless regards his hero's transformation as near complete. After an excursion about the North Korean mining industry and its model workers, he returns to the plot line to inform the reader that

> enveloped in this atmosphere Chaesu became like a different person in no time. They say one usually has to work in the mine

[108] *T'an'gaengch'on*, 94-95.

[109] Ibid., 101.

[110] G. Lebedev, quoted in Hans Günther, 86-87.

reclamation project, which stands, as in Yi Kiyŏng's *Land*, for the greater endeavor of socialism. The characters in the forefront of the narrative are presented as a random cross-section of the model community. All are positive figures, even Kŭmbok's mother and Yukkukt'ongsa; the former's reluctance to study is more than compensated by her exemplary hatred of the Yankees, while the latter's enviousness is belied by the special alacrity with which she delivers her "patriotic tax" to the authorities.

In a village so singlemindedly supportive of the regime there is no need for a party "organizer" like Sholokhov's Davydov or Ting Ling's Li Chang, nor for any extraordinary "positive hero" at all. The central protagonists of *Growing Village*, Yŏngmin and Kŭmbok, are singled out not for special revolutionary resolve or political consciousness, but because their very youth makes them the most suitable symbols of "typically Korean" *sobak ham* and innocence. They represent the concentrated essence, so to speak, of the village's collective virtues. It would thus be more accurate to posit them at the center of a circle (Fig.2) than at the top of Günther's diamond.

The negative camp consists solely of the widower Ch'oe. Isolated from the community both socially and geographically,[123] unaffiliated with any organized political opposition or coherent ideology, and posing no serious threat to the community as a result, he is a typical North Korean rural villain of the comic variety established by Yi Kiyŏng in *Kaebyŏk* (Creation, 1946).[124] Unlike Yi's character Hwang, however, Ch'oe is not doomed by landowner origins to eternal outsider status. Since his problems with the new order are grounded in minor character flaws—to be exact: "the bad habit of always distinguishing between *mine* and *other people's*"[125]—he can in time be persuaded to give up his antisocial ways and join the fun. In this sense he is a typical "reformable" outsider, like Suni's mother in Yi Kiyŏng's *Land*. ("Reformables" remain clearly negative figures until conversion. The DPRK's writers are too averse even to temporary ambiguities to allow such characters to hover between the positive and negative fields like the "undecideds" in Günther's diagram.)

The likelihood of such a cast producing any real conflict is slim from the outset. It becomes even more remote as Han uses the widower Ch'oe increasingly for comic relief, stressing his ridiculous marital designs on the young Kŭmbok. The town hall debate between Ch'oe and the united

---

[123] His land is on the hill slopes behind the village; *Charanŭn maŭl*, 260.

[124] *Kaebyŏk*, in the anthology *Kaesŏn* (Pyongyang, 1956), 16-38.

[125] *Charanŭn maŭl*, 266.

community might have been used to impart a little ideological bite to the toothless storyline, but Han chooses to restrict the discussion to a flurry of personal attacks on the widower, and then omits the latter's self-criticism entirely: Ch'oe's words were spoken in "an inaudible voice," claims the narrator.[126]

In *Growing Village* as in all his works, Han makes only the most desultory attempt to describe the visual world. Nonetheless, the village's social homogeneity, harmony, placitude and isolation (no one enters or leaves during the narrative) mark it as a product of the same New Tendency-tradition of ethnocentric pastoralism as Yi Kiyŏng's *Land*, a work replete with sugary idealizations of nature. It is important to distinguish North Korean pastoralism from the Soviet variety exemplified by writers like Fedor Panferov (1896-1960). Clark has shown that the latter is largely devoid of nostalgia, as it posits the idyllic world in the near future, in accordance with the dictate of *revolutionary romanticism*.[127] The North Korean writer, on the other hand, presents the contemporary village (in varying degrees of explicitness) as having already returned to a mythologized pre-colonial past, when the countryside was one great, benevolently naive *Gemeinschaft*. One could say that if the Soviet idyll is Elysium posited in the immediate future, its North Korean counterpart is Arcadia posited in the present.

In *Land*, for example, Yi is careful to portray the communal work on a reclamation project as a revival of the traditional Korean *ture* leagues, in which villagers would pool their labor and work on each other's plots in turn. The novel's tenant farmer hero even insists that the work day be patterned after Yi Dynasty custom, with songs and dances.[128] Han is never quite so blatant in *Growing Village*, except for one striking sentence:

> In the old days there may have been more, but nowadays there
> was no family as exemplary as Yŏngmin's.[129]

This statement may seem innocuous enough, but it violates socialist realism's old-vs-new opposition in two fundamental ways. First and most obviously, there is the implication that the villagers' ideal of conduct lies in the past—not in some Marxian *Urgemeinschaft*, of course, but in the village's pre-colonial days. Secondly, there is the absence of

---

[126] Ibid., 278.

[127] Clark, *The Soviet Novel*, 107.

[128] See *Ttang*, 3rd ed. (Pyongyang, 1960), 442-444.

[129] *Charanŭn maŭl*, 265.

on leaving the hospital and willing himself back to health, worker-heroes demonstrate a healthy contempt for doctors.[146]

Han's boundless respect for the medical world may be connected to his ignorance of the Soviet ideological shift to voluntarism in the mid-1930s (see *Mining Settlement*). Yet there is more than mere positivism at work in his depiction of the doctor-patient relationship. Wŏnju displays not only infinite faith in Dr Kriblyak's expertise, but also a childlike fear of incurring her displeasure. When she scolds a nurse on his account, his blood "freezes" and he wants to "crawl into the nearest termite hole."[147] Reproaching himself for having worried her by leaving his room, he resolves to follow her orders henceforth to the letter:

> Wŏnju took a deep breath and lay down in bed. From then on he never went in and out of his room without permission. While supine he would urinate and defecate in a bedpan. Even when he knew that Suni [his sister - B.M.] had arrived outside he would not go to the window, though it was practically under his nose.[148]

Like other contributors to the genre, Han is as intent on underscoring the pathetic nature of the Korean figures as he is on glorifying their benefactors. The gratuitous reference to Wŏnju's bodily functions serves this end in the same way as Yi Ch'unjin's description in *Anna* of a Korean woman vomiting on the doctor's golden locks.[149] Han also depicts his countrymen as reacting with amazement to the Soviets' most trivial acts of kindness, as if they had no right to expect humane treatment:

> [The doctor has told a young patient that he can go home - B.M.] But Pyŏngnok quickly said, "No, I'll stay with you, doctor." Seeing in his serious face that he wouldn't leave her for anything in the world the doctor turned around immediately, her face all smiles.
>
> "Really? Stay with me then. 'Cos I'll put you right for sure," she said, stroking Pyŏngnok's hair, adjusting his collar, and tucking him nicely into bed again. The doctor and Pyŏngnok had been conversing quietly, but an old patient had witnessed the

---

[146] See *Kak zakalialas' stal'* (Moscow, 1979), 565. See also Ernst Strittmatter's *Ole Bienkopp* (Berlin, GDR, 1963).

[147] *Nammae*, 176-177.

[148] Ibid., 178-179.

[149] *Anna*, 31.

scene. He had turned over unnoticed in his bed and was shedding secret tears at the beautiful conversation he had heard. In truth, Wŏnju felt like crying too.[150]

Like all Soviet-Korean friendship stories, *Brother and Sister* can be seen as a product of the same national inferiority complex that engendered the pro-Japanese literature of the colonial era. The image of the orphaned, childlike Wŏnju in the doctor's motherly care calls to mind Yi Injik's *Hyŏrŭi nu* (Tears of Blood, 1906), Korea's first *sinsosŏl* (lit., "new novel"). Yi tells of a young Korean girl separated from her family during the Sino-Japanese War, who finds shelter in the home of a kindhearted Japanese medic. A child-loving male colleague of Dr Kriblyak's, on the other hand, reminds one of the emperor's soldiers in Han's own pro-Japanese *Pagoda* (1940).[151]

The Soviets appear to have been embarrassed by these tributes, which far exceeded even East Bloc standards of obsequiousness. A 1957 Russian-language collection of Han's short stories published with Soviet assistance in Pyongyang pointedly omitted *Brother and Sister*.[152] A 1954 East German version of Han's short story *Ŏlgul* (The Face, 1948), and presumably the Russian translation on which it was based, left out a crucial scene in which a freed Korean lovingly strokes his Soviet liberator's face, greedily inhaling his new friend's "pleasant oily smell."[153]

Despite their special dual function, friendship stories like Han's *Brother and Sister* should not be seen as outside the mainstream of North Korean fiction. One would be hard put to find a figure as pathetic as Wŏnju in, say, a production novel, but he is a typical North Korean protagonist in that he is conceived not so much to inspire emulation (like socialist realism's *positive hero*) as to elicit emotional identification. For reasons we will discuss in later chapters, Wŏnju's childlike attributes are shared by most literary heroes. Soviet women like Dr Kriblyak may be rare in other genres, but their occupation and milieu are not. Even today it seems the model working woman is not a kolkhoz leader (as she was in the USSR)[154] or a

---

[150] *Nammae*, 196.

[151] Ibid., 185. See *T'ap*, vol. 5 of *Sŭlgi sosŏlsŏn* (Seoul, 1987), 208.

[152] *Khan Ser ia: Sbornik rasskazov* (Pyongyang, 1957). Elena Berman was one of the translators.

[153] *Ŏlgul*, in *HSYS*, 8:137-155 (quoted 153); *Der Freund*, in *Korea erzählt: Ein Einblick in die koreanische Literatur*, ed. J. Herzfeldt (Berlin, GDR, 1954), 84-92.

[154] Xenia Gasiorowska, *Women in Soviet Fiction 1917-1964* (Madison, 1968), 64-66.

the war to the Chinese, marked the occasion by holding impromptu talks with the group's top officials, to whom he stressed the need to "inculcate victory" into the minds of the people.[10] Han Sŏrya, who remained in the post of Federation chairman, took advantage of the occasion to exhort his fellow writers to carry on the struggle begun in the colonial era by KAPF.[11] A DPRK scholar later singled out the emphasis on the proletarian cultural movement as a striking characteristic of Han's speech.[12] This indicates that it marked the beginning of a new and more intensive stage in the glorification of KAPF.

Only days later Seoul fell once again to UN troops. After the seesaw battle around the 38th parallel had stabilized, Han Sŏrya and about one hundred and fifty other members of the KFLA's Writers' Union settled in a village east of Pyongyang. Though safe there from the incessant B-29 bombing raids, they were plagued by the same material shortages as their countrymen:

> There were no blankets or mattresses. There was no ink either, so you could hunker down in the cantine, pen in hand, and concentrate on writing as much as you wanted; it could hardly result in an actual work....In every house people tried to get by on maize gruel, but even that wasn't available in sufficient qualities, so one had to eat herbs, roots and bark to survive until the next day of distribution.[13]

Conditions were better for Han, who was allotted his own house (the others lodged with farmers) and secretary. In a few months he was able to complete *Sŭngnyangi* (Jackals), a virulently xenophobic novella about murderous US missionaries in colonial Korea that would become his most lasting work (see below).

On 30 June 1951 Kim Il Sung gave his first official talk on cultural matters since 1946. He began by apostrophizing the attendant writers and artists as "engineers of the soul," an old phrase of Stalin's that would become far more popular in the DPRK than it had ever been in the USSR. After praising his listeners for cultural achievements unparalleled in Korean history, Kim lamented that they had still failed to depict sufficiently the

---

[10] Han Sŏrya, "Kim Ilsŏng changgun'gwa munhak yesul," in *STP*, 230. For some reason the speech is not included in editions of Kim's works.

[11] Han Chungmo, *Han Sŏryaŭi ch'angjak yŏn'gu*, 299.

[12] Ibid., 299.

[13] Yi Ch'ŏlchu, *Pugŭi yesurin* (Seoul, 1966), 53.

"loftily patriotic" heroism of the KPA and the rear guard. Rather than comb newspapers for stories of extraordinary individuals and miraculous exploits, he said, they should reveal today's heroes as yesterday's workers and farmers who had lost none of their "deep emotions" and "humanity."[14] Kim's listeners will have instinctively understood what was meant by "deep emotions and humanity," but for posterity's sake the 1965 edition of the speech stated explicitly that writers must show "the guileless, benevolently naive (*sobak han*) ways" of the people.[15] The most often quoted part of Kim's speech concerned the "correct depiction of the enemy":

> Our writers portray the US imperialist invaders as cunning. This
> is of course correct. But there is a tendency to forget that they
> are not just cunning, but are also the cruelest and most repulsive
> barbarians. Where is the refined Yankee cunning in massacring
> our people, and devastating our towns and villages through
> indiscriminate bombing?....Having traded their crucifixes for
> rifles, the American missionaries who once came to Korea
> chanting "God" and singing "hymns" now gather large groups of
> pregnant women together and mow them down, and drive over
> little children with tanks. Those Wall Street "gentlemen," who
> arrogantly boast to the world of their "statue of liberty," today
> load naked Korean girls onto their tanks and drive around
> committing all manner of unimaginably infamous and inhumane
> acts. The peoples of the world must know of the Yankees'
> brutality. The crimes against humanity, the offense to our
> descendants must arouse hatred and curses for endless
> generations.[16]

It may seem paradoxical that Kim used the same speech to warn repeatedly against "narrow nationalism," but he clearly meant the phrase in its contemporary Chinese sense of failing to accord the USSR and other socialist allies the necessary respect.[17] He reminded his listeners that the assimilation of the "advanced culture" of the "great Soviet Union" was the *only* way to develop a people's culture in Korea, and he called for more literary tributes to the protective powers:

---

[14] "Chŏnch'e chakka yesulgadŭrege," in *Kim Ilsŏng sŏnjip* (Pyongyang, 1954), 3:242-244.

[15] "Uri munhak yesurŭi myŏkkaji munjee taehayŏ," in *Uri hyŏngmyŏngesŏŭi munhak yesurŭi immu* (Pyongyang, 1965), 4.

[16] "Chŏnch'e chakka," 244-245.

[17] Cf. Merle Goldman, *Literary Dissent in Communist China* (Cambridge, Mass., 1967), 88.

> In our literature and art the Soviet Union, the stronghold of
> world peace, and the Soviet people, the eternal friends of our
> people, have not been depicted enough; neither have the great
> Chinese People's Volunteers, who are fighting heroically at the
> side of the Korean People's Army, nor have the peoples of the
> democratic countries giving our masses international support and
> encouragement.[18]

The order in which the two allied nations are mentioned indicates the
continued primacy of the USSR in the DPRK's diplomatic hierarchy, despite
China's more important contribution to the war effort.[19] This hierarchy was
reflected in literature throughout the 1950s. Han Sŏrya, who wrote six
Soviet-Korean friendship stories in his career, saw no need to write more
than one clumsy article on the Chinese, and even then gave precedence to
the USSR whenever both countries were named.[20] Fictional works by other
writers on the Chinese-Korean alliance portrayed an equal relationship of
brothers-in-arms, not the mother-child bond of the Soviet-Korean friendship
stories.[21]

In his speech Kim also criticised naturalist, formalist and
cosmopolitan tendencies (without explaining just what he meant by them),
and indicated that sectarianism among critics was partly to blame:

> Unfortunately there has been a tendency among critics to try and
> "destroy" writers and their works instead of providing instruction
> and correction. This is not the kind of criticism we want. Rather,
> there must be a literary criticism which...is based on a spirit of
> mutual, comradely cooperation....On the cultural scene, therefore,
> we must fight mercilessly against all kinds of factional activities
> and tendencies.[22]

In the late 1940s Kim's hold on power had been too uncertain and
his talks on the arts too tentative for him to exert much influence on literary
development. The June 1951 speech, however, was immediately touted by
cultural officials as an event of major importance. Yi Ch'ŏlchu tells of being
reproached by a superior for not being familiar enough with it.[23] Thus began

---

[18] "Chŏnch'e chakka," 248.

[19] See also Scalapino and Lee, 1:415.

[20] See "Ch'insŏn," in *HSYS*, 14:190-198.

[21] See *Chosŏn munhak t'ongsa*, 2:239-240.

[22] "Chŏnch'e chakka," 247-248.

[23] Yi Ch'ŏlchu, 31.

an era in which Kim Il Sung participated actively in the North Korean literary discussion with all the authority of a wartime dictator. His injunctions derived added strength from the fact that they were simple and clear enough to prevent critics from enforcing them at will, as they could the vague postulates of socialist realism. Perhaps most importantly, however, Kim was preaching to the converted, in the sense that his own inclinations were those of a generation of Koreans raised on the same cultural diet of ethnocentric pastoralism. Whenever there was a conflict between his pronouncements and socialist realism, therefore, which was often, the former automatically took precedence, though everyone assiduously pretended that no such conflict existed. The literature of the DPRK thus began during the Korean War to drift further away from the Soviet aesthetic doctrine, which, while still enjoying ostensible authority, was reduced more than ever to a mere weapon of sectarian warfare.

The effect of all this is evident in the war fiction of the period, which is marked by a strident racism and cruelty at odds with Marxist internationalism. Soviet and Chinese writers tend to make clear distinctions of valuation between high and low-ranking enemy soldiers, Nazis and non-Nazis, soldiers and civilians, etc (see for example Fadeevs *Young Guard*, 1945-46).[24] Not so their Korean colleagues. In *Jackals* Han Sŏrya demonizes an American child, while in *Hwangch'oryŏng* (1952) he uses an enemy corpse and the wife's letter found on it for crude comic relief.[25] In *Miguk taesagwan* (US Embassy, 1951?) Yi T'aejun depicts the violent retribution inflicted by KPA soldiers on unarmed American prisoners.[26] While in line with the rhetorical overkill of Kim's remarks on the "correct depiction of the enemy," such stories appalled even sympathetic East European translators (see below), thus hindering the dissemination of North Korean literature in the "socialist realist bloc" at a time of unprecedented interest in the DPRK's culture.

Kim's stern call for unity in the June 1951 speech failed to prevent factional tension inside the NKFLA from increasing steadily during the war. Having lost their influential protégé Cho Kich'ŏn in battle in July 1951, and with vice-premier Hŏ Kai under official attack for wartime errors, the

---

[24] Even Dieter Boden, while critical of the jingoism of Soviet war fiction, admits that it observed a distinction between fascists and anti-fascists; see *Die Deutschen in der russischen und der sowjetischen Literatur* (Munich/Vienna, 1982), 68. See also Li Chi, "Communist War Stories," in *Chinese Communist Literature*, ed. C. Birch (New York, 1963), 139-157.

[25] *Sŭngnyangi* (Tokyo, 1954); *Hwangch'oryŏng*, in *HSYS*, 8:492-549.

[26] See the discussion of the book in *Chosŏn munhak t'ongsa*, 2:224.

Soviet-Koreans in the cultural apparatus—Pak Ch'angok (chairman of the Central Committee's propaganda and agitation section), Chŏng Ryul (the party's head of cultural affairs), and Ki Sŏkpok (editor of the *Rodong sinmun*)—were eager to shore up their position on the scene.[27] While continuing their patronage of the SKWP writers Yim Hwa and Kim Namch'ŏn, therefore, they devoted special attention to promoting the careers of Yim Hwa's newly arrived followers from Seoul, especially Pak T'aewŏn, who rapidly rose to prominence.[28] This only made Yim, whose sentimental poems of wartime separation were then enjoying huge popularity, even more unsatisfied with his symbolic post as vice-chairman of the Soviet-Korean Cultural Association's central committee. Yearning for greater influence, he began taking up-and-coming young poets under his wing, introducing them at private gatherings to fellow SKWP faction members Cho Ilmyŏng (Vice-Minister of Propaganda) and Yi Wŏnjo (vice-chairman of the Central Committee's propaganda and agitation section). This was in violation of a regulation according to which poets were to rely on the KFLA's poetry council alone for guidance.[29]

Wrangling for advantage and influence would hardly have been so intense had there not been widespread dissatisfaction with Han Sŏrya's leadership of the KFLA. While acknowledging his devotion to duty, colleagues generally considered him arrogant and standoffish. More importantly, they had very little respect for his writing:

> Whenever Han Sŏrya produced a novel other writers would cut it down behind his back. Han devoted almost all his works to the glorification of Kim Il Sung. That was all well and good, but he wrote clumsily and almost completely without the formal quality vital for a novel.[30]

In late 1951 the Soviet-Koreans began trying to undermine Han's position by harassing members of his inner circle. Their first target was Dance Union chairwoman Ch'oe Sŭnghŭi, the wife of Han's "right hand man" An Mak. In August 1951 her troupe won first prize at the World Youth Festival in East Berlin, whereupon a victory performance was scheduled for Pyongyang's bombproof underground theater in December. Hardly had Ch'oe returned from abroad, however, than the Propaganda

[27] Yi Ch'ŏlchu, 70.

[28] Ibid., 72.

[29] Ibid., 23, 32-33.

[30] Ibid., 23-24.

Ministry began demanding that she reduce her troupe's share in the program. The flamboyant beauty had long violated the DPRK's puritan moral code, and the Soviet-Koreans apparently hoped she would be too aware of her own vulnerability on this score to stand up to them. They guessed wrongly; Ch'oe turned for help to Kim Il Sung himself, with whom she was on an intimate footing. Kim promptly called in Han Sŏrya to rebuke him for neglecting to "look after" her, and the show proceeded as planned.[31]

In December 1951 Han departed for Vienna to attend the World Peace Conference. He then went to a sanatorium near Moscow, where he received treatment for neuralgia through January and February 1952. While in bed he began writing *Hwangch'oryŏng*, a rambling story about a nurse in a military hospital.[32] As if determined to exploit his absence, the Soviet-Koreans turned on another member of his coterie, Publications Bureau cadre and prominent critic Ŏm Hosŏk. In February Ki Sŏkpok published an article in the *Rodong sinmun* in which he scolded Ŏm for trying to "destroy" young writers instead of offering constructive advice. Quoting copiously from Stalin and Kim Il Sung to bolster his position, Ki strongly implied that an oppressive "royal family" was in place in the cultural apparatus.[33]

Meanwhile, on the political front, Kim Il Sung had grown convinced that Foreign Minister Pak Hŏnyŏng and his SKWP followers represented a danger to his rule. When Han Sŏrya returned to the DPRK in March 1952, he was promptly called to Kim's office, where plans were made for a purge of the Pak faction.[34] It was decided to begin with a campaign aginst Yim Hwa and Kim Namch'ŏn on trumped-up charges of literary transgressions. This would enable the regime to eliminate the two without alerting Pak himself. Kim was also aware that the Soviet-Koreans in the cultural apparatus were trying to increase their influence by promoting Pak's followers and harassing his own. Kim could hardly afford to offend the USSR in this difficult period by purging the Soviet-Koreans, but the critical campaign could be expected to "flush out" their patronage of Yim and other

---

[31] Ibid., 34-35.

[32] Han Sŏrya, "Ssŭttalinŭn uriwa hamkke sara itta," in *HSYS*, 14:199-211; idem, *Hwangch'oryŏng*, in *HSYS*, 8:492-549.

[33] Ki Sŏkpok, "Uri munhak p'yŏngnone issŏsŏŭi myŏkkaji munjee taehayŏ," in two parts, *RS*, 28 February 1952 and 1 March 1952. Ki's articles were ostensibly in response to Ŏm's article "Uri munhage issŏsŏŭi chayŏnjuŭiwa hyŏngsikchuŭi chanjaewaŭi t'ujaeng," *RS*, 17 January 1952, in which Ŏm had criticised the continued tendencies of factography and naturalism in Korean literature.

[34] Scalapino and Lee, 1:438.

writers; this could be used against them when circumstances were more opportune. For good measure it was decided to make vice-chairman Yi T'ae-jun, the Soviet-Koreans' protégé in the KFLA, a secondary target of the critical campaign.[35]

Ŏm Hosŏk set the ball rolling with an attack on Kim Namch'ŏn's *Kkul* (Honey, 1951), a short story about a wounded soldier nursed back to health by an old woman. Ŏm complained the author had violated *typicality* by insinuating that the KPA would have abandoned a wounded comrade.[36] As in 1949 with Kim Saryang's *Kaya Harp*, this vaguest of socialist realist postulates was again demonstrating its usefulness as a sectarian weapon. Han Sŏrya's *Chŏnbyŏl* (Soldier's Farewell), which had appeared the year before, also dealt with a KPA soldier forced to rely on an old woman's care, but it had aroused no controversy then, and was later mentioned approvingly in the DPRK's first literary history.[37]

Rodong sinmun editor Ki Sŏkpok rushed out an article in Kim Namch'ŏn's defense, claiming the events described in *Honey* were unavoidable in wartime and thus "typical" enough to merit depiction. Ŏm countered by pointing out—quite rightly—that *typicality* demands not the commonplace but the historically significant.[38] Ŏm went on to accuse Yim Hwa of sowing defeatism by portraying a soldier's mother as a helpless and lonely figure in a recent poem.[39] This too was a valid criticism from the standpoint of socialist realism, which advocates an optimistic emphasis on the surmounting of obstacles. Yet critics had hitherto been extremely receptive to tragic storylines. Two of the most effusively praised short stories of the period could as easily have been charged with defeatism, namely Han's *Jackals* (1951), which tells of a woman's failure to rescue her child from US missionaries, and Hwang Kŏn's *Pult'anŭn sŏm* (Island in Flames, 1952), which describes the last hours of a doomed KPA outpost during MacArthur's Inch'ŏn landing.[40]

---

[35] See Yi Ch'ŏlchu, 104-105.

[36] Ibid., 90-91. I have been unable to find these issues of the *Rodong sinmun*, but there is no reason to doubt Yi's version of Ŏm's criticism, which is duplicated in the official *Chosŏn munhak t'ongsa* (Pyongyang, 1959), 2:225.

[37] *Chŏnbyŏl*, in *HSYS*, 8:396-419; see *Chosŏn munhak t'ongsa*, 2:231.

[38] Yi Ch'ŏlchu, 92.

[39] The official *Chosŏn munhak t'ongsa*, 2:225, later echoed this criticism in reference to Yim Hwa.

[40] Han Sŏrya, *Sŭngnyangi* (Tokyo, 1954); Hwang Kŏn, *Pult'anŭn sŏm*, in *Mokch'ukki* (Pyongyang, 1959), 182-206.

In short, both Yim and Kim may have violated socialist realism, but they had conformed to *de facto* North Korean literary norms. Those like Scalapino and Lee, who (perhaps extrapolating from Soviet history) claim that Yim was punished for a refusal to adapt his art to the demands of the state,[41] forget that he was anything but an aesthete. (In the 1920s and early 1930s, it will be remembered, Yim had been the most militant of KAPF's writers.) One need only read his February 1952 poem *Kijie toragamyŏn* (When You Get Back to Base) to realize how conventional a propagandist he really was:

> To our beloved Leader
> To our proud People's Army
> To our dear Chinese comrades-in-arms
> To our yearned-for brothers and sisters
>
> Deliver the fervent February Eighth greeting
> That burns in our hearts in letters of flame,
> The fighting oath of us
> Who give our lives for the Fatherland.[42]

Kim Namch'ŏn, for his part, may have been well aware that a double standard was in force. In reference to one of Han Sŏrya's novels then enjoying the usual automatic acclaim, he is said to have posed the rhetorical question: "If my work is unrealistic, then what about *Taedong River?*"[43] Since Koreans are traditionally inclined to interpret conflict over issues in the context of interpersonal difficulties anyway,[44] one can be fairly certain that few if any in the KFLA's rank and file really took the campaign against Yim and Kim's literary "transgressions" at face value. This assumption is borne out by the continued popularity of tragic themes throughout the 1950s. As indicated above, Yi T'aejun also came under attack in this period, but Yi Ch'ŏlchu fails to expand on just what the criticism of his work was, and relevant publications are unavailable for study.

Han Sŏrya himself stayed out of the fray, choosing to spend much of 1952 bolstering his patron's new pose as Mao-like cultural arbiter. In the *Munhak yesul* articles "*Kim Ilsŏng changgun'gwa munhak yesul*" (General Kim Il Sung and the Arts, April 1952) and "*Kim Ilsŏng changgun'gwa*

---

[41] See Scalapino and Lee, 2:890.

[42] *RS*, 7 February 1952. The "February 8th greeting" refers to the day in 1948 on which the Korean People's Army (KPA) was established.

[43] Yi Ch'ŏlchu, 115.

[44] Norman Jacobs, 20.

minjok munhwaŭi paltchŏn" (General Kim Il Sung and National Cultural Development, August 1952) he tried to show the premier had played a decisive role in every stage of North Korea's literary development.[45] He also recounted various informal remarks Kim had made, presumably in his presence, about contemporary plays and novels. Though it is impossible to agree with Han that any of these asides bespeak "a profound understanding of the arts," a few certainly make sense from a socialist realist standpoint, such as Kim's criticism of a play for lacking thematic unity, or his complaint about the tendency to linger on American atrocities instead of emphasizing North Korean victories.[46] (Although in view of his own earlier guidelines on the "correct depiction of the enemy," this was a bit like the man of Korean proverb who gives the disease, then offers the remedy.)

Han also remembered the day in 1951 when Kim told the following "true story":

> "There was a unit which threw itself into the struggle for control of a hill, and won the battle the same day. Afterwards the commanding officer went to look in on his men...and asked them if they had any special needs. They replied, 'No, we just want the supreme commander [i.e., Kim Il Sung] to be in good health. Please deliver that message. That is all.'"
>
> Listening to the General as he told this story with a smile, we imagined with boundless joy the lovable figures of these patriots, *sincere without a trace of guile, as unspoiled as earth [hŭk kat'i sunbak hago], and as simple as truth itself*, these fighters who, while unyielding, are *filled with true virtue and love.*[47] (emphasis mine)

Han pretends to miss the point by interpreting the story in the context of the *sobak ham* cult, i.e., as another illustration of the Korean people's unique unspoiledness and virtue. A central myth of every socialist personality cult is that of the people's boundless love for their leader, which is meant to reconcile his dictatorship with democratic principles.[48] By telling this "true

---

[45] "Kim Ilsŏng changgun'gwa munhak yesul," in *HSYS*, 14:13-22; "Kim Ilsŏng changgun'gwa minjok munhwaŭi paltchŏn," in *HSYS*, 14:23-33.

[46] Ibid., 29.

[47] "Kim Ilsŏng changgun'gwa munhak yesul," 17.

[48] See L. Schapiro, *Totalitarianism* (London, 1972), 38-43, 95.

story" to a gathering of writers, Kim, as Han must have known, was calling for the treatment of this myth in literature.[49]

Especially interesting is the dictator's criticism of an unnamed writer for marrying the hero of his land reform-novel to a former concubine:

> "I'm no writer. But if I were, I would not have selected a woman who had been another man's mistress as a companion for this tenant farmer. Is there no woman who has lived a purer life and fought more for her rights? Even an old maid would do. Everyone likes pure water. I should like to give this tenant farmer, who has slaved and hungered so long in darkness and tyranny, pure water."[50]

Kim cares not that the former mistress in Yi Kiyŏng's *Land* (1948-49)—for this is clearly the work to which he is referring—"reforms" and becomes a community activist before tying the knot. Nor does he believe the tenant-hero's own failed colonial-era marriage should prevent him from marrying another virgin. All may want "pure water," but in Kim's DPRK, it would seem, only men have a *right* to it. Han interpreted this remark, which could not have been further removed from the ideological context of socialist realism, as "an amazing literary critique" revealing "lofty ideology" and a "deep love of the Korean people."[51]

Meanwhile, the campaign against Yim Hwa and Kim Namch'ŏn reached a new stage with accusations of "reactionary tendencies." Finally, in autumn of 1952, Kim Il Sung had Yim arrested. According to Scalapino and Lee the immediate pretext for Yim's arrest was a poem he had written with the words: "Forests were put to the fire/Houses were burned/If Stalin comes to Korea/there is not a house to put him up for the night."[52] While in prison, the poet apparently confessed under torture to having joined forces with fellow SKWP-faction members in conspiring against Kim Il Sung. Immediately following Yim's arrest, his friend Kim Namch'ŏn was apprehended and sent to a reeducation camp, from which he never returned. Other SKWP members outside the KFLA were also purged at this time, but

---

[49] Intent on getting his point across, Kim, with none of the publicity-shyness usually feigned by socialist dictators, would in later years explicitly exhort writers to write about the people's love and respect for him. See Han's "Suryŏngŭl ttara paeuja," in *STP*, 194-200, and Kim Il Sung's 1964 speech "Hyŏngmyŏngjŏk munhak yesurŭl ch'angjak halte taehayŏ," in *Uri hyŏngmyŏngesŏŭi munhak yesurŭi immu* (Pyongyang, 1965), 46.

[50] Quoted in "Kim Ilsŏng changgun'gwa minjok munhwaŭi paltchŏn," 28.

[51] Ibid., 28.

[52] Scalapino and Lee, 1:438.

Pak Hŏnyŏng himself was allowed to remain in office as Foreign Minister, no doubt to present a united front to the country's enemies.

On 15 December 1952 Kim opened the Fifth Plenum of the KWP's Central Committee with a diatribe against the "anti-party activities" of a small group of "factionalists" who had betrayed the revolution by constantly striving to secure top posts for their cronies.[53] The KFLA responded to the speech by introducing daily self-criticism sessions aimed at uncovering ties to Yim Hwa and Kim Namch'ŏn, who were referred to vaguely as "reactionary elements" until Pak was finally arrested in February 1953. These sessions continued until April. Many of those who confessed to social ties with the two writers were purged several months later.[54]

On 27 July 1953 a cease-fire agreement ending the Korean War was signed. A little over a week later Yim Hwa, Cho Ilmyŏng, Yi Wŏnjo and nine of Pak's other high-ranking allies (though not Pak himself) were indicted for participating in a US conspiracy to overthrow the government. This ludicrous charge was designed to deprive them of all legitimacy—and to absolve Kim Il Sung of the failure to reunify the country.[55] All defendants were found guilty and sentenced to death. The date of Yim's execution is still unknown, but it probably took place before 1955, when some of his codefendants retook the stand to testify against Pak.

On 26 September 1953 the First Congress of Writers and Artists convened in Pyongyang. It cannot have been a festive occasion, for the KFLA had lost some of its most promising members in the preceding years: in addition to Yim Hwa and Kim Namch'ŏn, there were Kim Saryang, Cho Kich'ŏn, Han Sedŏk and others who had died of war-related causes. In his keynote speech Han Sŏrya delivered a harangue against Yim Hwa and Kim Namch'ŏn, and exhorted his colleagues to fulfil the duty imposed on them a month earlier by the KWP's Sixth Plenum by assuming a "fighting" role in national reconstruction.[56] On the second day of the congress it was decided to follow the Soviets' example and dissolve the KFLA, making each union a separate entity directly answerable to the party and Ministry of Propaganda.[57] The KFLA's leadership was simply transferred to the Writers'

---

[53] Ibid., 1:439.

[54] Ibid., 1:440.

[55] Dae-Sook Suh, *Kim Il Sung*, 131; Scalapino and Lee, 1:451. A Japanese writer who accepted the North Korean line wrote a historical novel depicting Yim as a spy; see Matsumoto Seicho, *Kita no shijin* (The North's Poet, Tokyo, 1974).

[56] See Han Chungmo, 383; Yi Ch'ŏlchu, 173.

[57] Ibid., 172.

Union (henceforth WU): Han was named chairman, and Yi T'aejun vice-chairman.

Who would take the powerful secretarial post vacated by Kim Namch'ŏn? The appointment of a widely respected and factionally unaligned figure—Ch'oe Myŏngik, say—would have done much to restore harmony and show that Kim Il Sung's anti-sectarian rhetoric was serious. Instead Hong Sunch'ŏl was chosen, no doubt on the recommendation of his close friend and fellow Hamgyŏng-native Han Sŏrya. A former Japanophile mining agent, Hong had emerged after liberation with an anthology of declamatory verse, and gone on to earn special notoriety among his colleagues as a plagiarist and a lecher.[58]

Hong's appointment was the last straw for Yi T'aejun, who during the critical campaign against him had complained to associates that the cultural apparatus had become a "Han machine" more intent on serving the chairman's personal interests than literature itself. Yi believed (and rightly so) that the nascent glorification of the KAPF tradition was motivated in large part by the need to legitimize the leadership of a man who had amply demonstrated his own inability to break out of the old "proletarian" style of writing. Yi saw this as detracting time and energy from the real task at hand, namely the implementation of socialist realism through the intensive propagation of Soviet literature.[59]

The DPRK has never published a national bibliography, but indications are that Soviet literature was indeed being translated and published on a much smaller scale than Kim's effusive tributes to the "advanced" culture of the "great Soviet Union" would lead one to expect.[60] It apears too many socialist realist classics were incompatible with traditional Korean morals and reading tastes. Gladkov's *Cement* (1925) and Sholokhov's *Virgin Soil under the Plough* (1932), which were written in a hardboiled, unsentimental style that reflected the Marxist-Leninist discourse to a high degree (even to the point of condoning sexual liberation), had still not been translated in 1953, nor had Sholokhov's worldwide bestseller *The Quiet Don* (1928-40).[61]

---

[58] Hyŏn, 90-91; Yi Ch'ŏlchu, 184. This description was largely corroborated by Han and other North Koreans after Hong's fall from grace (see Ch4a).

[59] Ibid., 190-191.

[60] The official yearbook for 1954-55 merely states that 318 foreign works (*chakp'um*) were translated between autumn of 1953 and summer of 1954. See *CCY 1954-1955*, 460.

[61] They were finally translated in the late 1950s, though whether they were actually
(continued...)

In Korea the executive has traditionally succeeded in "monopolizing" ideology, reducing debate to squabbles over orthodoxy.[62] There was thus nothing strange in a former aestheticist like Yi basing his power bid on the claim that *he* could best implement socialist realism. It is of course unlikely that his supporters were any more sincerely devoted to the doctrine than he. The Soviet-Koreans, who had placed him in their debt upon his arrival in 1947, probably hoped to increase their influence on literary affairs under his chairmanship, while the writers of the now headless SKWP faction must have realized that under the *status quo* it would only be a matter of time before they were purged.[63]

Since a direct attack on Han's performance in office was out of the question, Yi and his backers decided to discredit him by focusing attention on the failings of his subordinates—a tactic rooted in Korea's Confucian tradition. Not surprisingly, the first target of attack was Hong Sunch'ŏl. In his first few weeks on the job the WU secretary had wielded his administrative powers with little restraint, imperiously dispatching writers to factories and farms, and even ordering them to take part in street repairs.[64] More fatefully, he had embarked on a series of indiscreet extramarital affairs. This provided a prime opportunity for Yi to garner support from the regime, which had made no secret of its dissatisfaction with the sexual permissiveness prevailing in the war's aftermath.[65] Yi lodged a formal complaint with the party, asking at the same time for a meeting to call publicly for Hong's removal. The party refused this request, perhaps aware of Yi's intent to link the secretary's excesses to the chairman's negligence, but agreed to look into the case.[66]

---

[61](...continued)
published is more difficult to determine. See Han Sŏrya, "Paltchŏn tosange orŭn chŏnhuŭi Chosŏn munhak," 118; also *CCY 1959*, 221.

[62] See Norman Jacobs, 26.

[63] Yi's supporters are said to have included Kim Kwiyŏn (one of the WU's few women), Paek Sŏk, Yu Hangnim, An Hoenam, Kim Sango, and former Yim Hwa followers like Yi Wŏnu and Kim Sangdong. See Yi Ch'ŏlchu, 192.

[64] See *CCY 1954-1955*, 459.

[65] Yi Ch'ŏlchu's account abounds in tales of sex scandals inside the WU. According to a private source who resided in Pyongyang at the time, public relief over the end of the war gave rise to what by DPRK standards was considered a festive nightlife, which continued for over a year in the face of both continued material hardship and a propaganda campaign aimed at restoring the old Stakhanovite ethic.

[66] Yi Ch'ŏlchu, 193, 185.

In the meantime the Soviet-Koreans turned their attention to their old foe Ch'oe Sŭnghŭi. Immediately after an open rehearsal of her new dance piece, Vice-Minister of Propaganda Ki Sŏkpok complained that it lacked thematic unity. Yi Ch'ŏlchu remembers the occasion as follows:

> "Comrade Ch'oe Sŭnghŭi, where have you located the center of conflict in this piece?....Is it a call for resistance against the Americans, or for struggle against indolent elements in post-war reconstruction? Come now, which one is it?"
>
> The penetrating questions which Ki Sŏkpok put forth in his clumsy Hamgyŏng dialect were on the mark. One could recognize what the choreographer had intended, but the piece itself was extremely diffuse....In front of all assembled, the highest cultural functionaries in North Korea, Ch'oe could hardly defend herself from the barrage of concentrated criticism, while [her husband] An Mak sat silently in a corner and listened with eyes closed.[67]

It is characteristic of the North Korean cultural scene that Ki's comments, though "on the mark," were immediately recognized by Yi Ch'ŏlchu and the others present as factionally motivated. Judging by Ch'oe's dumbfounded reaction, her ties to Han had hitherto afforded her a like exemption from criticism. Her mortified husband An seems to have recognised that as Han's "right-hand man" he would be the next in line for attack.

But Kim Il Sung had too great a stake in Han to sit idly by while the latter's stature in the cultural sector was undermined. After all, Han had only months before elevated the personality cult to new heights with *Ryŏksa* (History, 1953), the first full-length novel about the colonial exploits of the General and his band of anti-Japanese partisans.[68] In spring of 1954, therefore, Kim decreed another rectification campaign. Its ostensible function was to give writers and artists an opportunity to confess all errors and "thought crimes" committed during the war, but under Han's direction the daily self-criticism sessions quickly devolved into an extended polemic against Yi T'aejun, whose long-forgotten membership in the aestheticist Nine Man Group (*Kuinhoe*) of the 1930s was now trotted out as proof of lifelong reactionary tendencies. Writers were grilled on past ties to the writer, no matter how trivial. The poetess Kim Kwiyŏn confessed that she had once given him a few eggs during the war. Various Soviet-Korean and

---

[67] Ibid., 199.

[68] *Ryŏksa*, in *HSYS*, 9:1-360.

SKWP writers also came under attack for supporting him. Now it was the vice-chairman's turn to listen "quietly, with eyes closed."[69] The regime stopped short of purging or even demoting Yi T'aejun himself, however, apparently still afraid of a collision with his Soviet-Korean backers that might strain relations with the USSR. Of Yi's followers in the WU, only those who had already confessed to ties with Yim Hwa and Kim Namch'ŏn during the preceding year's rectification drive were purged. All others now began writing frantically to prove their allegiance to the regime.[70]

In December 1954, a year and a half after Stalin's death, the Second Soviet Writers' Congress convened in Moscow. While avoiding direct criticism of socialist realism itself, several speakers criticised the bureaucratization of cultural affairs, and demanded the freedom to present conflicts and contradictions still existing in Soviet life.[71] North Korean delegates to the congress, among them Yi Kiyŏng (who delivered a servile tribute to Soviet cultural leadership),[72] undoubtedly brought the report of the incipient "thaw" home with them. In January 1955 Han's Soviet counterpart Aleksei Surkov (1899-1983), a member of the reformist camp, visited the DPRK and gave a speech to assembled writers on such problems as the individuality of the author.[73] Yet there is nothing to substantiate Scalapino and Lee's claim that these developments created "by the spring of 1955 a literary controversy...[which] quickly became translated into a factional quarrel," nor is there any evidence that Yi T'aejun and his supporters launched an attack on Han Sŏrya from a reformist platform.[74]

The only echo of the trends in Moscow was in fact a March 1955 *Chosŏn munhak* article written by none other than Han-ally Ŏm Hosŏk, and it was speedily condemned by both factions. In "*Sahoejuŭi sasilchuŭiwa uriŭi munhak*" (Socialist Realism and Our Literature) Ŏm criticised a recent adaptation of a fairy tale which cast a landlord as villain and a tenant farmer

---

[69] Yi Ch'ŏlchu, 204-214.

[70] Ibid., 192, 222.

[71] Marc Slonim, *Soviet Russian Literature: Writers and Problems 1917-1977* (New York, 1977), 324-325.

[72] He is quoted by V.I. Ivanova in "Sovetskaia literatura v Koree (1945-1955)," *Problemy Dal'nego vostoka* 3 (11 1974): 192.

[73] Ibid., 192-193.

[74] See Scalapino and Lee, 1:493, 1:501. The historians seem confused about the time of the campaign against Yim Hwa and Kim Namch'ŏn, which had of course taken place three years earlier.

as hero. He felt this "narrowed" a story of the eternal conflict between good and evil, and created dangerous misconceptions:

> The formula that all landlords are bad and all tenant farmers honest does not entirely conform to reality. Because we know that in real life there are good and honest people, as well as selfish and bad people, among both tenant farmers and landlords....Conflicts between selfish and honest people are not confined to a society of landlords and tenant farmers, but are still common in our society, almost 10 years after the elimination of the feudal system of landlords and tenants. So by putting the story in the class framework of landlords and tenants, the adapters give the impression to our youngsters that since the only selfish people are landlords, and they have all been purged, then there are no selfish people in our society. This is harmful.[75]

From a socialist realist standpoint the first part of Ŏm's argument is untenable, for whether good landlords and selfish tenants exist is irrelevant; the question is whether they are "typical" enough to merit depiction. What Ŏm was ultimately getting at, of course, was that the complete absence of conflict in stories on topical themes, about which readers had begun to make their displeasure known, resulted directly from the disinclination of writers to acknowledge the continued existence of negative elements in DPRK society. Ŏm was particularly irked by the failure to depict domestic tension, which he considered more likely now than before, when women had acquiesced to their husbands' wishes as a matter of course. He ended his article by calling for the production of works dealing with real conflict in the workplace and the home.[76]

Though Ŏm was of course echoing his reformist Soviet colleagues, he would probably not have raised the issue had he not felt bolstered by the official KWP line, according to which the notion of a classless and conflictless socialist society was a chimera that could only induce a sense of false security. What he seems to have forgotten, however, was the regime's aversion to acknowledging that counterrevolutionaries were numerous enough to be encountered by the average citizen, lest this provide solace to such elements, or even give good people bad ideas. This was why Kim Il Sung, for all his talk of omnipresent class enemies, regularly claimed 100% support from the electorate—and why villains in stories about the

---

[75] Hong Sunch'ŏl quotes the article at length in "Küllojadŭrŭi kyegŭpchŏk kyoyanggwa munhak p'yŏngnon," *CM*, April 1955, 173. I have been unable to find the March issue itself.

[76] Ibid., 175.

DPRK would continue to be mere nuisances outside the great harmonious circle: clownish ex-landlords, for example, or cave-dwelling saboteurs who emerge at night in sheets to scare superstitious villagers.[77] As for conflict between husbands and wives, the Leader had made his male chauvinism clear enough in his criticism of *Land*.

In short, Ŏm's article was roundly condemned, both by Han crony Hong Sunch'ŏl *and* Soviet-Korean critic Chŏng Ryul. There had been enough conservative speakers at the Soviet Congress (e.g. Fadeev) to allow the claim that Ŏm had misinterpreted the general tenor of what had been said there. Chŏng called in a speech for a reaffirmation of socialist realist principles, and harshly criticised poets reluctant to fulfil the thematic tasks allotted them by the party.[78] To reinforce the impression that the Soviet reformers were a tiny minority, speeches by conservatives were translated, published, and approvingly discussed over the following months. The contemporary Chinese campaign against liberal dissident Hu Feng (1903-1985), who had attacked restraints on intellectual freedom the year before, was also given prominent place in literary magazines.[79]

The thirtieth anniversary of KAPF's founding fell in the summer of 1955. This was convenient for Han, who used the occasion to promote further a literary-historical myth legitimizing his chairmanship in the face of the Soviet-Korean challenge. The following is a distilled version of the myth as it was presented in articles and speeches by his cronies throughout 1955:

In 1925 KAPF was formed around the nucleus of Yi Kiyŏng and Han Sŏrya, and was immediately joined by numerous progressive writers. In the first two years Han demolished the *l'art pour l'art* movement with masterful critical articles before turning his pen against liberal KAPF members like Kim Kijin and Pak Yŏnghŭi. After KAPF's reorganization in 1927 Yi and Han began producing socialist realist masterpieces like *Wŏnbo* (Yi) and *Transition Period* (Han), which inspired other KAPF writers to reflect the growth of class consciousness and the struggle for national liberation in their own works.

---

[77] See for example Yi Kiyŏng's *Kaebyŏk* and *Ttang*, Han Sŏrya's *Ryongaksan* (Part 3 of the *Taedonggang* trilogy, 1955), and Yu Hangnim's *Sŏngsire taehan iyagi* (Pyongyang, 1958).

[78] "Tongmaeng che 17 ch'a hwaktae sangmu wiwŏnhoe," *CM*, June 1955, 207.

[79] See Kuo Mojo (kor. Kwak Maryak), "Ho P'ungŭi pansahoejuŭijŏk kangnyŏng," *CM*, July 1955, 172-181; also Ch'ae Ŭi, "Ho P'ungŭi purŭjo yusim nonjŏk sasangŭl pip'anham," *CM*, November 1955, 142-162. For more on Hu Feng, see C.T. Hsia, *A History of Modern Chinese Fiction 1917-1957* (New Haven/London, 1961), 333-336.

In the 1930s Kim Il Sung's guerilla struggle stimulated KAPF literature to an even higher stage of development. The Japanese reacted by stepping up their oppression of the group, finally dissolving it by force in 1935. The reactionary infiltrators Yim Hwa and Kim Namch'ŏn chose this moment to reveal their true natures. Together with bourgeois collaborationist Yi T'aejun and his Nine Man Group they began propagating naturalism and formalism.

All this only spurred the KAPF veterans on to new creative heights. Around this time Han's *Dusk* and Yi Kiyŏng's *Home Town* appeared, the most excellent works of the colonial period. Japanese oppression increased again, but led by Yi and Han the former KAPF writers continued their struggle until the liberation.[80]

The precedence given to Yi Kiyŏng's role was a clever touch. While it gave the myth a much-needed grounding in truth, it left Han's hold on power secure, for Yi, according to all reports, was known to have little interest in holding bureaucratic office.[81] The climax of the KAPF anniversary was a public ceremony on 24 August 1955 attended by the group's "founders and central activists, led by Yi Kiyŏng, Han Sŏrya, Song Yŏng, Pak Seyŏng and others."[82] The KAPF myth was presented in tributes by Yi Pungmyŏng ("Han Sŏrya and I"), An Hamgwang and Song Yŏng. Excerpts from *Home Town* and *Dusk*, which was republished in 1955 after an infusion of anti-Japanese rhetoric, were read aloud.[83] *Chosŏn munhak* published a few congratulatory telegrams from the Soviet Writers Union. These would be touted for years after as evidence of KAPF's international renown.[84]

Meanwhile Kim Il Sung had finally decided it was safe to move against the Soviet-Koreans in his government. In autumn 1955 prominent members of the faction came under attack as sectarian elements and began to be forced out of office. To defend themselves they entered into an alliance with the so-called Yenan faction. The ensuing struggle was reflected on the cultural scene:

> Writers and artists found themselves in the middle of the struggle
> between Kim Il Sung's Kapsan faction, [vice-premier] Pak

---

[80] Summarized from An Hamgwang, "Haebangjŏn chinbojŏk munhak," *CM*, August 1955, 171-181; "Sin'gan sogae: Han Sŏrya chak *Hwanghon* kaegan," *CM*, April 1955, 200. The falsehoods are too numerous to point out here; the reader is referred to Chapter 1 for the facts.

[81] Yi Ch'ŏlchu, 196.

[82] "KAP'Ŭ ch'anggŏn 30 chunyŏn kinyŏmŭi pam," *CM*, September 1955, 201.

[83] Ibid., 205.

[84] "Chakka tongmaengesŏ," *CM*, September 1955, 199-201.

> Ch'angok's Soviet faction, and Ch'oe Ch'angik's Yenan faction;
> they were criticised from this side, then from that side, and then
> the Yi T'aejun faction would be criticised, and soon all were
> shaking with fear.[85]

In November 1955 Kim clearly gained the upper hand. At the same time criticism of Yi T'aejun increased in intensity. In December 1955 the writer was finally purged and sent to work in a cooperative.[86] On 27 December 1955 a conference of KWP agitators and propagandists was convoked. Han delivered the opening speech, which appears to have been a harangue against the Soviet-Korean faction for its errors on the cultural sector. Unfortunately little is known of what Han said except that he criticised the *Rodong sinmun*'s editors for ignoring the important historical role of the indigenous proletarian movement.[87]

The next day, on 28 December 1955, Kim Il Sung delivered his famous *Chuch'e* (self-reliance) speech. The need to bolster Han's position appears to have played a larger role in the speech's formulation than historians recognize.[88] Indeed, it was probably the reason Kim had chosen to let Han precede him as a speaker. Kim criticised the Soviet-Koreans for a variety of transgressions, but at the top of the list was conspiring with the "reactionary bourgeois writer Yi T'aejun," and failing to accord the KAPF movement's prominent veterans the proper respect:

> When I asked Pak Ch'angok and his followers why they rejected
> KAPF, they answered that they did so because some renegades
> had been involved in it. Did they really mean to say that the
> KAPF of which Comrades Han Sŏrya and Yi Kiyŏng formed the
> nucleus was an organization of no importance? We must value
> highly the feats of those comrades in the revolutionary struggle,
> and *allow them to play the central role in the development of our
> literature today.*[89] (emphasis added)

---

[85] Yi Ch'ŏlchu, 222.

[86] Ibid.

[87] This is known from Kim Il Sung's references to the speech, which are dealt with presently.

[88] Scalapino and Lee refer to an edition of the speech that makes no mention of Han, having appeared after his purge. Considering the attention the historians devote elsewhere in their book to the DPRK's cultural scene, it is strange that they should dismiss the difference between this version and the original as "not significant." See *Communism in Korea*, 1:500.

[89] Kim Il Sung, "Sasang saŏbesŏ kyojojuŭiwa hyŏngsikchuŭirŭl t'oech'i hago chuch'erŭl hwangnip halte taehayŏ," in *Kim Ilsŏng sŏnjip* (Pyongyang, 1960), 4:329.

To underscore his support for the WU chairman, Kim made approving references to the speech Han had given the day before, and went out of his way to tell everyone that Han had joined him in opposing the Soviet-Koreans' bizarre scheme to enlist abducted writer Yi Kwangsu in the DPRK propaganda effort.[90] It was clearly not Kim's intention in this speech to glorify KAPF's literature itself (which he never even mentioned), nor to improve the standing of the already respected Yi Kiyŏng. Rather, Kim was determined to end the power struggles on the cultural front by legitimizing the leadership of Han—the only writer, one was to believe, with both the revolutionary credentials and the will needed to "play the central role" in North Korean literary development.

b)　Han Sŏrya's Fiction

Sŭngnyangi (Jackals, 1951)

Han's most lasting success in the DPRK has been the novella *Sŭngnyangi* (Jackals, 1951), a story of murderous US missionaries in colonial Korea. It is not difficult to guess the source of inspiration for the work, as tales of foreign clerics kidnapping local children for use in grisly medical experiments had been circulating in Korea since the late nineteenth century.[91] Though not a war story as such, *Jackals'* fiercely ethnocentric mix of anti-American and anti-Christian propaganda marks it as a typical work of the Korean War era. The plot is a simple one:

One day a little boy named Sugil finds a rubber ball near the American Christian mission where his mother, widowed since the death of her imprisoned union-activist husband, works as a charwoman. The boy and his friends play with the ball until they are interrupted by the missionary's fifteen-year-old son Simon, who claims it belongs to him, and then beats Sugil into unconsciousness for the "theft." The missionary watches the incident from afar, but worries only that his son may have soiled his "sacred" hands by touching the "filthy" Korean child.

---

[90] Ibid., 325, 329, 334.

[91] See Robert Scalapino, "The Foreign Policy of North Korea," in *North Korea Today*, ed. Robert Scalapino (New York, 1963), 37. Similar tales were widespread in Japan and China: see John Dower, *War Without Mercy: Race and Power in the Pacific War* (New York, 1986), 238; Joseph R. Levenson, *Confucian China and its Modern Fate* (Berkeley, 1968), 112.

Soon after, the missionary's wife Mary appears at Sugil's sick bed to assure his distraught mother that he will receive the best possible care at the mission hospital. He is promptly admitted, but the Americans are less interested in saving him than in covering up the incident. To this end they decide to inject him with bacillae, so he will appear to have died from a contagious disease. In the following days Sugil's mother becomes unsettled by ominous rumors about the hospital, and finally resolves to have the boy transferred to a patriotic Korean doctor's care. By then, however, the American hospital director has placed Sugil in quarantine, and refuses to let his mother see him.

Shortly thereafter a man arrives at her home and brusquely informs her of her son's death. Unable to believe what she has heard, she runs to the hospital, where an orderly hands her Sugil's cremated remains in a box. Only when offered a token consolation sum does she finally comprehend her misfortune. In a blind rage, she hurries to the missionaries' house, where she finds her enemies at the dinner table. In a flash of truth they appear before her as a pack of lupine monstrosities. An exchange of hysterical accusations and religious shibboleths leads to a tussle, during which Simon summons a policeman. "Just you wait," cries Sugil's mother as she is dragged away, "not all Koreans have died!"[92]

The characters of Sugil and his mother require no special explanation; like *Growing Village*'s Kŭmbok and Yŏngmin (whose name had been Sugil in the original *Village People*), they are typical North Korean heroes, designed not to represent a particular ideology or social class, but to embody "truly Korean" qualities, foremost among them *sobak ham*, with all its connotations of benevolent naivete, innocence, and spontaneity.

Like the heroes' positive qualities, so too are the negative characteristics of the eponymous villains to be understood as inborn. It is not their class origin, which is never indicated, nor their religion, which they acknowledge is a mere weapon of ethnic warfare, but their "typically American" desire to exploit and destroy other races which determines their actions. Han is so intent on making this clear that he presents the boy Simon, who exhibits none of his parents' religiosity or political awareness, as the most vicious character and the one most responsible for the central crime. The Americans' predatory nature is underscored throughout by extensive use of lupine and vulpine imagery, with the narratorial voice itself often referring to the missionary as a wolf, his wife as a vixen, and so on. In the book's last pages they are also called "evil spirits" (*angma*). There is no precedent for this kind of vilification in Korean literary tradition, nor in

---

[92] Based on *Sŭngnyangi* (Tokyo, 1954). This is the earliest version of the story I could find.

socialist realism. Han was most probably influenced by the conventions of
the anti-American propaganda with which he and his countrymen had been
bombarded during the Second World War. John Dower writes in *War
Without Mercy*:

> The marks of the beast [in Japanese propaganda] were claws,
> fangs, animal hindquarters, sometimes a tail, sometimes small
> horns—all of which, however, also marked a transition from the
> plain beast to the quasi-religious demon or devil. This latter
> stereotype was the dominant metaphor in Japanese propaganda
> against the enemy....Anglo-Americans were described as...*evil
> spirits (akki* and *akuma)*....A journalistic account...was
> accompanied by an illustration of *Uncle Sam as a sharp-nailed,
> sharp-toothed clergyman with the tail of a fox.*[93] (emphasis mine)

A Christian in a Japanese propaganda magazine's satire asks, "Is not peace
what occurs when all black men and yellow men serve us? Ah God! Has
God fallen asleep? Amen."[94] Han's "jackals" express themselves in similarly
half-diabolical, half-ludicrous fashion:

> "There are countless ways of dealing with the situation, are
> there not? I mean, just diagnose a dangerous contagious disease
> or something, and quarantine it [i.e., Sugil] at once. And don't
> let anyone near it, do you hear?"
> "Yes, that is what I was thinking."
> "Goooood. Spoken like a true American. We need our own
> virtues, not Korean virtues or any others for that matter." The
> director was silent. "Not only that: we have to demand our
> virtues from others. And if it hasn't got a contagious disease then
> we must give it an injection of bacillae and *make* it a contagious
> disease."
> "Let's just say it's for the sake of the American people—,"
> put in his wife again.
> "It won't be difficult."
> "Very good, director....The victory of the American people
> and its virtues requires more than just churches. God also gives
> us bullets, airplanes and warships. What do you think the bibles
> are, that we missionaries carry, or our doctors' syringes?"
> "They are weapons for America and its people," answered
> his wife with another twitch of her mouth....

---

[93] John Dower, 244-245.

[94] Ibid., 208.

"So I should dispose of the body entirely," said the director decisively.

"Ah! Right, right. Americans are wise. The day when America rules the world is nigh. May you be imbued with the glory of the American people." The missionary raised his hands and pretended to pray for a moment.[95]

Realism forces Han to provide the Americans with a few locals to help run the hospital, but he is determined not to let them complicate his racial message. They are "all Koreans in name only," one learns through the heroine, "inside they are no different from Americans."[96] Indeed, the fleeting glimpses of the "lackeys"—a few hospital workers and the son of a Reverend Yi—offer no insight into their treason, leaving the reader with the impression, reinforced by a whitish face here, a drooping nose there,[97] that they are simply genetic accidents.

The racist character depiction, the fairy-tale remoteness of the setting, and the triviality of the incident that sets the plot in motion (a children's squabble over a ball!) combine to disabuse the reader of hopes for a "social" storyline. In contrast to Chinua Achebe in the Nigerian classic *Things Fall Apart* (1958),[98] Han makes no effort to explore just *how* Christian missionaries serve as forerunners of Western imperialism, apart from the preposterous implication that the hospital doubles as a credit house. This is not to say that Han does not make his usual halfhearted nods at socialist realist convention. As the story unfolds, he describes in some detail the heroine's good friends (including a revolutionary comrade of her late husband), hints at the existence of an organized underground, and has the missionaries make frequent uneasy references to the Korean people's reckless courage. The reader is thus led to anticipate a village uprising of the kind so common in Chinese communist fiction. In the end, however, the idea of the heroine's total defeat, with its potential for tearful histrionics, apparently proved too tempting for the author. Just when the woman needs her allies the most, they disappear without explanation from the narrative: she must career towards her doom with minimum delay.

Yet it is questionable whether *Jackals* succeeds even as melodrama. Han is no Dickens, and thus cannot prevent the juxtaposition of conventional

---

[95] *Sǔngnyangi*, 50-53.

[96] Ibid., 63.

[97] Ibid., 5, 64.

[98] *Things Fall Apart* (London, 1958).

heroes and grotesquely lampooned villains from imbuing the entire story, the central tragedy included, with a surreal quality. The scene in which the dying Sugil promises his mother good marks in the coming school year is the sort of trusty tearjerking motif still popular in South Korean soap operas, but in the bizarre world of the "jackals'" hospital it seems almost to parody itself.[99] Later the dialogue between Sugil's mother, whose failure to grasp the tragedy is drawn out too long for effect, and the orderly, who implausibly treats the boy's death as a trivial mishap, takes on an equally incongruous Kafkaesque ring:

> "It's hospital policy. The rule says that to prevent contamination anyone who has died of a contagious disease must be cremated immediately. Therefore—"
> But Sugil's mother could not understand a word. "Where is Sugil?" she asked.
> "I shall give him to you." The man in the white medical smock went to the shelf and took down a little box wrapped in white cloth. Proffering it to her with both hands, he said, "Here is your son. Please." She gazed blankly at the box, but unable to comprehend what it was, did not even attempt to take it. "This is your son." Still she said nothing. "This is what was left after the fire. Please."
> "Fire?"
> "Yes, it's hospital policy."[100]

The author himself, however, appears beyond himself with rage at the story he is telling—so much so, in fact, that in the climactic scene of the heroine's hallucinatory anagnorisis he seems to lose all control over his craft:

> The old jackal's spade-shaped eagle's nose hung villainously over his upper lip, while the vixen's teats jutted out like the stomach of a snake that has just swallowed a demon, and the slippery wolf-cub gleamed with poison like the head of a venomous snake that has just shed its skin. Their six sunken eyes seemed to Sugil's mother like open graves constantly waiting for corpses.[101]

---

[99] Ibid., 38-42.

[100] Ibid., 68-69.

[101] Ibid., 72.

This overheated style is sustained until the end. Beside herself with anger and frustration, the heroine bites "so hard into her blood-caked lips that a stream of red blood [comes] spurting out."[102] Page after page of virtually unadulterated, shriek-filled dialogue (fleshed out in a 1960 redaction) follows until she is finally apprehended by a policeman.

This conclusion is reminiscent of the final scene in Gorky's *Mother* (1906), in which the Czarist policeman drags away the defiant Pelagaya. A more fundamental parallel consists in the fact that both stories chronicle a mother's transition from ignorance to knowledge, a process concluded in each case by the death of a son. Yet the two works differ in a way that is characteristic of the irreconcilability of socialist realism and North Korean literature. Gorky's story is the classic transposition of Lenin's spontaneity-consciousness dialectic into biographical categories: through rigorous self-indoctrination the heroine overcomes her naivete and attains political awareness. For Sugil's mother the process is quite the opposite. Over the years she has apparently acquired enough of a veneer of Christianity to oblige her employers and suppress her instinctive misgivings about working for them. The death of her son, for whose sake she has lived this lie for so long, finally induces her to slough off the remains of the un-Korean "consciousness" and heed her "spontaneous," i.e., ethnic aversion to the white race. In the climactic moment of truth the scales fall from her eyes, and in the scene quoted above she "reads" the missionaries' evil in the racial traits distinguishing them from her countrymen: long noses, sunken eyes, and large breasts.

In other words *Jackals*, for all Han's nods at socialist realism (and his debt to Japanese propaganda), belongs squarely in the New Tendency tradition. One is reminded in particular of Ch'oe Sŏhae's *Hongyŏm* (Scarlet Flame, 1926), the story of the Korean tenant Mun's exploitation by a Chinese landlord.[103] The latter is also characterized (albeit more skilfully) by grotesque bestial metaphors: his cheeks, for example, quiver "like an angry toad's stomach."[104] After a bad harvest, the Chinese demands and receives Mun's young daughter, a Sugil-like symbol of Korean innocence, as payment for debt. Like the charwoman's final confrontation with the "jackals," Mun's trip to the foreigner's house to visit his daughter is seen as a descent into hell. Shortly after crossing the gloomy threshold he feels "demonic eyes" on him—only here they gaze out from pictures on the soot-

---

[102] Ibid., 72-73.

[103] *Hongyŏm*, in *Ch'oe Sŏhae sŏnjip* (Pyongyang, 1963), 1:166-193.

[104] Ibid., 1:175.

blackened wall.[105] Like Han's heroine, Mun is arbitrarily refused access to his child. Thereupon Mun's wife dies of *hwappyŏng* (see Ch1). Blind with rage, Mun heads to the house of the foreign enemy. Here the similarities end: Mun splits the landowner's head open with an ax, rescues his daughter, and marvels at his own strength,[106] while Sugil's mother, as we have said, is dragged away before exacting even token revenge. This only underscores the impossibility of regarding Han's work as significantly closer to socialist realism than the first clumsy efforts of colonial proletarian writers.

Elena Berman, a Soviet translator hired by the North Koreans to prepare a Russian-language anthology of Han's short stories, found *Jackals* ideologically offensive enough to warrant a "translator's adaptation," i.e., a thorough rewriting.[107] While leaving plot and characters essentially unchanged, she eliminated the racial overtones entirely (effectively reducing the bestial imagery to the title), and tried to make the villains' actions appear more credible.[108] Critics in the DPRK, however, singled out the story's ethnocentric element for special praise, seemingly unaware of any conflict with socialist realism. Han Chungmo, for example, who described *Jackals* as one of the best works in all North Korean literature, extolled the clear contrast between the cruelty and violence of the American *personality*,[109] and the "deep love of humanity characteristic of the typical, benevolently naive [*sobak han*] Korean people."[110] Mary's snake-stomached vixen teats and the like compelled the same critic to disinter Mayakovsky's defense of the grotesque, though it had been rejected decades ago by Soviet literary theorists.[111] The story's tragic ending posed more serious problems, for Kim Il Sung had made his opposition to just this kind of literary pessimism clear.[112] As it was impossible either to ignore Kim or to fault the WU chairman, Han Chungmo bravely tried to show the story had an

---

[105] Ibid., 1:180.

[106] Ibid., 1:187-193.

[107] *Volki*, in *Khan Ser ia: Sbornik rasskazov* (Pyongyang, 1957), 143-160.

[108] In Berman's version the Americans try to save Sugil's life. When his death appears inevitable, they concoct the typhoid story to avoid a public relations disaster, but see no need to inject him with typhus. Han's talk of a bacillae injection must have been meant to tie in with the allegations of US germ warfare in the Korean War, but it makes no sense in the original, as the corpse is cremated anyway.

[109] Han Chungmo, 320.

[110] Ibid., 316.

[111] Ibid., 325; see Hans Günther, 70.

[112] See Han Sŏrya, "Kim Ilsŏng changgun'gwa minjok munhwaŭi paltchŏn," 29.

uplifting message, mainly by emphasizing the missionaries' *fears* of a village uprising and interpreting the heroine's last words—"But just you wait! Not all Koreans have died"—as a powerful threat.[113] The critic seemed not to care that the Yankees' fears prove completely unfounded, which in turn makes the heroine's parting shot sound downright pathetic.

A good way to find out how DPRK authorities really feel about a work by a high-ranking writer is to examine later redactions. A 1955 dramatization of *Jackals* indicates the authorities not only wholeheartedly approved of Han's equation of ethnic and moral categories, but even felt it should be made clearer to the public.[114] The local lackeys were thus replaced in the play by a naive Korean nurse, who takes a job at the hospital in good faith, but soon proves incapable of going along with the foreigners' schemes. On the other hand, recognition of the original's lack of a socioeconomic dimension led to the introduction of a rapacious US businessman as the missionary's houseguest. And sure enough, the final scene was changed to show the assembled villagers charging the mission while the terrified Yankees await certain death inside. Han, however, was his usual lackadaisical self when preparing the novella for republication in 1960, doing little more than tack on a short paragraph that depicts some sullen villagers following the policeman as he drags Sugil's mother away.[115]

Ryŏksa (History, 1953)

We have already said that the "master plot" of North Korean literature, like that of New Tendency fiction, is based on a virtual reversal of socialist realism's spontaneity-consciousness dialectic. The hero, in other words, does not master his willful self and become disciplined, like his Soviet counterpart, but instead goes from frustrated to liberated spontaneity. Perhaps nowhere is this "master plot" more clearly manifested than in Han Sŏrya's acclaimed novel *Ryŏksa* (History, 1953). The story, which is set in the 1930s, can be summarized as follows:

A leader of anti-Japanese Korean guerillas known as the General visits the school he has founded in the Manchurian mountains for the orphaned children of his fallen troops. No one is more excited by the visit than Kŭmch'ŏl, a fifteen-year-old boy yearning to avenge his father. The General has hardly begun to address the assembled schoolchildren when the lad stands up and

---

[113] Han Chungmo, 317-318, 334.

[114] *Sŭngnyangi*, dram. by Sŏ Manil and Yu Kihong, *CM*, January 1955, 6-67.

[115] See *Sŭngnyangi*, in *HSYS*, 8:420-491. This is the version known to South Koreans through *Kwihyang: Han Sŏrya chakp'umjip*, ed. by Song Hosuk (Seoul, 1990), 323-369.

requests permission to join the partisans. Though impressed by the boy's eagerness and pluck, the General feels he has not yet acquired the degree of hatred and fury needed to become a good fighter.

Soon the General returns to the forest to prepare for an attack on a Japanese barracks. Shortly thereafter Kŭmch'ŏl arrives at his tent. Though he has disobeyed an explicit order to stay in school, the General is secretly pleased that the boy now listens to his instincts. Soon, in an attack on a Japanese barracks, the boy gets a chance to prove himself, and his long-accumulated rage and hatred are released in a frenzy of violence. By the time a second battle ends in victory, Kŭmch'ŏl has become a regular fighter—yet he is still enough of a child to lament not having used all his grenades.[116]

Both the socialist realist and the North Korean "master plot" have the same point of departure: a young hero practically bursting with spontaneity. The headstrong fifteen-year-old presented to the reader at the beginning of *History* is thus similar to the character of Pavel in the first chapters of *How the Steel was Tempered*, Ostrovskii's classic *Bildungsroman*.[117]

The "educator" figures in the respective works, however, are as diametrically opposed as the directions in which they propel their young charges. Ostrovskii's are hardened father figures, who help Pavel attain revolutionary consciousness by propagating discipline and self-indoctrination. The General, on the other hand, is more of a mother figure, what with his fussy concern for the orphans' clothing and hygiene, his invitingly expansive chest, and his round and soft face, which, with its "pretty dimples" and "pretty side-teeth," conforms to the traditional Korean ideal of *feminine* beauty.[118] His dominant feature, and that which leaves the greatest impression on all who see him, is his smile, the expression of his indulgent nature. If socialist realism's fatherly educators confirm Jung's interpretation of the paternal principle as being on the side of discipline and consciousness, then Han Sŏrya's General clearly embodies the maternal principle on the side of the instincts.[119] Not once does he speak to the children of the need for discipline or political awareness. For him "schooling the mind" means channeling hatred and fury at the "Japs":

[116] Based on *Ryŏksa*, in *HSYS*, 9:1-360. Though the work gives the impression of having been written for a juvenile audience, it was treated by literary critics as a regular novel, in contrast to Han's later *Man'gyŏngdae* (1955). Cf. Han Chungmo, 269.

[117] Cf. Nikolai Ostrovskii, *Kak zakalialas' stal'* (Moscow, 1979).

[118] *Ryŏksa*, 28, 247.

[119] Cf. C.G. Jung, *Symbols of Transformation*, vol. 5 of *The Collected Works of C.G. Jung*, trans. by R.F.C. Hull (Princeton, 1956), 207-273.

> "Whenever you train, a Jap's mug must appear in front of
> your rifles. You'll never beat the enemy unless you school your
> mind in this way. With every step you must feel you are stepping
> on a Jap's skull. Every bayonet thrust must impale the hearts of
> ten, of a hundred of the devils. Only then can fame and glory
> return to the Fatherland."[120]

These words achieve the desired effect: as the children listen, a "wonderful
world" opens up before them in which "the apelike Japs roll down the
mountains like acorns."[121] The children become so excited they can hardly
sit still, but when Kŭmch'ŏl pleads to be allowed to join the partisans, for
fear that all "Japs" will be killed before he can avenge his father's death, the
General merely chuckles, promising to leave the boy his "share." He then
tells the tale of Nikita, a fifteen-year-old who pesters his parents for a rifle,
that he may do his part for the Reds in the Russian Civil War. The General
describes the lad's father as refusing the request, whereupon Nikita dreams
of his mother throwing him a rifle. As if that were not Jungian enough,
Nikita then uses his mother's key to steal his father's rifle from a chest.
Armed with his new weapon, Nikita singlehandedly dispatches a few White
soldiers, whereupon he is allowed to join the Red Army. Here the General's
story ends, with no indication that the lad's egocentric hotheadedness stands
to bring him into conflict with superiors.[122]

Naturally enough Kŭmch'ŏl who is also fifteen, feels encouraged by
the tale and begins to importune the General once more:

> "I'm really going to join the partisan unit this time."
> "Hahaha....So that's your 'special request'?"....As the General
> took another look at Kŭmch'ŏl, who seemed to him like an
> extraordinarily resilient rubber ball, he thought to himself: How
> quickly this boy will come running someday..."You're still not
> ready." Thus did the General speak, but in his heart he pictured
> to himself with pleasure how the boy would come running all the
> quicker for each setback he experienced.[123]

Far from valuing discipline, in other words, the General turns down his
request in the hope that the lad will disobey him and report for duty

---

[120] *Ryŏksa*, 37.

[121] Ibid.

[122] Ibid., 44.

[123] Ibid., 57.

anyway. Soon Kŭmch'ŏl and the other children receive another "training" session:

> Once more the General was certain that Kŭmch'ŏl could vividly see his parents' enemies before him; the boy's eyes sharply focused on the target expressed this clearly. But the General wanted to whip up the fire in the boy's breast a hundred, a thousand times.[124]

Then, during a school lesson in the General's absence, Kŭmch'ŏl draws a picture of a Japanese hit by a bullet. Under his teacher's watchful eye he stabs furiously at the likeness with the pencil, finally boring a hole in the paper. At last the reader feels certain there will be a few words about the need for discipline. But no: the teacher is deeply impressed by the boy's intensity, and believes he has learnt a valuable and humbling lesson from him.[125] The learning process of the socialist realist novel is thus reversed: naive willfulness is infused into the "conscious" educators!

When Kŭmch'ŏl finally runs away from school and reports uninvited to the partisans' mountain hideout, the General, not unlike the mother in Nikita's dream, rewards the boy's contumacy with a gun, ordering him to go and kill an enemy with it singlehandedly.[126] Kŭmch'ŏl wanders around in the woods for a few days but there are no "Japs" in sight, only little stray dogs which he dispatches with kicks to the stomach.[127] Recognising that his young charge's hatred and fury have finally reached boiling point, the General allows him to take part in the long planned attack on a Japanese barracks. The ensuing scene is not for the squeamish:

> Kŭmch'ŏl could feel his bitter heart begin to open, the heart that could only open at the sight of Jap's blood. A terrible storm was now raging inside him. "My father's enemies!" The long-accumulated hatred surged up in him like a mad wind. Half-insane he charged into a nearby room. There was still one Jap....
>
> "Filthy son of a bitch! So you want to live. But you enjoyed killing others, didn't you?" The Jap's neck glistening greasily

---

[124] Ibid., 126.

[125] Ibid., 149-150.

[126] Ibid., 216.

[127] Ibid., 220. As animal lover and appalled Korea-visitor Jack London would not have been surprised to learn, dog-kicking is not the infallible indicator of villainy in Korean literature and film that it is in the West. See "How the Hermit Kingdom Behaves in Time of War," in *Jack London Reports* (New York, 1970), 76.

like a pig's. When Kŭmch'ŏl saw it the fire in his breast raged
more intensely....He yanked the bastard up by the neck and
dragged him out of the box, where he fell down again. Then
Kŭmch'ŏl saw he had pissed on the papers in the box from fear.
Kŭmch'ŏl spat on his pale mug....Unable to speak, the Jap bowed
his head and pressed his hands together, pleading soundlessly for
mercy.
> "Son of a bitch! So you don't want to die?"....Kŭmch'ŏl
wanted to cut the swine's neck open with his own hands.[128]

The captive is able to get away for a moment, but

before having gone ten paces he fell over, his hands on his chest.
Kŭmch'ol had needed only two shots to bore a hole through his
heart. Almost simultaneously he caught up with him and dealt his
skull a furious kick. The eyeballs sprang out of their sockets as
the skull splattered against the barrack wall.[129]

This orgy of unrestrained savagery, which makes the New Tendency's
hunger-and-arson stories seem sophisticated, marks the climax of the hero's
"development." The second battle affords neither Kŭmch'ŏl nor the narrator
as much pleasure as the first, but the General, laughing as always, promises
plenty of future occasions for glory.[130]

History was regarded as one of the DPRK's greatest novels until
Han's purge. In his 1955 literary history Han Hyo accorded it more space
than Yi Kiyŏng's *Land*.[131] In 1958, five years after it was written, it received
the People's Prize, the DPRK's highest award for a work of art.[132] Most of
the acclaim had to do with the fact that it was the first long work of fiction
to deal with the guerilla struggle of Kim Il Sung—for the jovial General is
of course none other.

Rather than conclude a study of Han's fiction in the early 1950s
without discussing the period's dominant genre, let us take a brief look at
the glorification of spontaneity in Han's Korean War stories. One work
already mentioned is *Chŏnbyŏl* (Soldier's Farewell, 1951), the tale of a
wounded KPA man restored to fighting health by an old country widow.
Like the nursing mother-figures in Soviet-Korean friendship fiction she

---

[128] *Ryŏksa*, 254-255.

[129] Ibid., 255.

[130] Ibid., 349.

[131] Han Hyo, "Uri munhagŭi 10 nyŏn," 2:140-143.

[132] Song Hosuk, 402.

carries the hero around on his back. Her home is for him (in one of Han's trademark mixed metaphors) "a warm nest like a mother's breast."[133] Yet she is also a "spontaneity-mother" who stimulates the hero's fighting urges. Like Kŭmch'ŏl in his relationship to the maternal General, the hero must kill to prove himself worthy of his surrogate mother's love:

> Changsu's grandmother asked Yongju, "So, are you up to killing Yankees yet?"
> "Of course...Ma, what if I became your real son?"....
> "Be quiet, I already have a son."
> "Couldn't you use another one?"
> "I have enough trouble just raising one properly."
> "What do you mean, didn't he get a medal?"
> "Now listen, if I was a little younger, I'd go in the army and show you boys. You'd be no match for me. Sissies!....Can't you bring me fifty of those rotten sardine eyes on a line?" Her words were harsh, but they gave Yongju strength.
> "Ma, this time Yŏngik and I will bring you Yankees like sardines on a line, I promise. That would make me your son for sure, wouldn't it?"
> "Just eat your rice."[134]

Then there is *Haebangt'ap* (Liberation Tower, 1953), whose adolescent but motherly heroine Chŏmsun, a saboteuse in UN-occupied Pyongyang, is constantly striving to cultivate the spontaneity of her younger male comrades. Like the General in *History*, she is successful, making one young friend's mouth water with thoughts of "a thousand enemy throats slashed in one fell swoop."[135] Not surprisingly, the only problematic figure among Chŏmsun's friends is the one lacking spontaneity: gaunt, thin-lipped Sangnak, who spends too much time trying to raise his political awareness through self-education. His "reformation" to a spontaneous fighter forms an important subplot in the trilogy.

While war in socialist realism makes "conscious" men of "spontaneous" boys, the heroes of the Korean battlefield never lose their infantile willfulness—like the tank driver in Han's *Ttangk'ŭ 214 ho* (Tank 214, 1953):

---

[133] *Chŏnbyŏl*, in *HSYS*, 8:397.

[134] Ibid., 417.

[135] *Haebangt'ap* (Tokyo, 1954), 61.

The skin was dark, but the face was both noble and adorable, *like the face of a small child*. Chŏn Kiryŏn's expression didn't even change when he rolled over the enemy [with the tank]....Chŏn was a twenty-one-year-old *boy*. A voice within comrade Sŏ suddenly called out, "You kill people with a smile, *you little rascal*, you were born to beat the enemy!"[136] (emphasis mine)

The reader is reminded that the glorification of spontaneity had a tradition extending back to the New Tendency. Though not always as crudely expressed as in Han's work, it makes itself felt throughout North Korean literature—most obviously in a preponderance of juvenile or young unmarried adult heroes with a childlike innocence and playfulness. As a rule they are either orphans or reside with their widowed mothers, around whom they display a tendency to "play the baby," and who indulge them in return. Fathers, older brothers and teachers are conspicuous by their rarity (particularly considering Korea's Confucian tradition); when they do appear it is virtually never in the role of disciplinarian or consciousness-infusing figures. The few political cadres that appear are usually shown trying to implement party policy by affective means, so as not to diminish the *sobak ham* of their charges.[137]

---

[136] *Ttangk'ŭ 214 ho*, in *HSYS*, 8:563.

[137] See for example the cadres in Ch'ŏn Sebong's *Sŏkkaeurŭi saepom I* (Pyongyang, 1955), and in Yi Kiyŏng's *Ttang*.

4
Han's "Golden Age"
(1956-1961)

a)   The "Han Machine" and the Ch'ŏllima Movement

At an "enthusiasts' conference" held in Pyongyang from 23-24 January 1956, Han Sŏrya assumed a triumphal pose, apparently aware that Kim Il Sung's *Chuch'e* speech had rendered him virtually unassailable. After an introduction by An Mak, he launched into a lengthy diatribe against vanquished rival Yi T'aejun, condemning everything he had written during the colonial era as "reactionary," and denouncing his entire post-liberation oeuvre as part of the Yim Hwa/Pak Hŏnyŏng conspiracy to "propagate reactionary bourgeois ideology, weaken the revolutionary consciousness of the masses, and provide ideological assistance to the US invaders."[1] Han singled out Yi's wartime story *US Embassy* for special criticism, claiming it had slandered KPA soldiers by depicting them as bloodthirsty and undisciplined.[2] Those present must have been aware that this was a mere victory dance with little pertinence to real literary issues. After all, the Great Leader himself had once personally congratulated Yi on *US Embassy*,[3] and the story would not have been published at all had it not first been approved by the official censors in the Han-faction dominated Publications Bureau. In any case many writers, Han among them, had depicted equally unchivalrous orgies of violence in their war fiction (as we have seen with *History*). During the 1950s, however, it became ritual to subject a purged man's

---

[1] "P'yŏngyang sidang kwanha munhak yesul sŏnjŏn ch'ulp'an pumun yŏlsŏngja hoeŭiesŏ han Han Sŏrya tongjiŭi pogo," *RS*, 15 February 1956.

[2] Ibid.

[3] Yi Ch'ŏlchu, 235.

oeuvre, including works that had hitherto enjoyed official praise, to this kind of categorical execration. The critical apparatus failed to recognize that this tactic would further weaken the authority of socialist realism by making writers more confused than ever about what it really stood for.

Han then began excoriating Soviet-Koreans Chŏng Ryul and Ki Sŏkpok, whose expulsion from the WU presidium for "supporting and protecting the reactionary writers Yim Hwa, Yi T'aejun and Kim Namch'ŏn" had been announced two weeks earlier.[4] Han reminded his audience of Ki's support for Kim Namch'ŏn's controversial short story *Honey*, and of Chŏng's part in the infamous *Fragrant Scent* anthology of 1946. His main criticism, however, centered on the Soviet-Koreans' negation of the indigenous proletarian literary tradition. Chŏng, he fulminated, had dated the beginning of Korean socialist realism to 1945, while Ki had described the prose style of the colonial period as "critical realism." Their "anti-KAPF" campaign, Han claimed, had been part of a conspiracy to wrest control of the WU from its "nucleus" of KAPF veterans.[5] This last assertion is particularly interesting, amounting as it does to Han's admission that a) the KAPF myth was vital to his legitimacy as WU chairman and b) that his leadership had been a prime reason for the cultural sector's unrest.

It seems the party had taken the accusations against Hong Sunch'ŏl seriously when they were first raised in 1954, but had postponed his punishment to avoid the impression of subservience to Yi T'aejun and his backers. Now it decreed Hong's demotion (euphemistically couched in terms of a "transfer") from WU secretary to vice-chairman.[6] Six months later, in June 1956, he was demoted to the ranks.[7] Shortly thereafter the post of secretary was eliminated entirely, presumably to prevent future Hong-like abuses of power.[8] The discretion with which Hong was eased out lends weight to Yi Ch'ŏlchu's assertion that the secretary had procured women for

---

[4] See "Tongmaeng kigu kanghwawa chojikchŏk taech'aegŭl wihan kyŏlchŏng," *CM*, February 1956, 218-219.

[5] "Han Sŏrya tongjiŭi pogo."

[6] See "Tongmaeng kigu kanghwa," 219. The poet Pak P'aryang (1905-?) became the new secretary.

[7] See "Chosŏn chakka tongmaeng chungang wiwŏnhoe che 26 ch'a sangmu wiwŏnhoeesŏ," *CM*, June 1956, 209.

[8] At the same time the number of vice-chairmen was expanded to three. This may have been intended to prevent an accumulation of power similar to Yi T'aejun's. "Tongmaeng kakkŭp kigwandŭrŭi sŏn'gŏwa kak pusŏ sŏngwŏndŭrŭi immyŏng," *CM*, November 1956, 202-204.

Han, and was thus in a position to incriminate him.[9] (Official charges of Han's philandering were raised during his purge in 1962.) Only in 1957, after Hong had finally been expelled from the WU and sent to work in a factory, did Han feel safe enough to begin reviling his quondam friend as "a typical anti-party and reactionary element."[10] This time he was forced to forgo the usual calumniation accorded the writings of purge victims, as Hong's poems (which included a recent panegyric to Kim Il Sung in the *Rodong sinmun*) had always enjoyed the special praise of his own faction.[11] The best Han could do was claim, apparently not without justification, that others had written Hong's poems for him.[12]

The Third Congress of the Korean Workers' Party convened in April 1956. The criticism of the cultural sector contained in Kim Il Sung's opening report was quoted repeatedly in the following months, though it offered the usual, now ten-year-old formulae:

> There are still many cases of our writers and artists being removed from the real life and creative labor of the working class, which has had an extremely negative effect on their artistic activity....When writers and artists arm themselves better with Marxism-Leninism and penetrate deeper into the masses, they will be able to describe the form of our society correctly, and their work will fulfil the hopes and demands of our people.[13]

The congress marked the beginning of a sharp rise in Han Sŏrya's political stature. On the Central Committee roster he moved up from 24th to 18th place. A month later he was appointed Minister of Education[14]—a particularly influential post in communist countries, and one that placed him

---

[9] *Pugŭi yesurin*, 189.

[10] Han Sŏrya, "Uri munhagŭi saeroun ch'angjakchŏk angyangŭl wihayŏ," *CM*, December 1957, 17.

[11] See Han's "Paltchŏn tosange orŭn chŏnhuŭi Chosŏn munhak," *CM*, January 1955, 116; Hong Sunch'ŏl, "Saehae insa," *RS*, 1 January 1956.

[12] "Chŏnhu Chosŏn munhagŭi hyŏn sangt'aewa chŏnmang," in *Che 2 ch'a Chosŏn chakka taehoe: Munhŏnjip* (Pyongyang, 1956), 17. Similar claims were made by Pak Sŏkchŏng in "Hong Sunch'ŏrŭi chakp'ume taehayŏ," *MS*, 27 February 1958. See also Hyŏn Su, 90-91; Yi Ch'ŏlchu, 184.

[13] Quoted by Han in "Uri munhagŭi saeroun ch'angjakchŏk angyangŭl wihayŏ," 4-5. A rather inaccurate translation is offered in *Third Congress of the Workers' Party of Korea, April 23-29, 1956: Documents and Materials* (Pyongyang, 1956), 130.

[14] Dae-Sook Suh, *Korean Communism, 1945-1980*, 464. In August 1957 Han's title was changed (along with that of the Ministry itself) to Minister of Education and Culture.

in the best position to cultivate the Kim Il Sung cult. All the while he retained the chairmanship of the WU.

Yet clouds had begun to accumulate on the international cultural horizon. With each month it became harder to uphold the fiction that the forces of reform in the Soviet Union were a lunatic fringe. In February 1956, at the Twentieth Party Congress of the CPSU, Krushchev had publicly denounced Stalin's personality cult. Shortly thereafter world-famous author Mikhail Sholokhov had mocked the Soviet Writers' Union as a "union of dead souls."[15] The hardliner Aleksandr Fadeev, a personal friend of Han's and the most celebrated contemporary Soviet writer in the DPRK, committed suicide in May.[16] As if that were not enough, Mao Zedong chose the spring of 1956 to deliver his famous call to China's intellectuals: "Let a hundred flowers bloom together; let a hundred schools of thought contend."[17] Like the Chinese themselves, the Koreans needed a while for the full import of this slogan to sink in. During a WU presidium conference in July 1956 Han gamely echoed a little Hundred Flowers' rhetoric, complaining that administrative duties were keeping members from their literature, and even calling for an "atmosphere of free debate."[18] He dropped such talk as soon as it became clear that Mao was demanding nothing less than criticism of cadres and bureaucrats, and experimentation with a variety of writing styles.

Han thus found himself in a difficult position in October 1956, when he was faced with the task of delivering the keynote speech of the Second Congress of Korean Writers in the presence of Soviet and Chinese delegations. How should he pay the obligatory servile tribute to the cultural leadership of the neighboring countries, and still make it clear to his countrymen that there was to be no Korean "thaw" or "hundred flowers"? How was he to acknowledge the Moscow Party Congress without calling the indigenous personality cult into question?

Han sought refuge in an obfuscatory doubletalk that occasionally lent his speech an element of unintentional comedy. The long-time admirer of

[15] John and Carol Garrard, 72.

[16] Ibid., 73. Han may actually have believed the official Soviet line that Fadeev died of natural causes. See "A. P'ajeyebǔe taehan hoesang: kǔǔi sǒgǒrǔl ch'umo hamyǒnsǒ," in *HSYS*, 14:129-150.

[17] See C.T. Hsia, *A History of Modern Chinese Fiction*, 337.

[18] "Chosǒn chakka tongmaeng che 3 ch'a chungang wiwǒnhoeesǒ: pogo yoji," *CM*, August 1956, 184-185.

Stalin[19] began by welcoming "the end of despotism" in the USSR, and by asserting that in Korea too "a free debate" had exerted a positive influence on the creative process; people had begun to speak "more with their own voice."[20] In his very next breath Han took up Stalin's notorious term for writers, apostrophizing his audience as "engineers of the human soul."[21] He then promised to search out "in a free atmosphere...any signs of personality cult (*kaein usanghwa*) in our literature."[22] One can imagine the amazement of the assembled Koreans as the high priest of the Kim cult spoke these words. Han was quick to disabuse his listeners of any false expectations however, claiming only minutes later to have found evidence of just such a "personality cult" in some writers' inability to depict their protagonists' emotions convincingly.[23] Though he took pains to renew the call for assimilation of Soviet culture, he studiously avoided all mention of contemporary writers, praising only the dead Stalinists Ostrovskii and Fadeev, for whose "heroic-tragic story endings" the Korean reading public was allegedly clamoring.[24]

On domestic cultural matters, the chairman congratulated his countrymen on overcoming threats from the "reactionary Yim Hwa clique," which had rejected the need for "party spirit" in literature, and from "the national nihilists" (i.e., the Soviet-Koreans), who had denied the value of colonial "proletarian" literature.[25] True to form, Han could not resist taking this opportunity to lend new emphasis to the KAPF myth:

> As is generally known, KAPF was a union of progressive and revolutionary writers, who maintained close ties to the masses..., subscribed to dialectical materialism, and using the socialist realist method of artistic creation...produced magnificent works. In addition, the nucleus of KAPF struggled unceasingly beside

---

[19] See for example Han's "Ssŭttallinŭn uriwa hamkke sara itta," in *HSYS*, 14:199-211. In this article Han tells breathlessly how he once glimpsed Stalin at a movie premiere in Moscow; he was particularly impressed by the Generalissimo's refusal to occupy a front-row seat.

[20] "Chŏnhu Chosŏn munhagŭi hyŏn sangt'aewa chŏnmang: Che 2 ch'a Chosŏn chakka taehoeesŏ han Han Sŏrya wiwŏnjangŭi pogo," in *Che 2 ch'a Chosŏn chakka taehoe: Munhŏnjip* (Pyongyang, 1956), 6.

[21] Ibid., 7. Stalin: "You writers are also engineers—those who direct the construction of human souls." Quoted in Hans Günther, 11-12.

[22] "Han Sŏrya wiwŏnjangŭi pogo," 9.

[23] Ibid., 42.

[24] Ibid., 43.

[25] Ibid., 12.

the working masses for the realization of the revolution, despite
the Japanese imperialists' cruel oppression.[26]

Since Kim Il Sung in his *Chuch'e* speech (December 1955) had already
defined the "nucleus of KAPF" as Han and Yi Kiyŏng, this was particularly
crude self-aggrandizement—which must have made the ensuing attack on
careerism seem all the more hypocritical to those present:

> There are among us not a few comrades for whom personal
> advancement is more important than the development and future
> of party literature, who would rather defame others than take part
> in a debate conducive to literature....We writers, more than
> anyone else, must break the habit of harboring groundless and
> mean-spirited thoughts, of defaming, envying and attacking
> fellow writers, for this stands in the way of collegial and
> ideological unity.[27]

When it came time to take stock of the last three years' literary
production, Han made no effort to hide his disappointment. While singling
out a tiny handful of works for praise, he disparaged the rest as validation
of readers' growing complaints about "boring, monotonous, and
stereotypical" literature. The main culprits, he said, were "the harmful
tendencies of conflictlessness and schematism."[28] "Schematism" refers of
course to the sameness of literary works. "Conflictlessness," i.e., the absence
of noteworthy conflict in literature, had been sporadically propagated in the
USSR in the late 1940s as a desirable reflection of party-defined reality, but
even before Stalin's death it had become a catchword for all that was wrong
with Soviet literature.[29]

Criticism of these problems had of course dominated the Soviet
Writers' Congress in 1954. Han, however, did not put the blame on
bureaucratic meddling in the creative process, as his Soviet colleagues had
done, nor did he echo their demand for freedom to depict the contradictions
in a socialist state.[30] Instead, he diagnosed insufficient understanding of the
party line and of real life on the part of writers, editors and critics alike.
Han's remedy was the same old one: All were to "arm" themselves

---

[26] Ibid., 14-15.

[27] Ibid., 17-18.

[28] Ibid., 40.

[29] See Walter Vickery, "Zhdanovism (1946-53)," in *Literature and Revolution in Soviet Russia, 1917-62*, ed. by Max Hayward and Leopold Labedz (London, 1963), 117.

[30] Cf. Marc Slonim, *Soviet Russian Literature*, 325.

ideologically with Marxism-Leninism and penetrate more deeply into the masses.[31]

Pyongyang saw none of the drama of the Soviet Writers' Congress; Han's points were approvingly expounded upon by all succeeding speakers.[32] No one dared blame neglect of the formal aspect of writing for the readers' dissatisfaction (as Kim Kijin had done in KAPF days), because the official aesthetic doctrine permitted no such diagnosis. The best explanation for the congress' peculiar mixture of proud hyperbole, gloomy crisis mentality, and empty advice can be found in Slavist Maximilian Braun's diagnosis of this central *Konstruktionsfehler* of socialist realism:

> On the one side truth is separated from empirical reality, and thus subordinated to a rigorous formal principle, but in the same breath the quality of form is excluded as an independent criterion. Hence the amazing naivete of all official discussions on socialist realism. One claims to have the greatest and most progressive art of all time, one which arouses the envy and admiration of all peoples; at the same time one laments that the products of this art are justifiably rejected by the public as boring and irrelevant; and at the same time one forbids the artists to do anything to remedy the situation.[33]

After the congress had ended and the last foreign delegations had left the country, not another word was spoken of personality cult or free debate. On the contrary, the authorities began to do all in their power to enforce lip service to the orthodox Stalinist interpretation of socialist realism and to insulate Korean writers from foreign "revisionism"—which after October 1956 was mainly attributed to Hungarian reactionaries.[34]

Kim Il Sung's decision to launch a so-called "concentrated guidance campaign" against inner-party sectarianism in 1957 gave the authorities an opportunity to expose "revisionists" in the cultural sector, or at least intimidate them into inactivity.[35] This campaign was also aimed at cracking down on the moral permissiveness that had spread in intellectual and artistic

---

[31] "Han Sŏrya wiwŏnjangǔi pogo," 36, 45, 52-53, 60.

[32] Cf. Han Hyo, "Tosikchuǔirǔl pandaehayŏ," Yu Kihong, "Tosikchuǔiwa munanjuǔinǔn ssangdungida," in *Munhŏnjip*, 174-184, 292-296.

[33] *Der Kampf um die Wirklichkeit in der russischen Literatur* (Göttingen, 1958), 74.

[34] See for example Han Sŏrya, "Uri munhagǔi saeroun ch'angjakchŏk angyangǔl wihayŏ," *CM*, December 1957, 10.

[35] Scalapino and Lee, 1:515.

circles after the end of the war.[36] Flamboyant choreographer Ch'oe Sŭnghŭi was finally deprived of her seat in the Supreme People's Assembly, while her husband An Mak lost his position as dean of Pyongyang Musical College.[37] Han, however, was now too firmly entrenched for his friends' fall from grace to have a significant effect on his status.

At the same time the WU, in obvious imitation of Chinese developments,[38] stepped up its efforts to enlist new members from the proletariat, in the hope that these would be free of the "bourgeois tendencies" (sectarianism, aloofness from the people, etc) hampering the development of a true socialist literature. Han Sŏrya took it upon himself to select candidates personally, no doubt to win their loyalty for himself and prevent the formation of new factions. One of those interviewed was fertilizer factory worker Yi Hanggu, who became an editor for the WU's publishing house before defecting to South Korea:

> Han Sŏrya looked attentively at me from across the room, then directed a question at Yi Pungmyŏng, who was standing next to him. "What has this comrade written?"
>
> "Juvenile literature; a short story called *Safety Belt.*"
>
> "*Safety Belt?*" Han turned to look at me again. "This comrade here?"
>
> "Yes."
>
> "Why'd you write it?" Why did I write it?...
>
> "I wrote it because I felt an urge to."
>
> "What kind of urge?"
>
> "It's hard to say in a few words. If you read the work, sir, you'll probably understand."
>
> "Well, well—a smart aleck!" He glared at me for a while, then jutted his chin at Yi Pungmyŏng. "How many do we have if we include this comrade?"
>
> "Six."
>
> "Six? Not enough! We need three times that."....
>
> About two months later I received notice from the WU's prose department telling me to begin submitting the paperwork needed to join [the WU] as a candidate member, and to apply to

---

[36] Ibid., 2:901.

[37] Ibid., 2:885.

[38] Cf. Merle Goldman, *Literary Dissent in Communist China*, 244; Scalapino and Lee, 2:475.

take the test at the Pyongyang Literary Institute, which was due to be established soon.[39]

At this institute Yi and the others underwent a course taught by prominent writers; upon graduation they became full-fledged members of the WU.

A good indication of the chairman's stature at this time is provided by a friendly caricature in the New Year's issue of the *Munhak sinmun* in 1958, which shows an amiable, crewcutted Han at the head of a long parade of the WU's most prominent figures, leading a rather befogged-looking Yi Kiyŏng by one arm and showing everyone the way with the other.[40] A laurel wreath around his neck indicates that he had already received the title "People's Artist," the highest award for a writer. A ribbon on his chest (identical to one worn by Yi) may symbolize the "People's Prize" for *History*, though according to Song Hosuk he received this in 1958 proper.[41] By October 1958, when he was elected vice-chairman of the Standing Committee of the Supreme People's Assembly, Han had indeed, as Scalapino and Lee write, "reached the highest status accorded any orthodox intellectual both in the Party and the government."[42]

The late 1950s also saw the beginning of a drive to canonize Han's entire oeuvre. This was perhaps a natural outgrowth of the KAPF myth's two basic falsehoods. For if the group, in particular its "nucleus" of Han and Yi Kiyŏng, had produced socialist realist masterpieces, and if this "nucleus" had never wavered from the cause, then it was only logical to conclude that all of Han's colonial works, including the trivial romances of the 1930s, deserved a place in the literary pantheon. This is more or less what was claimed after about 1956, although critics and theoreticians thereby made a mockery of socialist realist principles. In 1957 Han's *Ch'ŏngchun'gi* (Prime of Youth, 1937) was republished with great fanfare. The novel's plot is worth recounting: Young T'aeho lives off his parents while waiting for a job worthy of a sociology graduate fresh from Japan. Though he himself does little but read books and go to movies, he cannot tolerate American vulgarity or the presence of indolent "*lumpen*," and longs for a moral renewal of his homeland. He falls in love with the beautiful doctor Ŭnhŭi and vice versa, but their chaste relationship is complicated by a benevolent millionaire, who also loves Ŭnhŭi, and his sister, who loves T'aeho. Tension mounts as the

[39] Yi Hanggu, "Pukhanŭi chakka taeyŏlsogesŏ," *Pukhan* 118 (1 1974): 242-244.

[40] *MS*, 1 January 1958.

[41] Song Hosuk, 402.

[42] Dae-Sook Suh, *Korean Communism, 1945-1980*, 376; Scalapino and Lee, 2:884.

hero overeats at a restaurant and must be carried by both female admirers to the hospital, where he nearly dies. He is finally hired by a newspaper, only to be dismissed later for insubordination, whereupon he suddenly disappears. While perusing a newspaper Ŭnhŭi learns that he has been arrested for an unnamed subversive activity. She promises to wait for his release.[43]

Though touted by North Korean critics as "a scathing indictment of the reactionary bourgeois lewd literature of the time,"[44] everything about *Prime of Youth*, apart from the last ten pages, is in fact typical of colonial penny dreadfuls: the hackneyed title, the meditative student-hero, the "modern"-but-chaste heroine in a prestigious job, the double love-triangle, etc.[45] Back in 1937, Han had begged his readers' forgiveness for the work (see Ch1). Now, in a proud preface to the new edition, he expressed the hope that all his young countrymen would emulate T'aeho and Ŭnhŭi. He also pointed out an ethnic dimension to the story:

> In this work I depicted the problem of love from all sides. But of course, this love is permeated with Korean morality, in contrast to the greasy love (*chibangjilchŏgin sarang*) of Westerners. I have no hesitation in saying that in this work I presented love with a Korean heart and grateful affection for the Korean way of life.[46]

Since Koreans have always cherished the belief that theirs is a uniquely profound love, it is not unlikely that the reading public (which seems to have been clamoring for romance fiction anyway)[47] accepted Han's portrayal of *Prime of Youth* as a cleverly disguised nationalist tract. The author's colleagues, on the other hand, cannot have failed to notice that the novel's heroes chatter endlessly of foreign novels and movies, and that one positive figure refers to the love between Dante and Beatrice (those greasy Westerners) as his ideal.[48] The reissue of the novel *in original form*, at the height of an official campaign against revisionism, "love for love's sake," and "insufficient ideological content" in art, must have provided the WU's

---

[43] Han Sŏrya, Ch'ŏngch'un'gi, vol. 2 of Han Sŏrya sŏnjip, ed. Kim Ch'ŏl (Seoul, 1989).

[44] Pak Ch'angnak, "Changp'yŏn sosŏl Ch'ŏngch'un'gi e taehayŏ," MS, 10 July 1958.

[45] Cf. Cho Tongil, Han'guk munhak t'ongsa, 5:334-335.

[46] "Hugi," in Ch'ŏngch'un'gi, 398.

[47] See a discussion of letters to the editor in "Tokchadŭrŭi p'yŏnjie taehayŏ," CM, March 1958, 144.

[48] Ch'ŏngch'un'gi, 291.

new proletarian recruits with a jarring introduction to the realities of the literary world. *Prime of Youth* was followed in 1958 by the republication of the courtesan-romance *Ch'ohyang* (Ch'ohyang, 1939; its original title, *Маймӱи hyangch'on* [Paradise of the Heart], proved too much even for the "Han machine") and the autobiographical *T'ap* (Pagoda, 1940), which was presumably purged of its loving depictions of Japanese soldiers. Also published for the first time was *Pagoda*'s sequel *Yŏlp'ung* (Hurricane), which he had allegedly been unable to publish in 1944, but this too can hardly have been the original version. Han's *Dusk* had already been reissued in 1955, when it had received a less than enthusiastic reception from Ŏm Hosŏk, who felt it might have devoted more attention to the problem of Korean independence.[49] Now, in a weighty tome entitled *'Kohyang' gwa 'Hwanghon' e taehayŏ* (On *Home Town* and *Dusk*, 1958), it was touted along with Yi Kiyŏng's *magnum opus* as one of the twin pillars of Korean socialist realism.[50]

In the spring of 1958 Kim Il Sung, impressed by China's Great Leap Forward, announced the birth of the Ch'ŏllima (lit. "thousand-*li* horse") Movement.[51] Like Mao, Kim hoped to effect a dramatic increase in the rate of economic progress by mobilizing all sectors of the population to work longer and harder.[52] Since the movement's success depended on mass enthusiasm, propaganda became the object of unprecedented official attention. The need for a sharp quantitative increase in literary output prompted Han in May 1958 to announce a five-year plan that called for the production of no less than 552 prose works.[53] In an indication of the ever-widening gap between the rhetoric of cultural diplomacy and the reality of Soviet-Korean literary exchange, the plan foresaw the translation of only 59 works from "the Soviet Union *and other foreign countries*" (emphasis mine) into Korean, while demanding that 226 Korean works be rendered into

---

[49] "Han Sŏryaŭi munhakkwa *Hwanghon*," *CM*, November 1955, 142-162.

[50] Yi Hyoun, Kye Puk, *'Kohyang' gwa 'Hwanghon' e taehayŏ* (Pyongyang, 1958).

[51] In Sun Tzu's ancient classic *The Art of War* and other Chinese works the term Thousand League Horse can indicate any stallion of exceptional quality, the idea being that such an animal would be able to travel a thousand *li* (about three hundred miles) without water or food. See Sun Tzu, *The Art of War*, translated and with an introduction by Samuel B. Griffith (Oxford, 1963), 67. North Korean artists, however, depict the Ch'ŏllima as a Pegasus-style flying horse; see, for example, the painting "Fatherly Leader Examines Designs of Chollima Statue" in *The Leader of the People* (Pyongyang, 1984), 112.

[52] Scalapino and Lee, 2:541.

[53] "Chosŏn chakka tongmaeng chungang wiwŏnhoe 5 kaenyŏn chŏnmang kyehoege kwanhayŏ," *MS*, 15 May 1958.

foreign languages.[54] On 14 October 1958 Kim issued an order to all on the cultural front to devote themselves wholeheartedly to the "socialist education of the workers."[55] Headlines in literary publications called upon their readers to "ride the Ch'ŏllima."[56] At a mass meeting in December the WU's members pledged not to disappoint their Leader.[57]

The Ch'ŏllima Movement brought few new literary ideas. In the center of all articles and speeches stood the same tired formulae about immersion in the masses, elimination of bourgeois thought, etc. There was, however, a new emphasis on depicting topical protagonists and industrial themes, in order to spur all on to greater heights.[58] Those who had written nothing or not enough in the past began to receive ominous warnings:

> It is not up to the writer whether he writes or not. Writing is what the party and the masses demand from him, and is therefore his duty. Whoever fails to fulfil this duty commits a crime against the people and obstructs the realization of the revolution.[59]

Every now and then lip service was paid to the need for literary quality, but this was vitiated by constant denigration of the skills needed to write:

> Literature is not something that only writers can create...Describe reality faithfully in the form of literature, and you have a literary work.[60]

To bolster this claim, the writings of working-class amateurs were published with increasing frequency.[61]

Han threw himself into the propagation of Ch'ŏllima spirit with great zeal, urging his colleagues again and again to produce works about party cadres and industrial workers surmounting genuine obstacles.[62] "We must

---

[54] Ibid.

[55] *CCY 1959*, 220.

[56] "Ch'ŏllimaŭi kisangŭro," *CM*, November 1958, 3-7; Kang Hyosun, "Urido ch'ŏllimarŭl t'aja," *CM*, December 1958, 3-7.

[57] *CCY 1959*, 220.

[58] See for example "Chŏllimaŭi kisangŭro," 5-6.

[59] Kang Hyosun, "Urido chŏllimarŭl t'aja," 6.

[60] Ibid., 7.

[61] See the anthology *Chŏlmŭn taeo: Kŭlloja chakp'umjip* (Pyongyang, 1960).

[62] Han Sŏrya, "Kongsanjuŭi munhak kŏnsŏrŭl wihayŏ," *CM*, March 1959, 12-14; "Kongsanjuŭi kyoyanggwa uri munhagŭi tangmyŏn kwaŏp," *CM*, May 1959, 24.

penetrate so deeply into the life of the workers," he wrote, "that their thoughts become our own."[63]

This rhetoric, however, stood in sharp contrast to Han's own literary output. He had not created a *bona fide* industrial hero since before the liberation, let alone written a production novel, and he showed no sign of doing so now. If the party was prepared to look the other way, some members of the reading public were not. Note the following exchange between Han and one of his audience at a literary evening devoted to *Mt Sŏlbong* (1958), his novel about a colonial peasant-union:

> **Q:** I don't suppose you're planning to write a novel on a work theme?
>
> **A:** Since I haven't got a clear plan yet, I can't say just what I'll write, but I promise right here that I'll definitely write one. This is an important task for all writers, so now many of the younger ones are taking part in industrial work. I will definitely write [on this theme], in socialist competition with these young colleagues.[64]

Han appears to have forgotten his promise. In 1959 he completed a long and sentimental South Korean family saga called *Sarang* (Love) and a sequel to the hospital story *Brother and Sister*.[65] In 1961, while continuing to scold his colleagues for avoiding industrial themes, he again indulged his lifelong predilection for hospital milieus in the novel *Sŏngjang* (Growth).[66]

Despite his flouting of the Ch'ŏllima guidelines, and the purge of his close allies An Mak and Ch'oe Sŭnghŭi,[67] Han proved strong enough to rebuff a power grab by Sŏ Manil, who had occupied one of the WU's three vice-chairman slots. Han's polemic in the May 1959 issue of *Chosŏn munhak* indicates, albeit in veiled terms, that Sŏ had tried to exploit the campaign against conflictlessness and schematism to push for his ouster, on the basis that he himself (who had studied literature in the USSR) was more

---

[63] Ibid., 24.

[64] "*Sŏlbongsan* tokcha moim," *MS*, 15 February 1959.

[65] *Sarang*, vol. 12 of *HSYS*; *P'yŏnji*, in *8.15 haebang 15 chunyŏn kinyŏm sosŏlchip* (Pyongyang, 1960), 5-16.

[66] *Sŏngjang* (Pyongyang, 1961). *Chŏngch'un'gi* (1937), *Sulchip* (1939), *Nammae* (1949), *Sŭngnyangi* (1951), *Chŏnbyŏl* (1951), *Hwangch'oryŏng* (1952), *Renindi ch'osang* (1957) and *P'yŏnji* (1959) all deal with sick people and/or hospitals.

[67] In spring 1959 An was placed under house arrest (Scalapino and Lee, 2:885). Han was quick to denounce his old friend in "Kongsanjudi munhak kŏnsŏrŭl wihayŏ," 5.

knowledgeable in socialist realist theory. Sŏ was of course doomed to failure, considering that there were no longer any government factions to support challenges to Han's leadership. In the same article Han asserted that others had also abused the campaign to indulge their "petit bourgeois individualism."[68] Thereupon he summarily declared the tendencies in question to be no longer extant:

> There can be no doubt: Not only has life-simplifying schematism been clearly eliminated, so also has the factography that simply records reality....The tendency of conflictlessness, which embellishes life, has also been overcome.[69]

This claim had no basis in contemporary North Korean literature, least of all in Han's own work. He had, it seems, only initiated the campaign against these tendencies in 1956 to give the impression of following the Soviets' lead. Now that it had brought unpleasant repercussions for himself, and lost its diplomatic relevance to boot—for cultural crackdowns were underway in Moscow and Beijing—it was to be terminated with equal arbitrariness.

Just how confident Han felt in these years is clear from the increasing intellectual and formal slovenliness of his writing. In his political journalism he began openly jettisoning the Marxist jargon he had never really understood. His phrenological observations of American POWs were presented in the rambling article "*Pabo k'ongk'ŭl*" (Idiot Contest, 1958) with striking matter-of-factness:

> [They] were skinny as beanpoles, bent over, frightening and hirsute. Their skulls hardly bore looking at, for mange had eaten away at their scalps, and their eyes seemed lifeless....The hide on their faces was so taut that the eyes seemed to have been drilled in.[70]

Han was not, of course, alluding to violations of the Geneva Convention, but instead preparing the grounds for his theory that the faces of Americans, in particular their "taut hide," manifest an inner "idiotization" (*pabohwa*):

> I got a closer look at [Eisenhower] during a newsreel in India. I could clearly see his eyes, which looked like punched-in holes, like the eyes of a demon. The mouth made the same impression

---

[68] "Kongsanjuŭi kyoyanggwa uri munhagŭi tangmyŏn kwaŏp," *CM*, May 1959, 15.

[69] Ibid., 9.

[70] "Pabo k'ongk'ŭl," in *HSYS*, 14:280.

of a hole bored into the taut hide....As expected, he showed the signs of an extreme "idiotization."[71]

These musings exerted a strong influence on Han's fiction; in the novel *Love* (1960) he even depicted an American baby with "taut skin" (see Ch4b). The writer's literary criticism was marked by a similar decline in intellectual rigor. While regularly attacking critics for failing to offer constructive advice, he saw nothing amiss in perfunctorily dismissing several works at a time in one or two short paragraphs, usually with stale slogans about "remoteness from the people."[72]

It seemed the more carelessly Han wrote, the more lavish the cult around him became. *Han Sŏryaǔi ch'angjak yŏn'gu* (Studies on Han Sŏrya's Work), a long and obsequious monograph, appeared in 1959.[73] The same year a collection of colonial writings by various KAPF authors was published, but not before Han's articles had been doctored to make their author appear to have been more of a censor-defying firebrand.[74] *Suryŏngǔl ttara paeuja* (Emulate the Leader), a collection of his prose on Kim Il Sung, was published in a massive edition of 100,000, apparently for use in schools.[75] (As Education Minister Han was of course in charge of textbooks.) Literary evenings devoted to his novels were staged routinely before hundreds of Pyongyang residents.[76] The tearjerking novel *Love* appeared in 1960 and was unanimously praised, despite its thorough incompatibity with the spirit of the Ch'ŏllima Movement.[77] Critic Yun

---

[71] Ibid., 292-293.

[72] See for example "Uri munhagǔi saeroun ch'angjakchŏk angyangǔl wihayŏ," 13-14.

[73] Han Chungmo, *Han Sŏryaǔi ch'angjak yŏn'gu* (Pyongyang, 1959).

[74] For example, in the original version of the article "Musan munyegaǔi ipchangesŏ" Han describes anarchist Kim Hwasan's theory as "an absurd, chimerical and empty theory" (*Tonga ilbo*, 20 April 1927). The 1959 version replaces this phrase with one charging that Hwasan's theory harbors "the extremely impure and evil intention of obstructing and destroying the proletarian movement by tearing it apart." See "P'ǔroret'aria chakkaǔi ipchangesŏ" (the original title has also been altered), in vol. 8 of *Hyŏndae Chosŏn munhak sŏnjip* (Pyongyang, 1959), 64.

[75] Han Sŏrya, *Suryŏngǔl ttara paeuja* (Pyongyang, 1960).

[76] See for example "Changp'yŏn sosŏl *Hwanghon* e taehan kamsanghoe," *MS*, 3 April 1958; "*Sŏlbongsan* tokcha moim," *MS*, 15 February 1959.

[77] Han Sŏrya, *Sarang*, vol. 12 of *HSYS*.

Sep'yŏng went so far as to call it "a groundbreaking product of our recent literature."[78]

The occasion of Han's sixtieth birthday carried his cult to its peak.[79] The private party in August 1960 was attended by the Great Leader himself.[80] The WU's publishing house set about issuing Han's Complete Works, including *Prime of Youth* and *Ch'ohyang*; it would take two years to publish all fifteen of the thick volumes.[81] Extravagant tributes began appearing in *Chosŏn munhak*. "*Han Sŏryawa na*" (Han Sŏrya and I), in which Yi Kiyŏng likened his colleague's pre-liberation criticism to a "knife" "plunged into the enemies' hearts," was typical of the melodramatic tone in which the KAPF era was now remembered.[82] Yi obligingly conceded that Han was "politically much more orthodox" than he himself, and called "the strong voice of political orthodoxy a characteristic of his novels."[83] Yun Sep'yŏng's "*Han Sŏryawa kŭŭi munhak*" (Han Sŏrya and his Literature) touted the writer as the one whose "name stands out the most" among all the contributors to the development of socialist realism in the DPRK.[84] Yun attributed to the writer a childhood strikingly similar to Kim Il Sung's: Han too had been a precocious and spunky lad, he claimed, with great sympathy for his weaker friends and an instinctive hatred of Japanese imperialism. His prison record was extended: now it was claimed he had spent three months in jail after the 1919 uprising and "more than two years" in the 1930s. Yun also claimed that Han had always endeavored to live like a proletarian.[85] (Yi Kiyŏng unwittingly contradicted this in his piece by referring to Han's "dapper" colonial attire.)[86] It had already been disclosed, in an obvious attempt to evoke comparison with Soviet martyr-writer Ostrovskii, that Han's neuralgia was in fact a life-threatening disease, against which he had

[78] Yun Sep'yŏng, "Widaehan hyŏnsil saenghwarŭi hwap'okkwa kongsanjuŭijaŭi chŏnhyŏng," *CM*, August 1961, 116; see also Yun's "Choguk t'ongirŭi chujewa changp'yŏn sosŏl *Sarang* ŭi segye," *CM*, January 1961, 91-106.

[79] In Korea, where calendar years were traditionally ordered in a sexagenary cycle (as opposed to the West's centenary one), a man's sixtieth birthday is still regarded as particularly important.

[80] Scalapino and Lee, 2:885.

[81] The complete set is advertised in *CM*, April 1962, 126.

[82] Yi Kiyŏng, "Han Sŏryawa na," *CM*, August 1960, 171.

[83] Ibid., 172.

[84] "Han Sŏryawa kŭŭi munhak," *CM*, August 1960, 173.

[85] Ibid., 173-182.

[86] Yi Kiyŏng, "Han Sŏryawa na," 170.

waged a long, hard struggle out of a sense of revolutionary duty.[87] At least
Yun's list of Han's various offices can be regarded as authentic:

> Today Han is chairman of the presidium of the Korean
> Writers' Union. An active person both on the domestic and
> national level, he has occupied the post of Education Minister,
> and been regularly voted into the Central Committee of the
> Korean Workers' Party as well as the Supreme People's
> Congress of the Republic; today he is not only vice-chairman of
> the Standing Committee of the People's Congress, but also
> chairman of the National Committee for the Protection of World
> Peace, and a member of the board of directors of the World
> Peace Council, where he works selflessly for international
> peace.[88]

In December 1960 An Hamgwang, the critic who had laid the foundation for
the Han myth in the 1940s, compared the work of the "leader of Korean
literature" with a

> sharply defined mountain range. There we find breathtaking
> summits, covered in luxurious forests, and smaller, cozier
> mountains with bushy young pines, seemingly lost in meditation.
> In such a mountain range it is difficult to decide which peak is
> the greatest and most beautiful.[89]

The regime's systematic promotion of Han did not mean that Kim Il
Sung was satisfied with the performance of the literary sector as a whole;
in fact the Great Leader found it lagging far behind the other areas of the
Ch'ŏllima movement. The main problem, as he saw it, was a lack of party
control, as he said in a speech in November 1960:

> In this area, it seems, the leadership of the party is weak, and the
> mass line has not been implemented....It is apparently necessary
> to unite the unions of writers, composers, dancers etc back into
> a Federation of Literature and Art, which like in the old days

[87] "Yŏlp'ung: Changp'yŏn sosŏl *Yŏlp'ung* ŭi ilbu," *CM*, September 1958, 86.

[88] Yun Sep'yŏng, "Han Sŏryawa kŭŭi munhak," 179.

[89] An Hamgwang, "Han Sŏryaŭi chakkajŏk haengjŏnggwa ch'angjojŏk kaesŏng," *CM*, December 1960, 107.

[i.e., before September 1953 - B.M.] will be kept under the party's direct control.[90]

In March 1961, in accordance with Kim's wishes, the KFLA was reestablished. Han Sŏrya, needless to say, was named to the post of chairman.[91] Now more powerful than ever, he was able to arrange Ch'oe Sŭnghŭi's reinstatement to the post of Dance Union chairwoman, though she had only been partially rehabilitated and her husband An Mak was still under house arrest.[92] Soon after, Han published the novel *Sŏngjang* (Growth, 1961). Despite its Ch'ŏllima-sounding title, it was little more than a throwback to the sick worker stories of the Soviet occupation period.[93] This flagrant violation of the voluntarist *Zeitgeist* was published in an edition of 15,000 as "a commemorative work in honor of the Fourth Congress of the Korean Workers' Party."[94] "In this work," wrote An Hamgwang in the *Munhak sinmun*, "the writer has shown the new visage, lofty spirit, and communist ideals of those growing up in the Ch'ŏllima era."[95] This was indeed, as Yi Chŏlchu writes, "the golden age of Han Sŏrya."[96]

b)   Han Sŏrya's Fiction

Sarang (Love, 1960)

During the 1950s North Korean authors began to write on life in South Korea, a subject which afforded them an opportunity to depict the kind of genuine conflict and variegated human experience that was otherwise permissible only in works about the colonial era. While the party reprimanded those who abused the theme to satisfy prurient interest, it was on the whole highly supportive of the trend. In August 1956 it called on

---

[90] Kim Il Sung, "Ch'ŏllima sidaee sangŭnghan munhwa yesurŭl ch'angjohaja: chakka, yesurindŭlgwaŭi tamhwa," in *Uri hyŏngmyŏngesŏŭi munhak yesurŭi immu* (Pyongyang, 1965), 30-31.

[91] See "Chosŏn munhak yesul ch'ongdongmaeng: Kyuyak," *CM*, March 1961, 150-152.

[92] Scalapino and Lee, 2:885.

[93] *Sŏngjang* (Pyongyang, 1961).

[94] See the advertisement on the back of September 1961's *Chosŏn munhak*.

[95] An Hamgwang, "Changp'yŏn *Sŏngjang* ŭi myŏkkaji hyŏngsangjŏk t'ŭksŏng," *MS*, 15 May 1962.

[96] *Pugŭi yesurin*, 236.

writers to devote special attention to South Korean campus resistance against conscription, perhaps intending to disseminate the finished product among the students themselves.[97] In 1957 Han wrote a medium length novel on the theme entitled *Uri kirŭn hanaida* (Our Road is One), which he then expanded to a full-length novel entitled *Sarang* (Love, 1960), the plot of which is as follows:

Kido and his girlfriend Ryŏnhŭi, students at the [fictitious] Hanyŏng University in Seoul, take part in demonstrations against student conscription. The day of Kido's call-up approaches regardless, and in desperation his middle-class parents decide to bribe the American dean of the university, a greedy old man named Anderson, into using his political influence to secure an exemption for the boy. A Korean university employee agrees to act as a go-between, but he puts half the bribe in his own pocket and has Kido's father arrested. The boy himself is then shanghaied into the army and brutalized by corrupt superiors.

Having lost their family savings, Kido's mother and younger sister Kiok are forced to move into the slums, where the former ekes out a living selling gruel. Soon catastrophe strikes again: on her way to school little Kiok is run over and killed by the Andersons, of all people. The hysterical mother later confronts the unrepentant pair during a church service, but is quickly dragged away by the police and beaten so severely that she loses her sanity. She is taken care of by Ryŏnhŭi, who loyally awaits her boyfriend's discharge.

One day Kido gets out on leave and arrives at the girl's window. After a tearful meeting with his mother, who fails to recognize him, he tells Ryŏnhŭi he will flee to North Korea when he returns to his post on the DMZ. The two pledge to meet again when Korea is no longer divided. Kido then dashes off alone: he wants to spend his last days in the South sightseeing in the historical town of Kyŏngju. While in prison Kido's father learns of his son's successful escape over the 38th parallel. Falling asleep, he dreams of the country's reunification under the DPRK flag.[98]

From a socialist realist perspective, *Love* goes irrevocably astray in the third chapter, when the narrator's attention shifts from the students' collective struggle to the unsuccessful efforts of Kido's parents to have him, and him alone, exempted from military service. A "social" storyline thus degenerates into a private family saga, and the reader is asked to believe that a middle class student's conscription into the peacetime army is a catastrophe more "typical" of the horrors of Rhee-era capitalism than, say,

---

[97] See "Chogugŭi p'yŏnghwajŏk t'ongirŭi chujee taehan hyŏbŭihoe," *CM*, September 1956, 183.

[98] Based on *Sarang*, vol. 12 of *HSYS*.

the daily hardship of the bark-eating rural poor (for whom military service probably constituted an improvement in living standards). As if intent on making the story even more "private," Han goes on to isolate the positive characters from all potential allies (except commiserating neighbors), and effectively reduces the negative camp to the Andersons. The latter are clearly meant as caricatures of Seoul's Underwood family.[99] By making them responsible for Kiok's death on top of everything else, and via an outrageous coincidence in the worst Korean literary tradition, Han finally robs the story of its last iota of sociohistorical significance. Here as in *Jackals*, it becomes clear that the author's prime goal is to move his readers to tears. Not unlike the bestial missionaries, therefore, the Andersons are allowed to go unpunished after their crime, leaving the long-suffering positive characters to give themselves over to their grief—which Han draws out for effect by letting only one character at a time learn of Kiok's death. (In the last one hundred pages characters swoon or burst into tears no less than eighteen times.)

The entire text bespeaks the absence of a clear compositional plan, and not just in the clumsy asides with which scenes are occasionally tacked together ("at this point we have to move the story back a little," etc).[100] Han lets a conversation between the Andersons and a US Army officer drag on until the latter has delivered mad-scientist-type pronouncements on everything from Dewey and Kierkegaard to India's Five-Year Plan and the Baghdad Pact. This rambling dialogue alone takes up roughly 10% of the entire novel. All pivotal events, on the other hand, such as the arrest of Kido's father, Kiok's death, and Kido's flight into the DPRK, must take place "offstage," whereupon they are reported in a a few dry sentences by the narrator or a minor character.

Love is thus a good example, if a rather extreme one, of the ramshackle, episodic composition characteristic of early North Korean novels, most of which had to be withdrawn or drastically streamlined after the cultural revolution of the mid-1960s. (Yi Kiyŏng's *Land*, for example, was whittled down to about 60% its original length.) To be sure, many South Korean critics consider a difficulty in structuring long novels to be a

---

[99] The Underwoods, an American family of Presbyterian missionaries, founded Seoul's Yŏnhŭi (now Yŏnsei) University in 1915 and have run it ever since. Anderson sounds like Underwood to Korean ears, and Han describes Hanyŏng University as having been built with Presbyterian funds. DPRK propaganda has demonized the family since the 1953 show trials, when Horace Underwood was named *in absentia* as an accomplice of Pak Hŏnyŏng. See Dae-Sook Suh, *Kim Il Sung*, 132, 135.

[100] *Sarang*, 459.

characteristic of Korean writers in general.[101] The North Koreans' problems are particularly noteworthy, however, in view of George Lukác's assertion that an aimless and unfocused structure in a literary work reflects the absence of a Marxist-Leninist *Weltanschauung*.[102] This would indeed seem to be the case in Han's literature, which one finds informed by a crudely moralist social criticism of the kind usually associated by Marxists with "bourgeois" critical realism.

In *Love* this worldview receives its first clear articulation in the form of an "epiphany" of Kido's mother after her husband's arrest, when she realizes she should have supported the KPA during the Korean War:

> But today her eyes and ears had opened. The beautiful and the ugly had parted clearly. How could I have failed to recognize such a clear contrast sooner? she wondered....Mansŏng's wife felt as clearheaded as if she had just woken from a long sleep.[103]

Later Professor Ro, an allegedly erudite left-wing economist, expresses himself in like fashion to his stepdaughter Ryŏnhŭi:

> "There are two great boards of judgement [*simp'andae*] in the world today. That is to say, there is that of the evil criminals [*choeindŭl*, which can also mean sinners—B.M.] and that of the virtuous people. Now, to die at the hands of the evil camp can of course be an honour for the virtuous. But he who is is called to judgement by the virtuous and put to death will never be able to expunge his shame, for such a person is no human being."[104]

Han's moralism, like Dickens', precludes a concrete political program to change society. The key to reform is a change of heart:

> Ryŏnhŭi reflected once more on the inner beauty of the women next door. I will make it my mission in life to spread the news of this beauty far and wide, she thought. It seemed to her as if there could be no holier duty. Only when her neighbors live in the hearts of everyone—when women everywhere, poker in hand, prepare meals in the kitchen, while their children play house and

---

[101] Cho Tongil discusses early Korean novelists' inability to follow a theme through to the end in *Han'guk munhak t'ongsa*, 5:430. Yi Yusik deals with modern writers' macrostructural problems in "Yŏkkarae nŭrigi sigŭn kollanhada," *Tongsŏ munhak* 170 (9 1988): 89-93.

[102] See Hans Günther, 75.

[103] *Sarang*, 376.

[104] Ibid., 609.

> card games; when they sing songs against the enemy, just as they
> sang to country circle dances back in the days of the Japanese
> invasion [in the late 16th century]—only then would the beautiful
> people win. And then all evil people would become beautiful, she
> thought. Will the beasts triumph with their evil, or mankind with
> its virtue? This is the struggle, and it's truly a terrible struggle to
> the death, she thought.[105]

This worldview is underscored throughout the narrative by heaven
and hell imagery, with emphasis of course on the latter. Syngman Rhee is
"the king of the underworld," his policemen "a hellish pack," and when Kido
is conscripted, "the raging sulphuric flames of hell" dance before his
mother's eyes.[106] The KPA on the other hand is a "dazzling," "righteous
army" which to the daydreaming woman seems "as if it would rescue her
from no matter what hell."[107] When the imprisoned father Mansŏng hears his
son Kido is in the DPRK, the author describes him as having "finally
received word from the paradise he had envisioned ever since arriving in
this hell."[108]

This almost Manichaean dualism may seem clear-cut if nothing else,
but in fact the author's lack of a more sophisticated *Weltanschauung* soon
leads him into difficulties—such as the problem of why, if the entire South
is a living hell, such a fuss is being made about Kido's conscription. As if
stumped for an answer, Han wavers between applying hell imagery to the
country as a whole and concentrating it on the army base (and finally
Mansŏng's prison); this indecision is evident in the above quotes. Ironically,
many inconsistencies reflect *positively* on the Rhee dictatorship and its
Yankee backers. Ryŏnhŭi, who since childhood has made no secret of her
fierce anti-Americanism, not only wants to study at Korea's "most
Americanized" university, but is allowed to as well—and is rewarded with
the highest marks in the class.[109] The same institution permits Professor Ro,
whose son broadcasts communist propaganda out of Pyongyang, to espouse
leftist economic theories in hugely popular lectures, and pays him so well

---

[105] Ibid., 667-668.

[106] Ibid., 471, 479.

[107] Ibid., 376.

[108] Ibid., 731.

[109] Ibid., 24-26, 52.

for his efforts that he can afford a maid (who, incidentally, receives as little attention in the narrative as a stablehand in a Jane Austen novel).[110]

Not a few South Koreans, one suspects, would gladly have traded the real Rhee dictatorship for this "living hell," especially as Han largely concentrates its evils (from rampaging G.I.'s to the black market) in Seoul and the army base, while presenting the countryside, in accordance with the usual pastoralism, as the largely undisturbed repository of the Good and Beautiful Korea. Kido's father tells him that he is only suffering in the city for the sake of his children's education; otherwise he would go to the country "and raise chicken or pigs."[111] In reality, the ROK countryside was in the throes of a severe food shortage in the late 1950s, but for a New Tendency disciple like Han rural poverty is always quaint—and *truly Korean*:

> The closer they got to the village, the better Ryŏnhŭi felt. Most of the houses were huts, which had almost completely collapsed, but they still looked adorable and happy. No doubt about it, those were *Koreans* in those houses....Ryŏnhŭi felt as if she had rediscovered the Korea she thought was gone for good.[112]

She would like to return to Seoul with these benevolently naive, neighborly countryfolk, who "almost all preserve the Korean spirit," that they may "wash away" the city's "filth."[113]

While a socialist realist would have illuminated the political and economic context of the alliance between the Rhee dictatorship and the USA, Han seems at a loss to explain just what the Yankees are doing on the peninsula. Kido, who is presented as well-informed, tells Ryŏnhŭi the US would be happy "if all Koreans died and the country were...turned into a completely flat, vacant space."[114] On the very next page, he warns her that America plans to include the Korean people in its ever-expanding "slave territory."[115] Rather than expound on the reasons for the US presence, Han prefers to concentrate on its bizarre and peripheral concomitants, especially those which result in the suffering of children. He returns again and again, for example, to the Yankees' alleged use of live Korean boys for shooting

---

[110] Ibid., 149.

[111] Ibid., 277, also 368.

[112] Ibid., 453-455.

[113] Ibid., 524, 526.

[114] Ibid., 296.

[115] Ibid., 297.

practice: "Herein lies the pleasure, the philosophy of the Americans," he intones.[116] East German scholar Hans-Joachim Bernhard once wrote that a literary preoccupation with children is the natural accompaniment of a moral criticism of society:

> In his tract *On Naive and Sentimental Literature* Schiller perceives childhood as a stage of integrity, and the child as the "embodiment of a relinquished ideal"....Schiller's antinomy of the child's ideal morality and the "ruined world" reflects...the necessary conflict between moral dictates and society's disregard for them, a conflict which takes on ever crasser forms as capitalist society develops. *It is this predominantly moral view of society that is responsible for the decisive import ascribed by critical realism to the ideals and worldview of childhood and youth.*[117] (emphasis mine)

And it is this which leads to the endowment of all positive characters in *Love* (except of course the mother figures) with the attributes of children:

> "Mummy!...I want to sleep with Mummy tonight, OK?" For the first time in ages Ryŏnhŭi wanted to play the little child again.[118]

> When Kido came home, he too behaved like a small child.[119]

> "Mummy...I'm hungry." said Mujin [a neighbor's son] childishly. He...still hung at his mother's breast. And as far as she was concerned, he was still her baby.[120]

> Her husband [Dr Ro]...was a man of childlike simplicity.[121]

In contrast to their spontaneity-embodying function in fiction on North Korean themes (see *History*), therefore, the children and infantilized adults in *Love* are intended to highlight the surrounding decadence with their purity and innocence. In one episode, for example, Mujin borrows money from a neighbor to buy medicine for his mother. When he gives it to her, she flies into a rage, thinking he has stolen the money for it—life in "hell" has conditioned her to mistrust even her own "baby." The neighbor soon tells

---

[116] Ibid., 626. See also 280, 317, 398, 449.

[117] Hans Joachim Bernhard, *Die Romane Heinrich Bölls* (Berlin, GDR, 1970), 177-178.

[118] *Sarang*, 14-15.

[119] Ibid., 39. See also 687.

[120] Ibid., 397.

[121] Ibid., 673.

her the truth, however, whereupon all three burst into tears.[122] As in Schiller's famous anecdote of the little girl who gives her father's wallet to a poor man, Mujin's pure action constitutes a "disgrace of the real world." So too, of course, does the central catastrophe, Kiok's death under the wheels of the Andersons' car. Like Dickens' little Nell, she is too good to survive in such depraved surroundings.

In accordance with their infantilisation the positive figures in *Love* are devoid of sexuality. Their abstinence is the effortless chastity of children, not revolutionary asceticism. It is thus only natural that Kido, directly after hearing his girlfriend's pledge of eternal love, should tell her he plans to spend his last days in the South sightseeing alone.[123] Such prudishness is common to all literature in the DPRK, which associates sexuality exclusively with negative characters. These are usually the same work-impeding temptresses that one encounters in socialist realism.[124] Han, however, is disinclined to present any Koreans, especially women, as promiscuous. Even the bar girls in the UN-occupied Pyongyang of *Taedong River* turn out to be chaste saboteuses in disguise. In *Love* as in virtually all of his post-liberation work, sexuality is the province of the bestial Yankees:

> "Amen," *bleated* Anderson in his *goat's voice*. Embracing Mary's torso greedily *like a vulture*, he raised his bent, skinny body onto its feet....*Like an octopus* he rubbed his *apelike* mouth against Mary's cheek....*Like a startled rabbit* Mary pulled back her neck, rolled her eyes, and giggled.[125] (emphasis mine)

Han's ethnocentricity finds its frankest expression ever in *Love*. The words above are, after all, those of the omniscient narrator, whereas the menagerie of animal metaphors at the climax of *Jackals* is at least extenuated by being presented as the heroine's hallucination. Even the

---

[122] Ibid., 402-410. Han had used an almost identical story in 1958's *Mt Sŏlbong*. It is significant that the tearjerking motif of the unjustly accused benefactor is also a staple of South Korean soap operas.

[123] *Sarang*, 714.

[124] Cf. Clark, *The Soviet Novel*, 185. See for example the temptress Yun Sŏngok in Yu Hangnim's *Sŏngsire taehan iyagi* (A Tale of Sincerity, Pyongyang, 1958), and Kaekkujang-manura in Yi Kiyŏng's *Ttang* (Earth, 3rd ed., Pyongyang, 1960). The North Koreans' prudishness even precludes the scenes of childbirth so common to Soviet and Chinese village literature. Cf. Gasiorowska, 57; C.T. Hsia, "Residual Femininity: Women in Chinese Communist Fiction," in *Chinese Communist Literature*, ed. Cyril Birch (New York, 1963), 171.

[125] *Sarang*, 174-175.

Andersons' baby is endowed with "tight skin"[126]—to Han the infallible sign
of Yankee "idiotisation"—and held up as an object of hatred. Towards the
end Mansŏng dreams in his cell of strangling it to avenge his daughter
Kiok's death:

> "Son of a bitch—" Mansŏng tried to twist the bastard's
> throat but there was no strength in his hands....Holding his hand
> like a knife, he aimed at the neck and brought it down with all
> his strength.[127]

The futile attempts to kill the baby take up four pages, in which the reader
is implicitly urged to share Mansŏng's frustration. Then the baby simply
disappears. (Even Han's bad taste, it seems, had its limits.) The dream ends
gruesomely nonetheless:

> [Mansŏng's] wife appeared. In her hands she was squeezing the
> corpses of the enemy pair [the Andersons]. The eyes of the bitch
> and the bastard looked like graves hollowed out by a fox, and the
> bestial blood gushed out of their muzzles like a river. Mansŏng
> was beside himself with joy.[128]

Love was received enthusiastically; in view of Han's stature at the
time, any other reaction would have been unthinkable. Far from criticising
the work's Manichaean worldview, critics singled it out for special praise.
Yun Sep'yŏng lauded the "sharp contrast of love and hatred, of darkness and
light," the contrast of the "repulsive bestial world" of the Americans and the
"lofty humanist world" of the positive characters, "our country's
benevolently naive [*sobak han*] average people."[129] Yun went on to call this
egregious violation of socialist realism's macrostructural guidelines the best
composed of all Han's North Korean novels.[130] He also praised Han for
"showing vividly the unbending struggle" of the South Korean masses
against Rhee and his US imperialists[131]—and this of a novel in which the
only resistance against the oppressor nation's feeblest representatives takes
place in a jailed man's dreams.

---

[126] Ibid., 165.

[127] Ibid., 740-741.

[128] Ibid., 742-743. Han had already used the eyes-like-graves simile in *Jackals*.

[129] "Uri naraesŏ changp'yŏn sosŏrŭi kusŏngsang t'ŭksŏnggwa chegidoenŭn munje," *CM*,
January 1962, 98.

[130] Ibid., 108.

[131] Ibid., 107.

Writings on Kim Il Sung (1946-1960)

"Without hesitation," wrote Han Chungmo in 1958, "one can say that Han Sŏrya is the writer who has devoted the most creative energy in his work to the depiction of the leader Kim Il Sung."[132] Indeed, the list of Han's works on the life and exploits of the so-called General is an impressive one, encompassing two short stories, a novel, a biography of the young Kim for child readers, and a score of newspaper and journal articles (though Han never wrote a single comprehensive biography comparable to that which appeared in the late 1960s under the name Paek Pong).[133] It is difficult to categorize this literature as fiction or non-fiction, for Han moulded Kim's life to conform to the "master plot" of the typical North Korean novel. A certain blurring of the boundary between biography and novel is also evident in the Stalinist literature of the 1930s, though of course the Soviet "master plot" differs strongly from its North Korean counterpart.[134] While Stalin's biography thus charts the usual socialist realist transition from an unruly childhood to a perfect synthesis of spontaneity and consciousness,[135] Kim's life story celebrates the total victory of "truly Korean" qualities. The following is a summary of this life story as it is presented in Han's various writings:

In the picturesque mountain village of Man'gyŏngdae the General (as he is referred to from the start) is born to a patriotic teacher and his wife. Recognising the child's potential for greatness in his upright, innocent actions, the father decides to raise him to become the liberator of his homeland. When the General is seven, his father is imprisoned for anti-Japanese activities. After his release the family emigrates to Manchuria, where the father opens a hospital for Korean liberation fighters and the General attends a Chinese school.

After his father's death the teenage General joins a communist youth organization, advancing quickly to the rank of secretary. Soon he is captured by Chinese troops and imprisoned for a year, but the experience only hardens his revolutionary resolve. In 1932 he organizes a band of Korean partisans and

---

[132] *Han Sŏryaǔi ch'angjak yŏn'gu*, 267.

[133] *Hyŏllo, In'gan Kim Ilsŏng changgun* (1946); *Kaesŏn* (1948), *Ryŏksa* (1953); *Adongdan* (1959); *Man'gyŏngdae* (1960), etc. Cf. Paek Pong's *Minjogŭi t'aeyang Kim Ilsŏng changgun* (Pyongyang, 1968). Considering the inherent looseness of the term, Scalapino and Lee are not wrong to describe Han's *Hero General Kim Il Sung* (Pyongyang, 1962; an English translation of *Yŏngung Kim Ilsŏng changgun*) as a biography (*Communism in Korea*, 2:203), but it is little more than a jumble of anecdotes.

[134] Cf. Clark, *The Soviet Novel*, 123.

[135] Cf. Henri Barbusse, *Stalin—Eine Neue Welt* (Paris, 1935); *Iosif Vissarionovich Stalin. Kratkaia biografiia* (Moscow, 1945).

embarks on a chain of unbroken victories against the Japanese, who try in vain to capture him.

In August 1945 Korea is liberated by the Great Red Army. Kim returns to the fatherland, delivering a victory speech in October before a rapturous crowd. Afterwards he meets his aunt, with whom he returns to his home village of Man'gyŏngdae, where he is accorded a rapturous greeting by his grandmother and the rest of the villagers.[136]

Han's depiction of Kim's father is in itself an indication of an important divergence from socialist realist convention. While Soviet biographers rarely mention Stalin's peasant parents, and even then only to stress the opposition of old and new, Han establishes the continuity of truly Korean values by presenting Kim Hyŏngjik as the exemplary product of a long line of "pure and naive [*sunbak han*] farmers."[137] With such a pedigree it is small wonder that his son, even as a toddler, is "happier, more upright and steadfast than the other children," with "the gleam of one fundamentally incapable of wrongdoing" in his "cute eyes."[138] Han devotes a huge portion of his biographical writings to episodes in which the child General demonstrates these and other positive qualities against the stylized landscape of Man'gyŏngdae, where blue mountains loom "like bouquets" and "cotton-like clouds" call out in friendship. The lad shows his courage by climbing the highest tree in the village, and ascends the highest peak to catch the rainbow—the first sign of his naive striving for the Beautiful and the Good. His healthy curiosity manifests itself in his taking apart a gramophone. These are happy times. Like a good North Korean educator (see Ch3b), his father "always strictly avoid[s] restraining the General's will."[139] Man'gyŏngdae, in accordance with the usual pastoralism, is depicted as largely free of Japanese influence and the negative effects of poverty—so free, in fact, that the General reaches the age of seven (when his father is arrested) before realizing that life does not consist solely of the Beautiful and Good. Only then does he exhibit another obligatory characteristic of every North Korean hero, namely a boundless capacity for vengeful rage, which, like Kŭmch'ŏl in *History*, he first vents on small animals.[140]

---

[136] Based on *In'gan Kim Il Sŏng changgun* (1946), in *Suryŏngŭl ttara paeuja* (Pyongyang, 1960), 5-81; *Hyŏllo* (1946), in *HSYS*, 8:3-31; *Kaesŏn* (1948), in *HSYS*, 8:110-136; *Ryŏksa* (1953), in *HSYS*, 9:1-360; *Man'gyŏngdae* (1955), in *HSYS*, 9:362-491.

[137] Ibid., 364.

[138] Ibid., 390, 396.

[139] *In'gan Kim Ilsŏng changgun*, 30.

[140] *Man'gyŏngdae*, 385.

A second series of episodes takes place at the General's middle school in Manchuria, where he invents a game called "Catch the Jap." Every day a different schoolmate (but never the General) is selected to be the "Jap," whereupon he is chased and beaten by the others.[141] Soon the General "develops" the game by fitting out the "Jap" in spectacles and buck teeth to add realism. Sure enough, the game becomes so much "more active" that the children sometimes get carried away and have to be restrained by the smiling General before they do serious harm to their disguised friends.[142] By the time the hero turns thirteen, however, he is in search of a more satisfying pastime. He finds it during a stay with his grandparents in Pyongyang, where his teacher encourages him and his classmates to throw rocks at the passing cars of "Japs."[143] The fact that almost all school episodes take place outside the classroom is consistent with Han's effort to downplay experiences that could be seen as having alloyed the General's "truly Korean" naivete or *sobak ham*. The reader thus receives no indication of books read by the General in these years. It is apparently a small and self-evident step from the infant's instinctive intuition that "working people are the best" to his decision at the age of nineteen to join the communist party.[144] Han skips Kim's party activities almost entirely, of course, as these too would necessitate showing him in cerebral activities incompatible with his spontaneous image.

By the time the reader meets up with the hero again, he has completed his character development, formed a band of guerillas, and embarked on an uninterrupted series of victories against the numerically superior enemy. Han's patent ignorance of military matters, his characteristic aversion to concretizing the environments of his stories, and his chronic underestimation of his readers' intelligence all combine to make the guerilla war appear as stylized as the games in the Manchurian schoolyard. One is asked to believe the enemy's best strategists were continually flummoxed by a simple hide-and-seek, and that the partisans would steal weapons by sneaking up on the Japanese and throwing red pepper in their eyes.[145] Fearful that the acknowledgment of even the mildest setback will make readers doubt the General's greatness, Han claims the partisan unit *never*

---

[141] Ibid., 408.

[142] Ibid., 424.

[143] Ibid., 449; *Ryŏksa*, 72.

[144] Ibid., 390.

[145] Ibid., 114.

lost an engagement.[146] Casualties are virtually nonexistent. In one hand-to-hand battle a thousand Japanese are killed, while not a single Korean is even seriously wounded.[147] The General is so confident of success that he likens war to fishing, and promises nervous soldiers on the eve of battle that they will not be hurt. (Needless to say, this does little to enhance suspense on the part of the reader.)[148]

Han constantly emphasizes, however, that the General is neither a God nor a superhuman being: "the great hero," he writes over and over, "is a great man."[149] Han disinters his favorite KAPF-era catchphrases to explain that the General's greatness springs from his unparalleled understanding of the omnipotent science of dialectical materialism:

> Equipped with Marxist dialectical materialism, the General knew that objects constantly find themselves in mutual relationship with appearances, rising and falling in constant motion and change; that quantitative change becomes qualitative change; and that history arises from the struggle between conflicts in the relationship between objects and phenomena. He could thus understand the enemy more profoundly and fundamentally than the enemy himself. As a result he was able to develop a surefire strategy of total victory before a battle. By adapting his strategies to time and place, he could remain undefeated in an everchanging war.[150]

Though rarely so clumsily expressed, this premise of "*rational* magic" (Bortoli) lies at the heart of all socialist personality cults.[151] In contrast to the Stalin and Mao myths, however, the General is said by Han to have arrived at his unique understanding of Marxism-Leninism not through intellectual discipline and consciousness, but through his immeasurable love for the Korean people. This love makes Kim's body one with his ideology, "and when they are one, miracles can happen."[152] This, then, is how Kim can know all without forfeiting any of his "truly Korean" naivete and innocence.

---

[146] *Yŏngung Kim Ilsŏng changgun*, in *STP*, 94.

[147] *Ryŏksa*, 257-258.

[148] Ibid., 242.

[149] *In'gan Kim Ilsŏng changgun*, 25, 81; *Yŏngung Kim Ilsŏng changgun*, 152.

[150] Ibid., 125. See also 120-121.

[151] See G. Bortoli, *The Death of Stalin* (London, 1975), 63.

[152] *Yŏngung Kim Ilsŏng changgun*, 137.

Nowhere are Han's efforts to downplay the cerebral, i.e., un-Korean aspect of his hero so striking as when he describes the General's strategic insights as spontaneous "creations" which rise up suddenly from his subconscious. Many of the General's best ideas, one is told, come to him when he is *asleep*:

> When the General...found a comfortable place, he closed his eyes and immediately fell into a short but deep sleep. During that time, new ideas bubbled up in him like a fountain. Sleep for the General was therefore not only a break to sooth fatigue, but also a process of creating new things.[153]

Again, the contrast to the Stalin cult is illuminating. Stalin is never described as sleeping. Henri Barbusse calls him in his biography "the only one on this earth who does not sleep," and the many poems about the never-extinguished light in the Kremlin window seem to confirm that this is indeed a man so "conscious," i.e., so in control of his bodily urges, that he can dispense with sleep altogether.[154]

Han strives to make the General's "creations" appear as folksy as possible, while at the same time presenting them as the expression of extraordinary insight. The incompatibility of these two aims is behind much of the unintentional comedy of his writing on Kim:

> The General reflected again on how he had let the big fish get away....In such a tiny space of time an insignificant fish had been able to escape. How much easier then, for a human being? And after all, Japs were humans too.
>
> "There's a Korean proverb, isn't there: Light your cigarette on the lightning bolt," said the General with a smile. Comrade Im, whose pained expression showed he was still mourning the loss of the fish, didn't understand and became embarrassed. "In other words, nothing is so fast that the human mind cannot grasp it. This is what our proverb teaches us. If one utilizes just the right moment—the moment within the moment—then one can solve any problem, conquer any enemy."
>
> Comrade Im was silent.

---

[153] *Hyŏllo*, 24.

[154] Barbusse, 286; V. Shefner, *Pereklichka*, in *Zvezda*, April 1950, 4; V. Gusev, *Stalin v Kremle*, in *Pesnia o Staline: Izbrannie stikhi sovetskikh poetov* (Moscow, 1950), 32. For more on Soviet panegyrics, see my "Personenkult und Poesie: Die Panegyriken der Stalin-Zeit," (M.A. thesis, Ruhr-Universität Bochum, 1989).

"If one underestimates the Japs, one misses the right
moment. Light your cigarette on the lightning bolt—that is the
way to think." Only then did Comrade Im recognise that the
General was again seeking truth while fishing....This is the
reason, he thought once again, why the General always wins
battles in advance: his brain moves faster than lightning.[155]

As we have seen in *History*, Kim, unlike the paternal, disciplinarian
Stalin, wants not to infuse consciousness in his followers but to cultivate in
them the spontaneous qualities he himself possesses in such abundance. As
if to confirm Jung's equation of maternal and spontaneous principles, Han,
as we have already remarked, endows Kim with the traits of a mother
figure.[156] His breast is invitingly expansive, while his face, soft and oval
with "pretty incisors" and dimples, conforms to the Korean ideal of feminine
beauty.[157] In striking contrast to Soviet panegyrists, who most often praise
Stalin's stern, shining eyes—the indicator of his intellect and a standard
attribute of a politically conscious socialist realist hero[158]—Han places
constant emphasis on Kim's laugh or smile. In *History* alone it is referred
to over seventy times, on an average of once every five pages, but
occasionally five times on one page. While Stalin is ascetic and controlled,
Kim likes to eat and sing, and he can suddenly cry (when he thinks of the
bicycle his mother gave him) or lose his temper (when subordinates
disappoint him), only to burst out laughing again.[159] Han puts it in a nutshell
when he calls the General a man of "unusual naive spontaneity." (*pisanghi
sobak hago...*)[160]

As the most positive of all positive heroes, Stalin belongs at the apex
of the diamond-shaped diagram which Hans Günther uses to rank the figures
of the socialist realist novel (see Ch2b). Soviet panegyrists themselves
constantly localize Stalin in the "high Kremlin," which Clark describes as
occupying the highest place in the "vertical cosmology" of Stalinist

[155] *Hyŏllo*, 27-28.

[156] This explains why the hero's mother, in violation of North Korean literary convention,
is assigned such an insignificant role in Han's writings; not even in his maternal qualities is the
General to be outdone by another figure.

[157] *Ryŏksa* 28, 247; *Kaesŏn*, 118.

[158] Myers, "Personenkult und Poesie," 55; Clark, *The Soviet Novel*, 141.

[159] *Kaesŏn*, 132; *Ryŏksa*, 80-85; *Man'gyŏngdae*, 423.

[160] *Kim Ilsŏng changgun insanggi*, in *STP*, 157.

symbols.[161] Kim, on the other hand, is the North Korean literary hero *par excellence*: the most spontaneous, the most naive, the most innocent, the most loving—in short, the man in whom the highest concentration of "truly Korean" virtues is embodied. For this reason he belongs in the center of the harmonious circle drawn in our discussion of *Growing Village* as a North Korean counterpart to Günther's diagram. It is no coincidence that Han himself refers to Kim as "the center" or "nucleus," a hero whom "we average people discover in our midst," and accordingly refuses to localize Kim in any edifice or city. He is everywhere, for he is at the heart of every Korean.[162]

Considering that much of Han's stature derived from his role as a curator of the personality cult, it is ironic that he was perhaps the person least suited to developing and propagating official myths. A more insightful writer would have instinctively recognised that the novel is a fundamentally irreverent genre incompatible with epic-scale reverence.[163] For this very reason the Soviets moulded Stalin's biography to fit the socialist realist "master plot" while stopping short of presenting his life in the form of a novel. Though one cannot know for sure how *History, Man'gyŏngdae* and the like were received by the North Koreans themselves, the absence of comparable panegyric fiction in the peninsula's tradition gives reason to believe that they will, at least at first, have found them as bizarre and ludicrous as does the foreign reader today.

Kremlinologist Leonard Schapiro once wrote that the true object of propaganda is "neither to convince nor to persuade, but to produce a uniform pattern of public utterance in which the first trace of unorthodox thought immediately reveals itself as a jarring dissonance."[164] Han's lifelong aversion both to planning his work beforehand and to checking it afterwards can therefore be seen as an additional factor unfitting him for the role of official mythmaker. In *History* the General exhorts teachers always to use Korean historical examples in their lessons—just after he has told the children a story about the Russian civil war, and just before he begins to talk about the October Revolution! There are also inconsistencies between the various texts. The hero's curiosity is roused in *In'gan Kim Ilsŏng*

---

[161] Myers, "Personenkult und Poesie," 55; Clark, *The Soviet Novel*, 141.

[162] *Yŏngung Kim Ilsŏng changgun*, 94, 152; *Kim Ilsŏng changgun insanggi*, 166-167.

[163] The projection of epic greatness into the novel's language of contemporaneity has always been used to *parody* lofty mythical models. See Mikhail Bakhtin, "Epic and Novel," in *The Dialogic Imagination: Four Essays by Mikhail Bakhtin*, 18-21.

[164] *The Communist Party of the Soviet Union* (New York, 1960), 472.

142 • *Brian Myers*

changgun (General Kim Il Sung, the Man, 1946) by his father's clock, and in *Man'gyŏngdae* by a rich landowner's.[165] Both *General Kim Il Sung, the Man* and *Kaesŏn* (Triumphal Return, 1948) describe the October 1945 reunion of Kim and his aunt, but the dialogues of the two versions diverge substantially.[166] Though they may appear trivial to outsiders, such inconsistencies may have helped hinder the establishment of a uniform pattern of personality cult propaganda, and perhaps raised even among sympathetic readers certain doubts about the veracity of the Kim myth. The fact that official censors were unwilling to subject even these texts of Han's to closer scrutiny, despite their enormous importance to the legitimacy of the regime, constitutes the most striking indication of the pervasiveness and authority of the "Han machine" inside the cultural apparatus.

---

[165] *In'gan Kim Ilsŏng changgun*, 32. *Man'gyŏngdae*, 366-367.

[166] To give just one example, the aunt in *In'gan Kim Ilsŏng changgun* (70) says to the General "I also fought against the Japs"; in *Kaesŏn* (123-124) she says instead, "though I've been stuck out in the rice fields until my hair turned white, I am one of the people who up to now have always acted in accordance with the will of the General and his father."

5

Han's Purge and Rehabilitation (1962-1969)

Even as the cult around the KFLA chairman reached its zenith, his detractors, apparently utilizing his frequent absences from the country, began petitioning Kim Il Sung for his removal.[1] Ringleader of the anti-Han camp was Kim Ch'angman, Kim Il Sung's erstwhile speechwriter and "ideological sidekick" (Cumings),[2] whose fall from grace in the early 1950s had coincided with Han's rise to prominence. Han had even replaced him as Minister of Education in 1956.[3] Though Kim Ch'angman had regained much of his earlier influence, he appears to have continued to regard Han as the usurper of his rightful place as Kim Il Sung's right-hand intellectual. In conversations with the premier, however, he would have been able to make an objective case for Han's removal on the basis of the patently declining quality of the latter's work, as well as the cultural sector's failure to fulfil the needs of the Ch'ŏllima movement.

Though Kim Il Sung refused to relieve Han, he appears to have been impressed by Kim Ch'angman's zeal, for he appointed him vice-chairman of the Central Party School in September 1961.[4] This allowed Kim Ch'angman to function as a kind of roving ideological watchdog among the various party institutions, including the KFLA. It is not unlikely that he was behind a leading article which appeared in *Chosŏn munhak* in November 1961. In it the anonymous writer lamented the failure of literature to meet the Ch'ŏllima guidelines, and sharply criticised the continuing tendencies of

---

[1] In February 1959 Han attended the World Peace Conference in Moscow, in April 1960 the Asia and Africa Conference in Guinea, and in March 1961 a writers' conference in New Delhi.

[2] Bruce Cumings, *The Origins of the Korean War II*, 310, 352-353.

[3] Dae-Sook Suh, *Korean Communism*, 464.

[4] Yi Hanggu, "Pukhanŭi chakka taeyŏl sogesŏ," 244.

factography and conflictlessness—tendencies, it will be remembered, that Han had arbitrarily declared nonexistent in 1959.[5]

More serious trouble for Han came during a conference of KFLA cadres in March 1962, when Kim Ch'angman attacked Ch'oe Sŭnghŭi (who had recently regained her old post as Dance Union chairwoman with Han's support) for carrying on an affair with one of the KFLA's vice-chairmen.[6] Kim also complained of the KFLA's failure to foster new talent, then closed the session with the ominous announcement that the organization would soon be purged of "several elements" presently limiting its effectiveness.[7] The vice-chairman and Ch'oe were promptly degraded, but the purge Kim had announced failed to materialize. In the next months Han, apparently distracted by this sword of Damocles, published next to nothing. Kim Ch'angman took this as an excuse to go to him and request his resignation. Han refused.[8] At around this time in summer 1962, Yi Hanggu, then an editor at the KFLA's publishing house, visited Han at his spacious home to request changes in the serial novel *Hyŏngje* (Siblings) before its publication in book form. Han was of course not accustomed to being treated like a regular writer:

> When he heard there were a few passages which needed correction he brusquely asked, "Whose opinion is that?" There was anger in his voice.
>
> "It is the opinion of the Publications Bureau's board of censors, sir."

---

[5] "4 ch'a tang taehoega chesihan munhak yesurŭi kangnyŏngjŏk kwaŏp," *CM*, October 1961, 4-15.

[6] Yi Hanggu describes the vice-chairman in question as Sŏ Manil, although Sŏ appears to have been purged in 1958. His name disappeared from the board of editors of *Chosŏn munhak* in November of that year, and he was subjected to intense vilification by Han Sŏrya a few months later (see Ch4a). The *Munhak sinmun* mentions Sim Yŏng and Yi Ch'an as KFLA vice-chairmen both in February and August of 1962, so one can be fairly certain that neither of them was degraded. See "Munyech'ong chungang wiwŏnhoe che 10 ch'a hwaktae chiphaeng wiwŏnhoe chinhaeng," *MS*, 23 February 1962; "Che 2 ch'a Asea, Ap'ŭrik'a chakka taehoee ch'amga hettŏn uri nara chakka taep'yodan kwiguk," *MS*, 2 March 1962; and "Munyech'ong kakto wiwŏnhoe chidojŏk kinŭngŭl chegohaja," *MS*, 3 August 1962. I have found no mention of Sŏ Manil in the few papers available from that time, but the reader will remember that three vice-chairmen slots were created in 1956 (see Ch4a). Since purges are not always final in the DPRK, it is indeed possible that Sŏ had returned to one of these slots by early 1962, but in the absence of an official list of the top KFLA hierarchy I would urge caution on this point.

[7] Yi Hanggu, 244-245.

[8] Scalapino and Lee, 2:885.

"They censor *my* work? People who don't know the first
thing about literature!"

"It's nothing, sir; it just needs touching up here and there."

"Hmph! You fellows can fix it up yourselves if you want."[9]

Yi goes on to tell how Han pointed to two drawings of him by different
artists, asking which one he preferred. When Yi diplomatically pointed to
the more flattering one Han replied, "Nonsense; the other catches the servile
part of my nature perfectly."[10] This story may seem farfetched, but there are
other indications that Han had indeed begun to feel he had made too many
compromises for the sake of his career. His introduction to *Love* in 1960
had shown a yearning for the psychological prose of his colonial works.

> For an engineer of the soul I have up until now only scratched
> the surface of the world of the human soul....It is my greatest
> aspiration as a writer to dig a little deeper in the future, if only
> inch by inch, into the world of the human soul.[11]

In another sign of creative restlessness Han had in the late 1950s
begun to write poetry—and in a lyrical style reminiscent of the colonial
Minyop'a (Folklore Group) at that.[12] Two of his poems dated September
1959 were finally published in the *Munhak sinmun* on 14 August 1962.[13]
The poet Min Pyŏnggyun is said to have responded by praising Han for
"moving in the right direction." Han answered him in a now famous letter.
Yi Hanggu and fellow defector U Kilmyŏng differ as to its exact contents,
but Yi appears to be more knowledgeable of the incident. According to him
Han expressed his intention of writing in the future "for himself," and
not—these were supposedly his exact words—"for one whose belly is filled
with fat."[14] Yi and U both assert, and there is no reason to doubt them, that
Han was alluding to his nemesis, the corpulent Kim Ch'angman. Kim Il
Sung, however, was also a fat man. Han's indiscretion proved fateful, for
the missive was intercepted by the Ministry of State Control and brought
before the Great Leader himself, either as proof of his old friend's treachery,
or more probably—as it is hard to believe Kim would not have understood

[9] Yi Hanggu, 246.

[10] Ibid., 247.

[11] Foreword to *Sarang*, vol. 12 of *HSYS*, 2-3.

[12] I thank Jörg Trappmann for pointing out the similarity to me.

[13] *Kŭmgangsan, Samilp'o* in *MS*, 14 August 1962.

[14] Scalapino and Lee, 2:886.

Han's true meaning—as evidence that the KFLA chairman had indeed grown too big for his britches. In any case, the letter seems to have finally convinced Kim to purge the writer.[15]

Shortly thereafter, in September 1962, a party session of the KFLA was called to discuss the quarter that had just ended. Directly after his opening report Han, to his great surprise, found himself under attack from *Munhak sinmun* editor Kwŏn Chongung. Yi Hanggu, who was present, remembers Kwŏn's criticism as follows:

> "The Federation's affairs have been handled sloppily and are thus in a state of stagnation. The achievements listed in the report were already brought up in the second quarter session. The Party asks us writers to stand at the vanguard of the ideological and cultural revolution and raise revolutionary art to a higher level of development, but we have been unable to fulfil our obligation. I cannot stand here and fail to criticise Federation chairman comrade Han Sŏrya for his lazy lifestyle and negligent leadership."[16]

Han thereupon interrupted Kwŏn with a storm of abuse, which the latter promptly held up to all present as evidence of the chairman's dictatorial nature. After Kwŏn had sat down, the young writer Pak Unggŏl stood up and continued the attack. When he too was shouted down by Han the session was adjourned.

On the very next day the case was brought before the Pyongyang municipal committee, a higher authority. "On this occasion," write Scalapino and Lee, "the full Party arsenal was brought to bear against Han," with Kim Ch'angman and others coming forward to enumerate his crimes, which

---

[15] Ibid. Distrust of all scholarship on the DPRK published in the anti-communist past and ignorance of everything written overseas on the subject have caused South Korean scholars to think up their own reasons for the purge. Kwŏn Yŏngmin claims Han was purged to make way for Kim Il Sung's *Chuch'e* literary theory (*Wŏlbuk munin yŏn'gu*, 44). This is highly unlikely. Han had already spent over ten years disseminating the Great Leader's pronouncements on literature, and there is no reason to believe such an ethnocentric writer would not have wholeheartedly supported the *Chuch'e* theory had he been asked to do so. In any case, the *Chuch'e* theory did not emerge until years after Han's banishment. Kim Yunsik, on the other hand, muses that Han was probably punished for remaining loyal to Stalin in the age of Krushchev ("Pukhan munhagŭi segaji chikchŏpsŏng," 203). This is absurd; the DPRK regime never looked back more nostalgically on the Generalissimo than in the early 1960s. More than a year after Han's purge some of Stalin's writings were published in Pyongyang in a book entitled *Sujŏngjuŭirŭl pandae hayŏ* (Opposing Revisionism, 1964).

[16] Yi Hanggu, 247.

included parochialism in the fostering of new talent.[17] The intercepted letter was finally exhibited to the assembled cadres as proof of Han's betrayal of the party and its leader. In the best Confucian tradition, Han's political and administrative errors were linked to private and moral failings, specifically his second marriage to a landowner's daughter and his affairs with secretaries (among them the daughter of famous playwright Song Yŏng).[18] His exalted position, it seems, had not exempted him from close scrutiny by the security apparatus.[19] The fact that his father had been a wealthy, pro-Japanese landlord (and not a Leninist patriot as he had claimed) was trotted out as confirmation that Han, like the various purge victims before him, had *always* been a reactionary element.[20] Even the writer's son Han Uk, a professor at Pyongyang's Kim Il Sung University, lent his voice to the denunciatory chorus.[21]

For days Han vigorously rejected all charges of wrongdoing, blaming them on the machinations of Kim Ch'angman. He had never been a particularly healthy man, however, and after several days of intensive criticism he no longer possessed the energy to defend himself. Finally, on the tenth day, he was stripped of his many offices and expelled from the party. (To add insult to injury, Kim Ch'angman ascended to the vice-premiership of the DPRK in October.)[22] In February 1963 Han was exiled to a remote village in the DPRK's northern province of Chagang. His possessions, which included a villa in the center of Pyongyang, a Soviet car, and a bank account worth 700,000 wŏn, were confiscated.[23]

In significant contrast to the preceding purges of Yim Hwa, Kim Namch'ŏn and Hong Sunch'ŏl, however, no mention was made of the case

---

[17] Scalapino and Lee, 2:886.

[18] Yun Kibong, another defector, offers a version of the heated exchange between Han Sŏrya and Kim Ch'angman in which Han points out that Kim too had discarded his first wife for a woman more in keeping with his high position. See *Naega pon pungnyŏk' ttang* (Seoul, 1973), 215-218. I find Yun a somewhat unreliable source, however, not least because he maintains Han's sixtieth birthday party was held in 1962.

[19] Scalapino and Lee, 2:886.

[20] Ibid., 2:887; cf. Han's "Reninŭi hoesanggi" (Remembering Lenin, 1957), in *HSYS*, 14:242-245.

[21] Yi Hanggu, 249.

[22] Dae-Sook Suh, *Korean Communism*, 482.

[23] Scalapino and Lee, 2:886-887. To put this sum into perspective one need know that the average North Korean citizen at the time was able to save no more than 10 wŏn a month. Ibid., 2:1412-1414.

148 • *Brian Myers*

in either the literary or the national press. Han's name was simply removed from circulation, thus making him the first nonperson in the history of the DPRK. This can doubtless be attributed to his longtime role as curator of the personality cult. To denounce him in public as a reactionary element and an enemy of the people would have raised serious doubts about the veracity of the official myths he had propagated. While the *Munhak sinmun* therefore discreetly announced the appointment of novelist Ch'ŏn Sebong (1915-1986) as new KFLA chairman,[24] the authorities set about the Herculean task of removing all of the disgraced writer's works from bookshelves across the country—and from every schoolchild's desk as well, for as Education Minister Han had made sure his Kim writings were included in textbooks.

A rectification campaign was implemented on the cultural scene in spring 1962 to purge it of "the remnants of Han Sŏrya's ideological poison."[25] KFLA members were forced to spend every weeknight from mid-March 1963 to the end of the year criticising themselves and each other. The campaign's first victims were close Han associates like Min Pyŏnggyun, critic Yun Sep'yŏng, literary scholar Kye Puk, and comedian Sin Pulch'ul. Han Uk's betrayal of his father could not prevent him too from being purged.[26] According to a South Korean source the purge eventually claimed ninety members of the KFLA.[27] The effect of this turmoil on literary production can be imagined. Publications were hard put to find new material to print, and the *Munhak sinmun* was even forced to suspend publication temporarily.[28] Unfortunately there is little information on the role played by literary issues *per se* during these criticism sessions. According to Scalapino and Lee, however, charges of traditionalism and liberalism were raised against Han.[29] This would seem to indicate that his lifelong flouting of socialist realist guidelines was finally "exposed" and held up for critical discussion. A spectacular climax to the campaign was provided by the torching of Han's writings in a courtyard behind KFLA headquarters, where the members of the WU had been summoned. The bonfire burned for over three days.[30]

---

[24] *MS*, 19 October 1962.

[25] Yi Hanggu, 250.

[26] Ibid., 251-252.

[27] *Pukhan taesajŏn* (Seoul, 1974), s.v. "Han Sŏrya."

[28] Yi Hanggu, 251.

[29] Scalapino and Lee, 1:520.

[30] Yi Hanggu, 252.

As for Han, he is said to have spent his years in exile tilling his garden.[31] He must have been startled at the changes taking place in North Korean culture from about 1966 in the wake of the Sino-Soviet crisis, which had convinced the DPRK of the need to reduce its dependency on its socialist allies. These changes were dramatic and far-reaching enough to warrant being called a cultural revolution, though one without the hysteria of its more famous Chinese counterpart. Its most important development was the sudden efflorescence of the cult of Kim Il Sung, who was now claimed to have liberated the country in 1945 without foreign help.[32] Needless to say, this myth required an even more extensive rewriting of books than had Han's purge. Starting with Cho Kich'ŏn's epic poem *Paektusan* (Mt Paektu, 1947), virtually all canonical works had made grateful reference to the Great Red Army and its commander-in-chief Stalin. All were withdrawn, and only the minority was prepared for republication in amended versions. At the same time Kim Il Sung's motley pronouncements on literature were tricked out as a coherent literary theory which, though still ostensibly socialist realist, was said to be suited to the unique needs of the Korean people.[33] This served both to legitimize and widen the already irreconcilable differences between North Korean literature and the Soviet aesthetic doctrine. Literary exchange between the DPRK and the rest of the communist bloc, which had in any case been steadily declining since the Soviet occupation period, now dwindled almost completely away.

Other changes came about as a result of the regime's desire to bring harmony to the literary scene once and for all by stamping out vainglory and egotism among writers. Ch'ŏn Sebong, the KFLA's new chairman, was denied the degree of official veneration that Han had received, though he remained in the post for almost twice as long (from 1962 to his death in 1986). The KAPF cult, which had served to exalt a small clique of writers over their colleagues, disappeared without a trace.[34] Long acclaimed works by KAPF veterans were at last subjected to objective scrutiny and found wanting, particularly in macrostructural respects.[35] More and more novels began to be produced by authorial teams. This was especially the case with books related to Kim Il Sung, for the regime was clearly determined never

---

[31] Scalapino and Lee, 2:887.

[32] Dae-Sook Suh, *Korean Communism*, 203-208.

[33] See Hong Kisam, *Pukhan munye iron* (Seoul, 1981).

[34] Ibid., 25.

[35] Yi Kiyŏng's long-touted *Land* was thoroughly rewritten, apparently by a different author or authors, and republished in a much shorter version. See *Ttang* (Pyongyang, 1973).

again to link its legitimatory myths to the name of a single writer. The first comprehensive biography of the premier, 1968's *Minjogŭi t'aeyang Kim Ilsŏng changgun* (Sun of the People, General Kim Il Sung), was almost certainly written by a collective, though it appeared under the name Paek Pong. This was said to be the pseudonym of a historian conducting research in Japan.[36]

But purges in North Korea are not always final, as the career of Ch'oe Sŭnghŭi has already shown us, and sure enough, Han Sŏrya's name suddenly reappeared on the roster of the KWP's Central Committee in 1969.[37] Kim Il Sung, who had purged Kim Ch'angman the year before, appears to have felt the writer had been treated a little too harshly. Yet his ranking was much lower than before the purge, and he was not reappointed to any of his old posts. This is by all appearances the last mention of Han as a political official. His name is absent from the roster of the Fifth Party Congress in November 1970, and from all rosters thereafter. It is hard to believe that Kim Il Sung would have been so capricious as to rehabilitate the aging Han only to purge him again a few months later. It is likely therefore, though by no means certain, that Han died sometime between late 1969 and late 1970 at the age of 69 or 70. Perhaps a rapid decline in his health had prompted Kim to rehabilitate him in the first place, as a last favor to the man who had devised the iconography of his personality cult.

[36] Paek Pong, *Minjogŭi t'aeyang Kim Ilsŏng changgun* (Pyongyang, 1968); see also Dae-Sook Suh, *Kim Il Sung*, 339.

[37] Scalapino and Lee, 2:887.

Conclusion
Han Sŏrya's Legacy

How was Han Sŏrya, an undistinguished veteran of the proletarian culture movement, able to dominate North Korean literature in its formative years? The absence of an uncompromised, Gorky-type hero on the leftist literary scene, combined with the personal support of Kim Il Sung, who may have sensed a soulmate in KAPF's "country bumpkin," made it possible for Han to ascend to the chairmanship of the Federation of Literature and Art in 1948. Once in office, however, the patrimonial functioning of the cultural apparatus gave his career a momentum of its own, by ensuring that both his administrative and literary performance would be exempted from adverse criticism. Subservience to Han became even more imperative after the Soviet-Koreans and others capable of dispensing career privileges on the cultural scene were purged. As a result his works were praised more extravagantly with every year, even as they declined in formal quality and became increasingly removed from the official doctrine of socialist realism.

The other main factor in Han's rise to the top consisted in his being, in Han Chungmo's words, the "writer who devoted the most creative energy to depicting the leader Kim Il Sung."[1] Yet it would be wrong to think in terms of a simple *quid pro quo* for Han's panegyric services. Rather, it seems the regime's strategy was to enhance the authority of the Kim myths by exalting the man under whose name they were disseminated. Parallels can thus be found both to the systematic celebration of octogenarian folk-panegyrist Dzhambul during the Stalin era, and to the minor cult of Mao's right-hand man Lin Piao.[2] Alas, Han was a clumsy mythmaker, and his writings on Kim Il Sung were fraught with gross inconsistencies that must

---

[1] *Han Sŏryaŭi ch'angjak yŏn'gu*, 267.

[2] Cf. A. Avtorkhanov, *Zagadki smerti Stalina* (Frankfurt am Main, 1976), 281; James T. Myers, "The Political Dynamics of the Cult of Mao Tse-Tung," in *China: A System-functional Reader*, ed. Yung Wei (Columbus, 1972), 91.

have been noticed even by sympathetic readers. The cultural apparatus, however, exempted even these works from objective criticism. Like a true patrimonial bureaucracy, its first loyalty was to its boss, not to official ideology.[3]

By the early 1960s, the writer was so firmly entrenched in office that he could only be removed from above. But though chronic factional unrest had proven Han to be a destabilizing and demoralizing influence on the cultural scene, Kim Il Sung refused to purge him. While considerations of friendship doubtless played a role here, Kim must have most feared bringing into disrepute the myths legitimizing his rule—myths which by that time had become linked in the minds even of schoolchildren with Han's name. Only when the writer's arrogance could no longer be overlooked was he purged, and even then with a discretion unprecedented in the DPRK's history.

It is difficult, regardless of one's ideological standpoint, to conclude that the formative development of North Korean literature benefited from Han's chairmanship of the KFLA. The very appointment of the little respected writer appears to have sent an early signal to colleagues that their careers would depend less on performance than on access to power. This in turn helped create an atmosphere in which many promising writers paid less attention to their work than to the attainment of cultural offices which in other socialist countries were imbued with little real authority and even less prestige.

Han's special position certainly militated against the implementation of socialist realism, which was defined in North Korea, as in the USSR, primarily by a list of model novels. By canonizing Han's work despite its gross violations of socialist realism, while applying pedantically strict standards to less favored writers, critics effectively reduced the doctrine to a mere weapon of sectarian conflict. This in turn helped facilitate its displacement by Kim Il Sung's own folksy pronouncements on literature, which were in any case more compatible with the traditional inclinations of the intellectuals themselves. One wonders of course to what extent Kim (who has never been known to be a voracious reader himself) allowed his views on literature to be shaped or even formulated by these very intellectuals in the first place, in particular by Han Sŏrya. Considering all the empty chatter reproduced in Kim's *Selected Works*, it certainly seems odd that one must turn to Han's writings to find so many important remarks made by the Leader on literary matters during the 1950s. Whether or not

---

[3] Cf. Norman Jacobs, *The Korean Road to Modernization and Development* (Urbana/Chicago, 1985), 18-19.

Kim's views on literature were his own, it seems safe to conclude, at the very least, that the North Korean party's attitude to established cultural values was similar to that of its Stalin-era Soviet counterpart in that it was "more often deferential than destructive. As party values penetrated culture the cultural values of the old intellegentsia penetrated the party."[4]

While colleagues like Yi Kiyŏng and Hwang Kŏn at least made some effort to bring their literature in line with socialist realist dictates, Han unabashedly demonstrated his allegiance to colonial-era traditions from the spontaneity-glorifying *Path of Blood* (1946) onward. The fundamental incompatibility of his writing with the Soviet doctrine is perhaps most obvious in *Jackals* (1951) and *Love* (1960), both of which reflect a moralist and ethnocentric social criticism far removed from the Marxist-Leninist *Weltanschauung* a socialist realist literature is obliged to reflect.

It is ironic that the cultural matrix informing Han's works should have triumphed so completely in North Korean letters after his purge, with the propagation of the so-called *Chuch'e* (self-reliance) theory of literature in the late 1960s. If Han were in fact still alive in 1973, he would doubtless have been gratified by the appearance of *Chosŏn munhwaŏ sajŏn* (lit., A Dictionary of Korean Cultured Language), which listed "imperialist invader" as a second definition of the word *sŭngnyangi* (jackal). The suspicion that Han's 1951 novella of the same name influenced this entry is strengthened by the example sentence given: "US imperialists are 20th-century barbarians, two-legged *jackals* and bloodthirsty murderers."[5]

But perhaps the real triumph of Han Sŏrya's legacy came in the mid-1970s with the canonization of *Kkot' p'anŭn ch'ŏnyŏ* (The Flower Girl), the product of an authorial collective.[6] This crude tale of benevolently naive villagers groaning under the Japanese colonial yoke exhibits the same ethnocentric, prudish moralism, the same emphasis on the ideals of childhood, and the same curious mix of sentimentality and brutality that marked Han's fiction. The eponymous heroine is even falsely accused of stealing money to buy medicine for her mother—just like the angelic children in Han's *Love* (1960) and *Mt Sŏlbong* (1958). As one of the

---

[4] Sheila Fitzpatrick, "Culture and Politics Under Stalin: A Reappraisal," in *Slavic Review* 35 (12 1976): 213.

[5] *Chosŏn munhwaŏ sajŏn* (Pyongyang, 1973), s.v. "sŭngnyangi."

[6] The story, which was claimed to have been staged by Kim Il Sung himself in the 1930s, appeared as an opera in 1973 and as a novel in 1977. *Kkot' p'anŭn ch'ŏnyŏ: purhuŭi kojŏn myŏngjak 'Kkot' p'anŭn ch'ŏnyŏ' rŭl kaksaekhan hyŏngmyŏng kagŭk* (Pyongyang, 1973); *Kkot' p'anŭn ch'ŏnyŏ* (Pyongyang, 1977).

154 • *Brian Myers*

DPRK's three most highly touted works, *The Flower Girl* has proved to be more effective in spreading Han's literary ideals than Han himself had been.[7]

This is fine by some intellectuals in the ROK, who claim North Korean novels like *The Flower Girl* evince a more "purely Korean" style than most of what is written at home.[8] It is difficult to agree with such praise. Pyongyang's authorial collectives have clearly abandoned the most Korean characteristics of New Tendency-KAPF fiction—its boldness and vitality—while retaining the foreign-influenced elements it shared with the rest of the colonial era's mass-oriented literature: the chocolate-box settings, the stilted melodrama, the Pollyanaish, orphaned heroines. (The very motif of the flower girl seems somehow inauthentic, not so much an evocation of real life on the peninsula as a throwback to the colonial Korean theater's craze for Victorian-inspired Japanese schmaltz.) What else but the anachronistic un-Koreanness of this literature—in form if not in message—can explain its failure to interest more than a handful of academic readers in the South? The contrast to the popularity of East German writers like Anna Seghers and Hermann Kant in West Germany makes one wonder whether socialist realism's vague postulates and updatable canon might not have allowed writers in the DPRK to pursue more genuine and progressive forms of national expression—and thus made the much-invoked task of Korean literary unification a less daunting one than it appears today.

Considering the triumph of Han's literary ideals in the DPRK, it was perhaps inevitable that official literary scholars would someday begin to move tentatively toward his rehabilitation. Finally, in 1986, there appeared a book entitled *Chosŏn munhak kaegwan* (An Outline of Korean Literature), which mentioned Han and three of his works in a positive context.[9] A little over a page in the book deals with *Dusk* (1936), which is said to possess "literary historical significance as a pre-liberation novel comprehensively depicting the working class."[10] In contrast to Yi Kiyŏng's *Home Town*, however, with which it had always been coupled in the literary historiography of the 1950s, the novel is not granted its own subheading. On

---

[7] The other two works are *P'ibada* (Sea of Blood) and *Han chawidanwŏnŭi unmyŏng* (The Fate of One Member of a Self-Defense Unit).

[8] South Korean novelist Chŏng Tosang confessed to having been moved to tears by *The Flower Girl*. See Kim Ch'ŏl et al, "Pukhanmunhwa paro ilkkiŭi ipmun," *Munye chungang* 12 (3 1989): 274.

[9] Pak Chongwŏn and Yu Man, *Chosŏn munhak kaegwan* (Pyongyang, 1986).

[10] Ibid., 2:62-63.

the other hand, two full pages of the *Outline of Korean Literature* are devoted to *Jackals* (1951), which comes in for especially high commendation as a "brilliant work" exposing the "true murderous nature" of American missionaries. The plot is lovingly retold, and excerpts from the villains' dialogue ("syringes...are weapons for America and its people") are quoted to demonstrate Han's skill in character depiction.[11] The survival of *Jackals'* reputation indicates that not all of Han's fiction was granted model status as a result of his special position in the cultural apparatus, but was in some cases canonized because it genuinely did—and still does—conform to official guidelines and tastes. That this should be true of an openly racist work, which a Soviet translator found offensive enough to warrant a complete rewriting, is in itself sufficient cause to challenge the prevailing view that *Chuch'e* culture is "nothing more than a variation of socialist realism."[12]

The *Outline of Korean Literature* also praises Han's *Kaesŏn* (Triumphal Return, 1948) as "the first short story to describe the Great Leader as he appeared after the liberation."[13] In this case, however, Han's authorship of the work is left unspoken, a clear sign that the authorities remain disinclined to associate Kim Il Sung with a writer who fell from grace even temporarily. This is ironic, of course, for Han's imprint is still clearly evident on the personality cult as it exists today. True, the Kim biography produced under the name of Paek Pong is more sophisticated than anything Han ever wrote on the subject. Countless little inconsistencies have been ironed out, and one notices a desire to impart a more well-rounded image of the Great Leader than that which prevailed during the 1950s. Kim's more recent claim to be the world's leading interpreter of Marxist-Leninism has made it impossible to continue presenting him as the embodiment of unadulterated *sobak ham*. Yet he remains overall a spontaneous, unascetic and maternal figure, in contrast to the objects of other socialist personality cults. These and other distinguishing characteristics of the Kim myth, such as the emphasis on his pure peasant lineage, can all be traced back to Han's writings of the late 1940s and early 1950s. And if the DPRK's efforts to convert foreigners to Kim Il Sungism have succeeded only in making a proud people into an international laughing stock, then Han must bear a good part of the blame, for the myth's insulting

[11] Ibid., 2:167.

[12] Youngmin Kwon (Kwŏn Yŏngmin), "Literature and Art in North Korea: Theory and Policy," *Korea Journal*, 31 (Summer 1991), 64-65.

[13] *Chosŏn munhak kaegwan*, 2:121-122.

patronization of its audience (as in the wildly improbable depictions of Kim's military exploits) and the unintentionally comical touches so often ridiculed overseas (such as the paeans to Kim's dimples) are also the legacy of his unique style. Though no longer acknowledged in the DPRK to be a major writer, therefore, Han has lost none of his importance. On the contrary; since the Kim cult has steadily grown until it has virtually *become* North Korean culture itself, Han can be said to be more important than ever.

JACKALS (1951)
by Han Sŏrya

Note: I am offering a complete translation of Sŭngynangi *over other works mainly because it is the most acclaimed of Han's stories in today's DPRK. In presenting a novella that makes no mention of Kim Il Sung, I also hope to counteract the widespread misconception that the personality cult has always dominated North Korean culture to the extent it has since 1966-67. The Concerned-Asian-Scholarly implication that the UN side had a virtual monopoly on racist propaganda during the Korean War (cf. Halliday & Cumings'* Korea: The Unknown War, *1988) also needs challenging, if only to help explain KPA misconduct without resorting to cliches (themselves racist) about typically Asian brutality.*

The translation is based on the earliest edition of Sŭngynangi *I could find, one brought out in 1954 by a Tokyo publisher. Though marred by typographical errors, this is clearly the version referred to by Han Chungmo in his* Han Sŏryaŭi ch'angjak yŏn'gu *(1959), and there is no reason to believe it was not the version read by North Koreans throughout the 1950s. In 1960 a slightly expanded version of* Sŭngynangi, *which attempted to bring the original more in line with socialist realism, was published in Han's* Selected Works *(HSYS, 8:420-491). I have referred to this redaction, whose emendations may or may not be the work of Han himself, only to help clarify phrases that make no sense at all in the 1954 version—though one might say that these very inexplicabilities make the latter a more authentic document of the author's unique style. I have no more aimed for a polished literary translation of this story than Han, who prided himself on writing very quickly, aimed for a polished literary original. The reader will thus find* Jackals, *like so much of Han's work, to be riddled with mixed metaphors (usually of the bestial variety), logical inconsistencies, long stretches of tautologous dialogue and confusingly abrupt transitions. I have diverged from Han's style only when allegiance to it would have produced an English significantly more unwieldy or confusing than the Korean original. —B.M.*

1

In a puddle behind the missionary's cowshed little Sugil found a huge rubber ball. It was a little old all right, but there was something special about its pleasant feel, and the way it had been worn down all nice and smooth.

"This must be my lucky day!" Sugil was so happy he jumped up and down for a while. Then he tried throwing the ball into the air with all his might, bounding after it with long strides to catch it as it came down. It wasn't always that easy, but he felt a foolish pleasure just chasing it, and that one time in five when he managed to jump up and catch it right away. Then he tried kicking the ball. Watching it fall and roll away he wished someone was on the other side to kick it back. He thought of the schoolchildren playing soccer in the schoolyard. Sugil looked around and around in the hope that some children from the village would appear.

But in fact the place had been set up so that children couldn't easily get in. The missionaries' long fence went all the way around, with barbed wire wrapped thickly around the tree trunks, so outsiders did not dare show themselves. Why, not even the boldest pranksters considered trespassing, for everything was on the missionaries' property, from the cowshed to the fruit trees on the slope beneath it—to say nothing of the missionaries' residence itself, which nestled in the dark woods high at the crest of the hill.

Sugil's mother was the missionary's charwoman. She did the laundry, cleaned out the cowshed, helped milk the cow at times, and picked fruit in the autumn. She lived with Sugil in a little hut attached to the cowshed. One room there was set aside for Mr Ch'oe, the old odd-jobs man. He had originally been a farmhand for the landowner "Piggy" Kang. He had been so naive as to handle "Piggy" Kang's night soil every day for ten years, a job which in the village earned him the nickname of Old Sewer-Soaked Ch'oe. But as he got older and his back grew bent, it became clear he would be cast aside despite his years of service. As fate would have it, he had previously cleaned out the missionary's stable, so it was here that he came to work for good. As a result his status in the community rose somewhat, and soon people began referring to him simply as Mr Ch'oe. It was through this old man that Sugil's mother had come here to work. Unlike Mr Ch'oe she was tough and shrewd, but since they were both kindhearted people they got along as well as poor neighbors can, without any major differences.

All in all, there were a lot of poor people living around here. The missionaries had purchased the area for twenty wŏn upon arriving in Korea twenty years ago. Since then they had turned it into a scenic summer retreat, on which Reverend Yi and one or two newly-rich families had recently erected neat brick houses. But far from benefiting from this, those who had always lived here in their rock huts just became more inextricably enmired in poverty as time went on.

At least here (as in all poor neighborhoods) there was no shortage of children. Sugil had begun to mingle with them soon after his arrival, and he enjoyed nothing more than joining them in games. So today too he dashed out of the yard, taking his unexpected new toy with him. The children all took a turn holding the ball before beginning to discuss the best way to play with it. Then they started to throw it up in the air, knocking their heads together in their haste to get to it first. A boy on this side would punch it with his fist, whereupon a boy on the other side would punch or kick it back. It was fun no matter what they did. Even the children who did not usually play with Sugil came by to take a look, like the orchardist's son, who always walked around with his hands in his silk jacket, removing them only to sneak cookies and candies into his mouth. Reverend Yi's son Yohan,[1] who had a little ball which he always played with alone, also tried to join in. But Sugil cried out, "You can't play! Yesterday when I asked you for a candy you just gave me the wrapper!" Unable to take part in the game, Yohan was forced to stand and watch. Sugil could not abide this fellow. He would turn his pale white face away whenever Sugil asked him for a cookie, saying "Out of the way, your manure smell makes me sick."[2]

Even after Sugil got home, he could not stop thinking of what had happened. He talked to his mother to get it off his chest. "Today that Yohan fellow sure left with a red face," he said, still savoring the ball's pleasant touch.

"Yohan? You mean Reverend Yi's boy?"

"That little squirt thought he could kick my ball."

"You mean you didn't let him?"

"Of course I didn't."

"Now we're in for it! Reverend Yi is supposed to be a good friend of the missionaries. And what's that school called, the mission school you'll be starting this spring? They say he's more important there than the principal, that his power is second only to the Westerners'. You think you'll be able to go if Yohan tells his father what happened?" At this even Sugil felt a stab in his stomach. Already at the sight of the mission's primary school he had

---

[1] Yohan is the Korean version of the biblical name John.

[2] Note that right after introducing the orchardist's son as a hoarder of cookies and lemon drops, the author has Sugil accuse the *reverend's son* of refusing to share precisely these treats. This is but one of the trivial but glaring inconsistencies which riddle Han's prose. This one, at least, was spotted; in the 1960 version the attributes of the orchardist's son and Yohan are reversed (see *HSYS*, 8:423).

begun saying to himself "*my* school," his body literally tingling at the happy words. Since his mother worked for the missionaries, he had taken it for granted that he would be admitted.

"Do you think any other school would take such a poor child," said his mother in a flash of temper, "and one without a father at that—" She stopped herself in time, unwilling to voice the thought which weighed constantly upon her: the thought that she was without a husband, and her only son without a father. Her husband had been seized by the Japanese in connection with the revival of the —— Peasants' Union,[3] and after four and a half years languishing in pretrial custody had been sentenced to seven years hard labor. One cold winter, with only one year left, he died suddenly while hauling bricks, before he could even once call Sugil's name, the name he had longed to call.

While he was in prison his wife, with Sugil on her back, would make the ninety *li* trip from her farming village to visit him. Each time she was accompanied by old women of the village whose sons had also been arrested. Without Sugil's plucky, fast-talking mother with them they would have just stood helplessly before the foreboding prison gates. It was not out of the ordinary for one journey to prison and back to take four or five days, so they would make millet cakes and tie them to their waists when they set out. They always slept huddled together on dark roadsides. Too old-fashioned to impose on someone else for shelter, especially since they had nothing to offer in return, they would seek out a cozy mountain bend or something and spend the night dozing fitfully. Once these women slept in this way at the foot of the hill behind the missionaries' house. That was when Sugil's mother chanced to meet Mr Ch'oe, who arranged for her to become the missionary family's charwoman.

Whenever she went to the prison, her husband earnestly asked her to raise Sugil well. Once she brought Sugil along although he had come down with whooping cough, causing her husband to scold her sharply. "Don't come again until Sugil is better. No need to worry about me—just take good care of the child," he said angrily. Her husband had always been a stern man, and even then his face showed no sign of sadness, but she knew well how much the thought of Sugil's illness pained his resolute heart. When she visited him shortly before his death, she intuitively felt that something was wrong with him. He was no more than skin and bones, and he had difficulty holding his

---

[3] While it may seem antiquated to Western readers, the practice of leaving out names of places, institutions, etc, instead of creating fictional ones is still widespread in the literature of both Koreas.

head up. When she asked about his health, however, he simply replied, "I'm not sick. I've been a little under the weather after injuring my finger on a brick a few days ago, that's all." Showing her a finger on his right hand, he gazed attentively at Sugil on her back. "The spring after next Sugil will go to school; a year and a half to go," he said with a satisfied expression. Sugil could already walk on his own, but she kept him on her back, for the infernal wardens would otherwise prevent him from entering the visitors' room with her.

A few days later a young man with a pale and worn face came to see her at home. When he took off his cap in greeting, baring his shorn head, she immediately thought of her husband. This man has just got out of prison, she thought; the leucoderma on his skin was the unmistakeable mark of a prison stay.

"You're Sugil's mother, aren't you?"

"Yes I am. Where...?" She tried to control her racing heart as she spoke.

"I was together with your husband."

"Really? When were you released?" The hope that the day would come when her husband too would appear like this shone before her like the sun and moon combined.

"I've been out a few days now. I would have come sooner...your husband is all right, but he worries about Sugil at times."

"Sugil!" She called, for rather than answer questions about the boy she wanted to show him to her husband's friend right away. But Sugil had gone somewhere to play. "Sugil's doing fine...but why don't you come in for a while?"

"No, I'll come back again. I'm staying nearby."

"But where...?"

"Just in front of that house with the brick chimney."

"Ah, I see, and who...?"

"My name is Yi Tonggŏn," he said. After giving her the latest news about her husband he left.

It was only a few days later when, like a bolt from the blue, she received the news that her husband had died in prison. Tonggŏn was the first person she went to see then, and he was the one who went with her to prison to claim the corpse. From then on he was the first person she turned to whenever she was in difficulty. For a time she contemplated returning to her home village, but her fervent desire to have Sugil receive a good education made it hard for her to leave. There was no school near her hometown, and there was no way that scratching furrows in the barren mountain fields would enable her to send Sugil away to study. After mulling over every alternative she went to see Tonggŏn, who agreed with her that it would be best if she stayed on as the missionary's charwoman.

During these visits she got to know Tonggŏn well. He had started out as an errand boy at the provincial hospital, where his diligence and intelligence had enabled him to rise to the post of assistant pharmacist, before he was sent to prison in connection with the Pacific Workers' Union incident that had so surprised everyone.[4] While in the hospital he had passed on communications between comrades, used hospital medications to heal them, and engaged in enlightening others. When a comrade had been injured by a bullet while fleeing from police, Tonggŏn had taken him to an abandoned mine in the mountains, saving his life with his treatment.

Instead of taking time after his release from prison to recuperate properly, he immediately set about looking for a job. After a while he told Sugil's mother he had begun commuting by train to the —— Chemical Factory, where he had found work. She wondered why a man of such talents would take a job as a simple worker, but she continued to address him as "sir." When she had gone to see him a few days earlier about entrance examinations for her child, Tonggŏn had been as concerned as if it was his own affair. He said there were still some of his old comrades among teachers in other primary schools, but was not particularly hopeful that anything would come of these connections, and said it would be easier to get Sugil into the mission school. While regretting his lack of contacts in the church, he reassured Sugil's mother by saying, "But Sugil is so bright, he'll end up getting in. Go to the school and keep after the people there. I'll go too."

Sugil's mother resolved to continue where her husband had left off and raise Sugil well. As she stroked his hair, the hope swelled in her that someday the door would be thrown open to a bright new future for her too. She taught the boy to count to a hundred. She found out the missionary's address and taught Sugil that it was his address too. She also found out what other questions the teachers asked in entrance examinations and taught him the answers. For all this she never ceased worrying, and had finally resolved that she would go to the missionary himself and plead with him no matter what. But now, having heard Sugil had offended the son of the influential Reverend Yi, she felt as if her threadlike hope had been snuffed out like a candle in the wind. Then she thought "But it's still the missionary's influence

---

[4] It is not clear what incident is meant here, particularly as we are never told just when this story is taking place, but Han is probably referring to the most famous Korean strike of the colonial era, that of the dock workers in the Pacific port of Wŏnsan (in present-day North Korea) in 1929.

that decides everything..." and deep inside she continued to place her hopes on Sugil's admission after all.

2

Right after Sugil got up, he ascended one of the mountain ridges near his home. The golden sunlight seemed to make the mountains and streams near and far glow in a dim green hue. It was a fresh morning of the kind that made one want to fly from sheer restlessness. North of this road the mountain ridge rolled gently until it neared the S— river, where it suddenly grew more jagged, throwing a peak high into the air. As it sloped downward it formed numerous little pleats, ridges, hills and valleys. Everything but the bare high peak, which seemed to be wearing a Buddhist wimple, was covered with trees. Scattered through the ones at the base of the mountain were the somber white and red buildings that housed the church, the mission hospital, and the mission school. Below the wimpled peak that faced the S— river the base of the mountain stretched right and left like two arms, its embrace forming a wide and concave shell. At the base of the peak, which stuck up like the shell's crest, was a grove in which the missionary's white house could be seen nestling. Surrounding it were apple, pear and peach trees, which separated the pine forests on the neighboring ridges. The trunks of the apple trees were a purplish-red color in places, as they had been even in winter. Even more striking were the whitish apricot trees on the west corner of the missionaries' house, which were clustered together so thickly that they already made one think of the blaze of laughing apricot flowers to come. Looking at all this while he walked the ground suffused with golden spring sunshine, Sugil was overcome with an almost unbearable happiness that made him want to run around and play as he pleased.

Sugil hurriedly ate his breakfast of millet, spilling half of it in the process. He then hurried with his ball to see the children who lived in the houses down below. This day too was spent kicking the ball around with his friends. As the children played, they became much more skillful in passing and receiving it. Some of them, trying to imitate the middle-school students, kicked the ball with a very self important air. Some dribbled the ball, while others stood aside, then dashed in and kicked it away from them. One child, who had watched the middle-school students play, tried to head the ball, but as he did so he slammed into the boy standing next to him. Both tumbled down on the spot.

Seeing the ball drop behind them, Sugil ran and tried to kick it too quickly. He twisted his ankle and hopped back holding his leg. "You're lucky I don't have shoes on," he boasted, massaging his feet, which were caked black as a crow's with dirt. He got to his feet again, limped to the ball, and was just about to kick it when someone quickly snatched it away.

"Who stole my ball?" It was the missionary's son Simon. His eyes livid with rage, he glared contemptuously at the children. None of them said a word, but one or two inadvertently looked at Sugil. Simon reacted by clamping his strong hand like a kite's claw on the back of Sugil's neck. Sugil at once drew his head in like a turtle. Simon's fist struck Sugil under his chin with a crack, sending him flying to the ground, where he struck his head and rolled. As his head rebounded off the ground, Simon's boot came crashing down on it so hard that even Sugil's legs shook. The other children's blood turned cold at the sight, and like little spiders they scurried away in search of a hole to hide in.[5] With the bursting vigor of one fattened on milk—the milk brought everyday by Sugil's mother—Simon dealt Sugil another blow to the chin that knocked him out entirely. Then he looked around for the others. They had scattered. They had the fixed notion that they couldn't possibly lay a hand on the fifteen-year-old Simon, although they did not understand who had given him and his kind the right to do such things in Korea. With the ball in one hand, Simon calmly began shambling home on his long, grasshopper-like legs.

"Simon!" Surprised to hear his name called, the boy turned his head sharply in the direction of the voice.

"Father!" he shouted back, breaking into a run.

The missionary, who had just handled some matters at the church, had watched the incident unfold while walking home up the hill. He stopped to wait for Simon to catch up, pulling in the leash of his bulldog, which was straining to run forward.

"What've you got there?"

"It's a ball. That thief from the cowshed stole my ball."

"Stole it?"

"Yes, so I took it back."

"What, something those children have kicked and handled? Yech, how filthy! Throw it away at once; there might be germs on it." He watched as his son threw it down. "Now Simon," he said, adopting the grave voice he used when praying, "it is for God to punish thieves. We Americans must not touch filthy people with our sacred hands, is that understood?"

---

[5] The imagery is inappropriate, implying a criticism of the Korean children which Han obviously does not intend. The metaphor is absent from the 1960 version, which describes the fleeing children as continuously looking behind them to see how Sugil is faring (*HSYS*, 8:435).

"But father, we Americans have the right to beat blacks to death, don't we? God forgives us for doing that."

"That's because blacks aren't sons of God..."

"And Koreans are?"

At this the missionary hesitated a while, then said, "There are some sons of God among Koreans: Reverend Yi, Reverend Kim, Elder An..."

"Are they really sons of God?"

"Yes, because they swore they would become His sons, and because God has forgiven them. And after all, God has very many sons..."

"But isn't it true that thieves can't become God's sons? Just like blacks can't?"

"For thieves...we have dogs. Just as a dog kills a thief with his teeth, you know, one mustn't beat niggers with bare hands but with sticks. In the same way..." Slackening the bulldog's leash, the missionary began walking again.

While he and his son were entering the house in the misty woods, Sugil was lying unconscious, attended to by no one. Blood streamed from his nose. After a while a boy named Kyedŭk and his friend timidly approached, but, afraid to touch Sugil, they ran home. Shortly afterwards Kyedŭk's mother came running out. She too was a widow, and a friend of Sugil's mother, with whom she always spoke her mind. Seeing Sugil's bloodied face she thought of Kyedŭk, her only son, and she felt a needle stabbing deep into her own flesh. "Will Kyedŭk end up like this someday?" She felt a wave of terror and pity rush over her. Carrying Sugil firmly in her arms, she returned to her house. She squeezed out a cold wet cloth, wiping his nose and cooling his forehead with it. His body felt as if it were on fire. Under her fingertips she could feel his child's heart racing softly like a little chick's. In a flash a searing thought occurred to her, and tying Sugil firmly to her back with a little quilt she ran without resting to his mother's house.

"I thought only the Japs kill people," she kept thinking, "but the Americans too..." Unable to give voice to such thoughts, she could only cluck to herself as she ran. "The way Koreans are being killed from all sides there won't be any of us left." The future she faced, raising her only son in this harsh world, seemed to her as gloomy as the longest of moonless nights. All the time she prayed to herself. "Don't die, please don't die. Whatever happens, you've got to live. The heavens can't stay so indifferent forever."

3

No matter how Sugil's mother turned things around in her mind she could not control the rage inside her. Her request to have Sugil admitted to school—and the hope that this might still be fulfilled despite everything—had prevented her from running up the hill right away and wringing Simon's neck, but after pacing back and forth for a while she could bear it no longer. After all, what use was the school if Sugil died? In the twinkling of an eye her precious only child had been reduced to this state. Whether I live or die, I'll get to the bottom of this, she thought. She half-ran, half-stumbled up to the missionary's imposing house. The emotions bottled up inside her made her want to smash boulders with her bare hands.

Then she thought, "He isn't going to die, is he?" Her surging thirst for revenge subsided somewhat before her desire to save her boy's life no matter what. But as soon as the missionary threw open his heavy front door the words burst out of her in an angry rush.

"My son is dying!"

At this the missionary blinked, as if poked in his sunken eyes with a fresh leaf. Then, raising his hand to block the way, he assumed a stately air.

"Uhh..."

"My son is dying because of your son," she cried, her arms trembling violently, "now bring him out here!"

"Uh, what on earth are you talking about?"

"I love my child like everyone else. And in Korea we don't beat someone to death for picking up a rubber ball that's been thrown in a filthy puddle!"

"Oh, the devil has gotten into you. Go away."

"The devil? The devil is the one who attacked an innocent person, that's who the devil is! Hurry up and bring the bastard out here, I said. The son of a bitch, I'll..."

Still blinking his sunken eyes, the missionary pulled his head back, as if slashed in the throat by her sharp, hate-filled voice. Just then the missionary's wife came running in.

"My dear, what is going on here?"[6] She was as cunning a fox, and now her fear made her adopt a gentle expression as, gushing "my dear," she placed herself between her husband and Sugil's mother.

---

[6] In the original the missionary's wife uses a respectful if somewhat untranslatable form of address, namely, *hyŏngnim* (lit., honorable elder sister). I have translated this as "my dear" to convey the tone of hypocritically polite familiarity which I believe Han intended, but it is worth noting that Sugil's mother is older than the American woman, which makes the injustice later done to her even more shocking to Korean readers raised on Confucian values.

"As if you don't know? Go ask your son. Is this the way all the sons of God are? My son has been beaten almost to death, I tell you, beaten by your son!"

"That's impossible. Punishment awaits those who tell lies."

"Lies? Who's telling lies? Let's have the village court decide!"

"We have nothing to do with those people. Our Simon is a son of God."

"Is it right for a son of God to go around attacking people? Hurry up and bring him out here. Bring out the vicious bastard, I tell you!"

"Oh, my dear! Your son will be punished." Glaring down with her thin, foxlike eyes the missionary's wife said, "Please go back home. We will pray to God for your son. If you cause a fuss it will only harm him."

Suddenly everything went hazy before Sugil's mother, and she saw in her mind a vision of her stricken son. It seemed to her as if her son's life was draining away while she stood here, taking to task people with hearts so stony they wouldn't shed a drop of blood if jabbed with a needle. She also envisioned her neighbor [Mr Ch'oe], so sympathetic to her despite his own poverty. Even more vivid was Tonggŏn's form, which rose before her like a lamp in the midnight darkness.

"Just you wait, I have people on my side too. You think all Koreans are dead?" Her eyes flashing, Sugil's mother turned and began to leave, but unable to suppress her rage after all, she cried, "You'd better hope my boy doesn't die. You think I'd let your son go on living the good life if he did?" Her head held high, she stomped out past the couple, swinging her clenched fists.

Arriving home, she felt Sugil's forehead and body, then rushed over to see Tonggŏn, who had just returned from work. She was greeted cheerily at the door by his old mother and younger sister, but she was not in the condition to exchange pleasantries. "Our Sugil has been beaten so hard he's going to die!" she burst out.

"Hold it, what are you saying?"

"I never thought I'd live to see such a thing!" She told them roughly what had happened. "Sir, please go and take a look at him. I have no one else to turn to in the whole wide world."

"All right, let's go." With that the two hurriedly left. As soon as they reached the entrance of the orchard, Tonggŏn espied the missionary's wife looking down from the balcony of her house. She seemed to have seen him too, for she craned her neck and peered down intently before going back into the house. Upon entering the charwoman's home, Tonggŏn felt Sugil's forehead and body. Apart from the traces of blood under his nose no exterior wounds were visible, but his face was ashen and he lay completely still, as if devoid of any energy. He was obviously bleeding internally. For a while Tonggŏn simply gazed down at the boy in silence. Not a word escaped his lips. It was frustrating to see unfold before him yet another of the scenes he had hoped never to see again. This was the kind of thing that could have been committed only by people who never consider the consequences of their actions, let alone assume responsibility for them. "Are they allowed to do this because he is Korean? Must Koreans always suffer murder at the hands of others? Damn it, what gives them the right?!" The more he thought about it the more furious he became. Here these people were, thrusting knives under the noses of his countrymen at will, as if to say, what's the problem with killing one lousy Korean?

"Sons of bitches!" Tonggŏn murmured the words that rose up in him almost of their own will. Then, turning to Sugil's mother, he said, "It's better to have him admitted to a hospital than to keep him here."

"A hospital?"

"Yes, let me think...I know a doctor. I'll probably have to go and see him."

"Oh, could you?"

"Then again, I've already caused him trouble so many times, even to where he's been dragged around and harassed..." The man Tonggŏn had in mind was Dr Yu. The son of a penurious carpenter himself, Dr Yu understood the situation of his poor patients, and refused all compensation from those in particularly dire straits. He had also treated for free several members of the underground, for which he had not infrequently been called to the police station and interrogated. Just then the sound of someone approaching broke into Tonggŏn's thoughts.

"My dear?" said a strange voice, as the door opened with a creak. It was the missionary's wife. She held a white cloth to her nose with one hand, as if reluctant to enter a room whose smell offended her so. In her other hand she ostentatiously brandished a transparent wax-paper bag of cookies. "My dear, I've come to offer my prayers." She had adopted a gentler tone.

"Prayers?" Sugil's mother could make neither head nor tail of the woman's words.

"Yes, God...saves all people, every one."

Sugil's mother said nothing.

"We are all God's children." Saying this, the missionary's wife softly laid the bag of cookies next to Sugil's head. Unsettled at the sight of a strange man entering the servants' quarters, she had asked her husband what to do. The missionary, just as uneasy, had sent her down to check on things.

As far as they were concerned, Koreans were not to be taken lightly. They had been hacked into pieces by the Japanese oppressors, to be sure, but each of those pieces still seemed to be throbbing. Back during the 1919 uprising the Japanese infantry and cavalry had soaked the streets with blood.[7] Even the firemen had taken part, swinging their fire-axes down on people's heads and yanking them back as if smashing their way through burning houses. But the Koreans' procession never stopped. When sabers struck the heads of the vanguard those behind them tore their own overcoats for tourniquets to stanch the flow of blood. The crowd then linked hands to carry the vanguard, forging ahead in defiance of the bayonets. Jabbed in their hindlegs with steel prods, the mounted policemen's horses charged off through the fences of an adjacent house. Knocked off the road by the angry wave of people, the cops flailed their way back and forth in the open sewer.

But it wasn't just the people on the streets. Students and citizens arrested by the police before the event kept their promise to the nation, and began shouting "Long live an independent Korea!" at the same time as those outside. At their forefront were middle school students, including some members of the mission school. One student, who had spent the night under brutal interrogation by the cops, leapt onto a chair and removed a flag from under his clothes. Waving it, he began yelling "Long live Korea!" and immediately all in the interrogation room stood up as one and took up the cry. The detainees kept in the policemen's judo hall and the other interrogation and detention rooms quickly followed suit, rattling the roof-tiles with their shouts.

The chief cop and his counterpart in the military police lashed about with their swords as if to cut through the forest of hands that had risen with the cheers. While the other cops brandished their guns, the judo bastards hurled the detainees to the ground as if killing fish. Blood flowed, arms and legs were broken, but still the cheering knew no end. One student was hit in the back of the head so hard that one of his eyes fell out, but he just pushed it back in and continued shouting. The police sent many to prison. They rounded others up at random on the streets, trussed them up like herrings, then beat them in the fire station's pump room before throwing them out.

But things weren't over. The Korean people never gave up. Only a year and a few months later there was a funeral for a mission middle-school

---

[7] On 1 March 1919 a declaration of Korean independence from Japanese rule was read at a park in downtown Seoul. This set off months of disturbances in which over a million people from all areas of the country participated. "The police response to the demonstrations bordered on hysteria, and by May, military reinforcements had been summoned to help quell the rioting....The Japanese reacted to subsequent gatherings with an orgy of arrests, beatings, and even village burnings." Carter J. Eckert, Ki-baik Lee, Young Ick Lew, Michael Robinson, Edward W. Wagner, *Korea Old and New: A History* (Seoul, 1990), 279.

student who had died after being imprisoned in connection with the uprising. Students trailed the bier holding up two streams of white cotton cloth. They were in turn followed by ordinary citizens. Claiming they were blocking traffic, the police repeatedly ordered them to disperse, but the line always formed again quickly. On that day too, the missionary had stood on his balcony and watched the procession passing over the bridge on the S— River. He considered them savages for not fearing death, but to ingratiate himself with the locals he would say, "The Korean people are really quite magnificent. During the uprising I went to the police station and protested on behalf of my Korean brothers and sisters. I said, those Koreans' heads aren't on fire, so why are you using fire-axes on their heads?" For all this the missionary still had to wait five years before he could summon Reverend Yi back.[8]

But of course things never really settled down. On the contrary; as time went on the wind spread, blowing with ever-increasing force. Even stronger was the wind that swept in over the Tumen River.[9] No one knew what would happen, or when and where it would take place. This atmosphere had prevailed to this day.

The missionary couple was of course aware that Sugil's father had died in prison after a long incarceration. They found this somehow unsettling. Mary stole a glance at Tonggŏn and Sugil's mother to assure herself they had no weapons in their hands or on their bodies. Then she gently bowed her head, pretending to close her eyes.

---

[8] It is unclear what is meant by this sentence, which is absent from the 1960 version (cf. *HSYS*, 8:446). It is likely that Han, who was never one to review what he had just written, mistakenly believed that in the preceding text he had made Reverend Yi responsible for the student's arrest. Han's point would thus seem to be that it took five years for the villagers' anger to subside enough for Yi to return.

Han's excursion into the missionaries' reaction to the 1919 uprising serves an important propagandistic function. The legitimacy of the Korean communists' rule rested largely on the claim that they alone had provided meaningful resistance against the Japanese. It was no secret, however, that the uprising, which had posed a far more important threat to Japanese rule than all Kim Il Sung's exploits combined, had been organized mainly by Christian and other religious leaders (see *Korea Old and New*, 277), with the Korean Marxist movement then too small to play a significant role. Thus Han's effort to try to "expose" the missionaries and their local converts as hypocrites whose true sympathies had rested with the Japanese.

[9] Both China and the Soviet Union lie to the north of the Tumen River, but the Russophile Han is almost certainly referring to the influence of developments in the latter country. Well into the 1960s it was the custom in the DPRK to credit Russia's October Revolution with sparking the 1919 uprising and the nationalist unrest that followed it. (The influence of Mao's struggle on colonial Korea was only rarely acknowledged.)

"Oh God our father! Save this poor person. Forgive the sinner. Though he may have sinned, he has repented."

Sugil's mother, still eager to have Tonggŏn visit the hospital he had mentioned, cleared her throat and said "sir" in a low voice. At this the missionary's wife instinctively stole a sidewards glance at Tonggŏn and Sugil's mother. Just then she saw their gleaming eyes meet, as if they were making a silent pact of some sort. For an instant disconnected images rose in her mind. She saw an iron hammer, a kitchen knife, the shovel in the stable, the rake and the pickaxe in the storage room...then she saw all these things in the hands of Sugil's mother and Tonggŏn as they set upon her. The flash of images before her eyes made her confuse her words and thoughts.

"God our Father! From tonight the front and back doors must—" The missionary's wife caught herself with a start. She had almost voiced her intention to have vicious dogs guard the front and back doors from that night on. She regained her composure and continued. "Bestow fortune on this young child. Make him healthy and strong."

But Sugil's mother was already completely deaf to such talk. Turning to face Tonggŏn, she murmured, "Sir! This child has to go to the hospital quickly...if we keep standing around..." She pressed her hand on her chest, unable to finish.

"All right, I will go down and see. As long as there's a vacant bed, I will do all I can." With that Tonggŏn left.

The missionary's wife glanced sideways again, then quickly closed her prayer with an amen. There might be a hue and cry, she thought, if Sugil were to die tonight and be submitted to a Korean doctor's autopsy—or even if he were to remain alive in a Korean hospital for a while. "Relax, my dear. He will soon be well again. There are good medicines and good doctors." After these reassuring words she said, "This room is not clean. It's bad for the patient. He should be admitted to hospital."

"As a matter of fact I just—"

"Ah, but our mission hospital is the best. It has expensive medicines that one can only get from our country. They can even bring the dying back to life." Hearing this, Sugil's mother seemed to calm down a little. "I will talk to the people there. I'll see to it they take care of the boy for free."

"Well, that would certainly be—"

"We are all God's children, all brothers and sisters in the same family. We have to love each other." As soon as the old fox had convinced herself that her ruse had worked, she left the room and ascended the hill to the mission hospital, shaking her fat, goose-like posterior as she walked. She walked straight into the office of the director, Mrs Mack, and told her roughly what had happened.

"Now, under no circumstances can we speak of a contusion; he must be said to be suffering from some kind of disease," she instructed, "so instead of letting another doctor see the boy you must always tend to him in person."

"I understand."

"First, administer an emergency injection and let a day or two go by. After that say it has some different kind of fever, is that clear? Then there won't be any trouble if it dies."

"Don't worry. Once he's here we will have all kinds of ways to handle the situation."

"Well then, send an ambulance immediately."

So that evening Sugil, still unconscious, was laid on a soft hospital bed for the first time in his life. Gloom had descended unexpectedly on him and his mother, but that night the missionary gave thanks to God for his beneficence, and vigorously embraced his wife as if she were a young bride.

"God made you especially wise," he said admiringly. "We have been truly blessed." As they went to the dinner table they sang of the "beautiful world" they lived in, where they could take life with impunity.

4

That night an injection helped Sugil regain consciousness. His stomach was so empty that he ate almost the entire bowlful of the hospital's white gruel. He then asked for something cool and sweet to drink. His mother went to borrow some money from Kyedŭk's mother, then bought a can of pineapple juice down in the village.

"Just get well quickly and I'll buy you anything you want to eat," she said.

"But we don't have any money. I don't want anything to eat anyway."

"Come now, no matter how poor we may be, we can buy what you want to eat." Whenever she thought of her husband starving to death in prison she resolved anew not to let Sugil ever want for anything. Even now she didn't think there was anyone as obstinate as her husband had been. During one of her first prison visits she had promised to arrange private meals for him, but he had flown into a rage at the idea, admonishing her to raise the boy well rather than worry about such trifles. Back then one such meal cost only fifty chŏn, an affordable amount even for a woman in her position, and all the other prisoners' wives were having food sent. But her husband refused to listen, even as he was gradually reduced to skin and bones. She knew that he was only thinking of Sugil and herself, but it was still a source of eternal, ineradicable regret for her. The only way for her to come to terms with her husband's death was to raise her only son Sugil well.

"Mother, how many more nights must I sleep until I start school?" Sugil asked suddenly.

"Well, there are still more than thirty nights to go."

"Thirty?" Sugil counted to thirty on his hands, then went on to count to a hundred.

"You don't have to worry about getting into the school, because Christian schools actually *prefer* poor children." She said this with a knot in her stomach, well aware now that the Christian schools were no different from the others.

"When I get into school, I'll be at the top of the class."

"Of course you will, you think there's another child like our Sugil?"

They were so immersed in their conversation that they did not notice nightfall. But after midnight Sugil began to complain of a stabbing pain in his head again. Unable to bear it, he ground his teeth violently until, too exhausted to continue, he lapsed back into a coma. After a while the nurse entered and peered at him. "He has fallen asleep now, so you mustn't wake him." Having said this, she left the room.

Unable to sleep a wink, Sugil's mother kept watch over his bed all night. Sugil's pain-wracked form was worn and pale. The muscles in his discolored face and around his mouth were twitching violently. Something was definitely very wrong indeed. Sugil's mother suddenly placed her hand on her chest. She felt a jabbing pain from the pit of her stomach down to her toes, as if a needle was stabbing into her flesh and bones. But she was sure it was not her own pain but Sugil's that she was feeling. She gently laid a hand on Sugil's head. Feeling the sharp heat deep in her flesh, she told herself she was drawing his pain out of him. With one hand on his forehead and the other supporting the back of his head she cried out silently. "I don't care how much it hurts me, just as long as you live!" Then she bent down over the bed, resting her forehead once again on Sugil's cheek. Closing her eyes gently, she murmured, as if in prayer, "What is my pain, after all; I can die for all I care. If I can save Sugil that way, I'll gladly die right now." Her eyes misted over with tears.

During the next morning's round of visits the female doctor gave Sugil two more shots. These may have been why Sugil was able to regain consciousness shortly after. Though his body remained exhausted and limp, and his face dull and expressionless, his mother was happy that he was conscious at all. When his eyes finally opened it seemed to her as if a dark door had been thrown open to let in the morning sunlight.

"Sugil, do you know who I am?"

"Of course I know."

"How about an apple?"

"I'm not hungry."

How much like his father he is, she thought. Last year Sugil had had to go the hospital for an eye ailment. After he had seen his mother's empty purse one day, he had stubbornly refused to go back there, so following the hospital's instructions she had had to heat a flat stone and massage his eyes with it herself. His father too had been stubborn until the day he died. "He was worth a hundred men, but that didn't stop the Japs from getting him, did it." The thought vexed her no end. And now Sugil, who was to have followed in this rare man's footsteps, had been reduced to this by those American vermin. She could no longer see or hear anything; she was blind and deaf to the outside world. Guns, knives, and the sound of cannonfire formed one lament in her dreams. Her body was like a hard bullet that would explode like a lightning bolt on contact with anything in its path. "What bastard could do this to my son...no! They can't kill my son!" She cried out to herself. From somewhere, faintly, she seemed to hear an answer.

The injections still enabled Sugil to regain consciousness now and then. For some reason the old director looked in regularly on the boy, and, perhaps because he was in more serious condition than the other patients, often gave him his shots in person. "They're feeling guilty for what they did," thought Sugil's mother. Whatever the reason, Sugil was able to cling to life like this for over a week. His condition didn't seem to be getting better, but neither was it deteriorating significantly. After a few days, however, he would sometimes start talking in his sleep after his shots, then would open his eyes a little and come to. His mother was happy just to hear his voice; she saw it as a sign of recovery, which she attributed to the injections.

One day, leaning against the cold radiator, she managed to rest her tired eyes for a while. Half awake, she felt as if she was holding something in her arms. Certain that it was Sugil, she tightened her embrace. Then she realized it was an icy cold boulder. Death! The consciousness of it suddenly sent a horrid fear running down her spine. In vain she tried to cast off this feeling. Just then she was jogged by a pitiful call from somewhere.

"Mother...ahh mother..."

She opened her eyes with a start. She began to let out a sigh, but the terrifying sound of another cry stifled it. She could hardly bear the tightness in her chest.

"Mother...that bad guy, that bad guy..."

Pressing both hands hard against her chest, she almost threw herself on Sugil's bed. A fire raged inside her throat, as if the sigh trapped inside her would explode.

"Simon, it was Simon...that guy..."

"Sugil," cried his mother, embracing him tightly, "Sugil my child..."
Only when she could feel that his body was still warm was she freed of the
tightness inside her, and she let out a long sigh. But Sugil, lying there as
limp as a wilted leaf, now lacked even the strength to talk in his sleep.

At times his mother was gripped by foreboding, but she didn't know
what to do. The women in the village only added to her uneasiness. They
would say "What, you think they take good care of non-church members
there?" or "How well do you think they're taking care of him for free?" Such
talk made her hair stand on end and her heart sink. An outsider could not see
behind the scenes at the hospital, said another woman, but one could imagine
what it was like simply by looking at doctors who had established their own
practices after working there for a long time. As if by a conspiracy of some
sort these doctors, whether Dr Ham or Dr Ro, would first find out if a patient
had money, and if so how much, before treating him. If a patient had no
money they would boot him out, telling him to go to a different hospital,
even if he was on the verge of death. At night they would see no patients at
all, devoting themselves to a different kind of business—in most cases, usury.
It was said that they would place church members in their debt, and if the
money was not repaid in time they would seize property as payment, saying,
"Sons of God mustn't lie, for God will punish them." Why, they had even
taken a gold watch off someone's wrist.

"And you think people so obsessed with money will be nice enough
to take care of someone with none at all?" By way of contrast the women
would say how good other hospitals were, or how this and that doctor
virtually raised people from the dead. Of all those mentioned, Dr Yu was said
to be the best. "They say that gentleman has a lot of good medicines, so with
one injection he can cure people who'd need three injections somewhere else.
And it's inexpensive too."

"In the village down there someone's son started thrashing his head
around and rolling his eyes, but they say that doctor just extracted water from
his spine and gave him a shot, and he was well again."

Sugil's mother ran to see Tonggŏn and told him all that she had heard.
She then asked if it wasn't too late to have Sugil entrusted to Dr Yu's care.

"Well, last time he said he'd take him, but it's a question of how the
church hospital will react...You go on up already; I'll go and have another
talk with Dr Yu, and then I'll come up after you." Somewhat relieved, she
returned to the hospital. After a while Tonggŏn arrived, telling her she could
begin the formalities of discharging the boy, as Dr Yu had agreed to take
him. Sugil's mother immediately sought out a nurse and told her of her plans.
She had not anticipated any difficulty, but the nurse, with a dignified
expression, told her she would first have to get the director's approval.

"Wait a minute, he's my son and I'll take him where I want," said Sugil's mother. Tonggŏn told the nurse to communicate this to the director. The nurse returned from the director's office with a grave look.

"The director says that not even a parent can discharge a patient at will after he has been admitted." She turned around and began disinfecting needles, as if to preempt any further questions. Sugil's mother and Tonggŏn went straight to the director's office.

"Now really, even if he is to be released I will have to take one more look at him first." The old director's face was unexpectedly friendly. "As I've already said, he seems to be showing symptoms of a different illness...and now that he's with us he's my responsibility. It's too late today, so tomorrow morning I will take one more good look at him, and after I give him the appropriate treatment...anyway, please leave things as they are for tonight." Feeling a little reassured, Sugil's mother decided to wait until the next morning. Little did she dream that on that accursed night Sugil was hastening towards his doom.

5

That night the missionary listened a little to what the director (Mrs Mack) had to say. Then, excitement creeping into his prayer-voice, he said, "You are an American. For what have we Americans come to Korea to work, for what do we bestow God's grace on Koreans?"

"For America," said his foxlike wife, picking up where he had left off, "for the American people."

"And what is the life of one Korean child when weighed against the glory of the American people? I tell you, why concern yourself any more with a life that even God knows nothing about?"

"One discarded by God is like a flea-bitten beggar," chimed in his wife once more.

"I know; that's why I didn't let it leave," said the director.

"You did well. But what's the point of simply refusing to let it leave? A doctor has certain rights, certain methods."

"Well, that's why I always said it wasn't a contusion, but another disease that had manifested itself."

"But the ignorant are brave. What do you plan to do if they come in at night and smuggle him out?"

At this his wife's mouth twitched. "That's true," she said, butting in again, "they could steal him away. Where's your American wisdom? You mustn't become a Korean, I tell you, you mustn't be contaminated by their ignorance. American wisdom, bravery and virtue are vital."

"We must be decisive. There are countless ways of dealing with the situation, are there not? I mean, just diagnose a dangerous contagious disease or something, and quarantine it at once. And don't let anyone near it, do you hear?"

"Yes, that is what I was thinking."

"Gooood. Spoken like a true American. We need our own virtues, not Korean virtues or any others for that matter." The director was silent. "Not only that: we have to demand our virtues from others. And if it hasn't got a contagious disease, then we must give it an injection of bacillae and *make* it a contagious disease."

"Let's just say it is for the sake of the American people—," put in his wife again.

"It won't be difficult."

"Very good, director! But we have to think of an even better method. A contagious disease is all well and good, but if it has to die within an hour no time can be wasted. There are several good injections for such a contingency, are there not? Well, are there no such injections in our hospital?"

"Yes there are."

"Good. I should hope so. The victory of the American people and its virtues requires more than just churches. God also gives us bullets, airplanes and warships. What do you think the bibles are, that we missionaries carry, or our doctors' syringes?"

The director said nothing.

"They are weapons for America and its people," answered his wife with another twitch of her mouth.

"He who forsakes his rifle and is then shot by someone else is a pathetic fool. You have to use your weapon first. You must take precautionary measures. If you don't, your weapons are useless."

"I understand, sir."

"Good. If that's the case I will, as God's representative, ask you one question: What happens if the corpse of a patient who has died of a contagious disease is subjected to a thorough autopsy by another doctor—by a Korean doctor, shall we say?"

"Who is there who would do that?"

"You never know. Koreans are ignorant, and ignorant people are brave. Their lives mean nothing to them. If they can fight the rifles of the Japanese with their bare hands, they can certainly spirit off their own son's corpse. In that respect they're braver than people who respect laws and policemen."

"So I should dispose of the body entirely," said the director decisively.

"Ah! Right, right. Americans are wise. The day when America rules the world is nigh. May you be imbued with the glory of the American people." The missionary raised his hands and pretended to pray for a moment. Then he continued. "Have the body cremated immediately, do you hear. A doctor has the right to do that. The Japanese police won't interfere."

"Yes sir." The director stood up. The missionary and his wife followed suit.

"God our Father!" cried the missionary. "Bestow glory on the American people. Aaamen."

"Bestow fortune on Director Mack. Aaamen," prayed his wife, as if to supplement her husband's prayer.

The following morning Sugil's mother went home to eat breakfast, then rushed back to the hospital. When she got there Sugil was already gone. A vile antiseptic smell stabbed her nostrils. As if to escape it a pleurisy patient in the neighboring bed had covered himself with his blanket. Hearing someone enter he poked out his face.

"Hey, where's my boy?" she asked him.

"Well, they say he has a contagious disease. I was just lying here and it was like a bolt from the blue. There was a real commotion." Just then a nurse with a huge hood-like mask on her face came running in, accompanied by a man in a medical smock. They brusquely grabbed hold of Sugil's mother and sraightened her up, then sprayed her with a foul-smelling disinfectant. It stung her nose and made it difficult for her to breathe.

"Listen, where has my Sugil gone?" she shouted sobbing. The pungent disinfectant stabbed her tongue. "Our Sugil is—"

"Your son has a contagious disease. That's why we're disinfecting you."

"Contagious disease?"

"He's been taken to the isolation ward."

"Where's that?"

"You can't go there."

"Well, where is it anyway?"

"I said you can't go there, so just hurry up and go home." With that, the two left.

For the life of her Sugil's mother could not make head or tail of this. Her stomach churning with fear, she half-ran up the stairs to the director's office, only to be told that the director was out. Not knowing who to turn to, she wandered around in confusion for a while. With nothing better to do she headed back in the direction of the sick ward. She staggered up and down the hall on her shaking legs until she finally encountered a nurse who looked familiar.

"Excuse me miss, where is my boy Sugil?" She pleaded.

"Sugil, you say?" The nurse looked at her for a while. Then, as if suddenly remembering something, she said, "Hold on, isn't he in that ward?"

"Well, they said something about a whatchamacallit, an isolation ward—"

"Ah, I see...well, you can't go there." The nurse tried to get past but Sugil's mother blocked her way.

"No, please, just tell me where it is." Sugil's mother drew close to her as if to grab her sleeve.

"Go home and stay there. Patients are well taken care of in this hospital. Please calm down and leave."

"Just let me be with him in his room, I beg you."

"That's not allowed; you would be contaminated."

"No I wouldn't. And I don't care if I am contaminated and I die, just let me be with him. I'll do anything you want."

"That's impossible. If the police find out they will take you away." With that the nurse disappeared into another room.

These medical people are all in it together, thought Sugil's mother. Not knowing who to turn to or what to do, she felt her chest tighten even more. She had no choice but to leave out the back door of the sick ward. She walked around for a while peering into the various buildings, but there was no way of knowing what was what. Squatting next to the flight of stairs that led to the director's office, she waited for Mrs Mack to turn up. It was afternoon when she finally saw the director returning from some business outside. Like a mad woman Sugil's mother ran up the stairs and blocked the way to the office.

"Director! Where is Sugil?" Her eyes pleaded even more forcefully than her voice. A little startled at first, the director looked at those eyes. Then she quickly regained her composure.

"Your son has a contagious disease. He has gone to the isolation ward." She tried to get past, but Sugil's mother, sticking to her like a magnet, forced her to stop.

"Director! Please let me go there, please."

"That's impossible. No one else is allowed there."

"Then bring Sugil out to me."

"That's not allowed. A patient suffering from a contagious disease is not allowed to go anywhere. Please go home."

"No! Director!"

"Please get out of the way."

"Director, give me Sugil. Let me have him and I'll see he gets better, I promise."

"I said no; now get out of the way before the police take you away."

"No. He's my child, and I can take him away if I want."

"I told you no."

"Director! Whether he lives or dies, let me be the one...please."

"That's impossible. Please get out of the way or I'm calling the police."

"I'll take my child away if it's the last thing I do. You can kill me, but I'm not leaving here without him."

"I told you to get out of the way. Hey, somebody over there!"

"No! Do you think I'd allow someone to kill the child I raised? I won't allow it, I won't."

"Get out of the way I said! Hey, over there!" Straightening up as as if to deliver a kick, the director again tried to slip away.

"No," cried Sugil's mother, grabbing hold of her sleeve.

"Oh my goodness!" the old director struggled to break free, her eyes wide-open in surprise like a trapped rat.

"Let me have my boy, let me have him!"

"Isn't anyone going to help me?"

"Not so fast! I've asked you where you've hidden my Sugil. Let me have him!"

"Hey, there's a crazy person here! Is anyone there?" The lifelong spinster bleated meanly, unable to find a hole to escape. Her head bobbed around like a puppet's. By now her spectacles had slid to the end of her nose and her sleeve had been pulled almost completely off her shoulder.

"I'm taking my child with me...hand him over, hand him over!"

Just then two nurses and a janitor ran up and latched on to her. The man grabbed her wrist, while one of the nurses tried to pry her fingers loose. The director managed to slip into her room. Looking down from her window she saw the janitor and a guard pushing Sugil's mother out the door. Only then did she let out a sigh of relief, and begin scrubbing her hands and her sleeve with disinfectant. "I wonder if I'll ever get the dirt and the smell out..." Scrubbing her skin raw in the places Sugil's mother had touched, she thought to herself, "It will have to be done tonight...and he must be gone early tomorrow morning."

Having been pushed and shoved to her home, Sugil's mother waited for the hospital workers to leave. Then she went to Tonggŏn's house, but he was not at home. She returned straight to the hospital, only to be pushed away again by the doorman. Climbing to the top of a hill behind the hospital, she gazed down blankly at the redbrick buildings. Somewhere in there Sugil was lying all alone, gasping for air. She envied the birds flying overhead. Then she briefly clung to the phantasy that she could be taken on as a hospital maid and be allowed to see Sugil without any problems. Above her the spring sky darkened with clouds, and the telephone cables hummed. Just then she saw someone walking up the steep road. It was the hospital's pharmacist. She had sometimes seen him coming out of church with a bible under his arm, and he had always seemed very dignified to her.[10] She had seen him a few times since then in the hospital. She quickly caught up with him.

"Excuse me sir!" After calling him a few times he slowly turned around. He was on his way home from work. After listening indifferently to her trembling voice, he said in a prayer-like tone: "Being entrusted to American doctors is like being entrusted to God."

"But sir! What do you mean, entrusted to God?!" If anything, the pharmacist's words only unsettled her more. How could even the greatest god compare with a boy's own mother?

"Americans don't lie. Take a look around you. In Korea they build hospitals, establish schools...doctors come, and preachers..."

"But sir!" Just gazing down at the hospital buildings that contained her son was better than listening to this talk. All the Koreans who worked in the hospital, all of them, were Korean in name only. Inside they were no different from Americans. They seemed to her like people from a completely different world.

That night she went to see Tonggŏn again. Listening to the day's events from start to finish he thought there was definitely some unpleasantness afoot, but he had no way of knowing just what was being planned. But he promised her that, no matter what happened, he would accompany her to the director's on his way home from work the next evening.

After almost an entire day and night without sleep, she was finally able to close her eyes at dawn and doze off for a bit. No sooner had she done so than she began to dream. She was being chased by a terrifying thief. She tried to flee but was unable to run. After struggling for a while she saw the thief before her eyes. But suddenly someone took a sharp dagger and went and stabbed the son of a bitch. It was a welcome sight indeed. She was sure her rescuer was her husband, but when she looked closer she saw it was

---

[10] The news that Sugil's mother had a favorable impression of a bible-toting churchgoer is significant. Judging from the other villagers' comments earlier in this chapter, it seems that Sugil and his mother were not actual members of the church. But while reluctant to tarnish his heroes by depicting them as *bona fide* Christians, Han knew he could not ask his readers to believe that a missionary would employ a woman who was completely unsympathetic to the religion.

Tonggŏn. She woke, streching herself with a deep sigh of relief. Now she could hear the sound of a nightingale from somewhere. "What does today have in store?" She thought, with a tightening of her heart.

That afternoon a strange man came to see her. For some reason her heart sank as soon as she saw him. He was a villanous looking man, with a dark face, droopy eyelids, and a nose that hung down like a steer's testicles in June. She was sure he was either a security guard or a janitor she had seen at the hospital. Rocking on his heels as if he would go back before communicating his message, he asked, "Is this Yi Sugil's home?"

"Yes, what is it?" She ran out of the house in her bare feet, placing her hand gently on her breast to still her pounding heart.

"You're wanted at the hospital."

"At the hospital? But what—"

"Someone from this house was in the hospital, right?"

"Yes, that's right."

"They say he died."

"Di..." Sugil's mother head began to spin. Her legs gave way and she sank down into a crouch then and there. The man shambled off without so much as another word. "Su— Sugil!" With a loud clap of her hands she ran after him, without even bothering to put on her shoes. But she hadn't gone far when she felt her throat constricting tightly and a wave of sadness rushing over her. She sank down again onto her haunches. "Sugil's dead? What do they mean he's dead?" As she struck the ground with her hand she began to wail. She was racked so hard with sobs it seemed she would cease breathing altogether. Then anger rose up in her like a bludgeon. Everything was clear to her now. Those missionary jackals and that bitch of a director had killed Sugil. "All right, so that's the way it is. You sons of bitches, you've all conspired to take my child from me, but I won't let it happen, I won't." She took up a pole that had been lying around in the field and struck the ground with it with all her strength. "You can't get away with it, you can't. You sons of bitches can't take an innocent person and say he has a contagious disease...you can't, you can't. Make him well again, make him well again, or I'll make short work of you sons of bitches, do you hear me?"

She broke into a run again. The vision of Sugil's corpse battled strangely in her mind with the image of Sugil still breathing laboriously. She plunged on, unaware of the movement of her feet or the lay of the road beneath them, and arrived at the hospital before the security guard. As she entered the lobby, someone called to her from the reception desk, but hearing nothing, she hurtled down the long corridor.

"Sugil, Sugil!" she cried.

"Hey, hey!" A man in a white smock caught up with her and grabbed her firmly by the arm.

"Where is my Sugil?"

"Don't make such a racket. You'll startle the patients."

"Listen—where is my Sugil? Just let me see him quickly."

"Come this way please."

She was led into a room in a dark and gloomy corner. But Sugil wasn't there either. "Where is Sugil? Please hurry up and let me..." She turned and tried to run out the door, but the man grabbed her again and pulled her back.

"Please sit down here," he said, trying to sit her down on a stool.

"I can't, I have to go—"

"Yes, well, just sit down. I will let you see him shortly." With that he forced her down onto the stool. "Are you Yi Sugil's mother?"

"Yes. Sugil's still alive, isn't he?"

"With our hospital's warm prayers your son has gone to the eternal world."

"Gone, you say?" Blue lights flashed before her eyes.

"He has returned to God's embrace."

"God?" She rose with a start, then sank back down again.

"The illness became so severe that we didn't even have time to contact you at home."

Sugil's mother was speechless.

"It's hospital policy. The rule says that to prevent contamination anyone who has died of a contagious disease must be cremated immediately. Therefore—"

But Sugil's mother could not understand a word. "Where is Sugil?" she asked.

"I shall give him to you." The man in the white medical smock went to the shelf and took down a little box wrapped in white cloth. Proffering it to her with both hands he said, "Here is your son. Please." She gazed blankly at the box, but unable to comprehend what it was, did not even attempt to take it. "This is your son." Still she said nothing. "This is what was left after the fire. Please."

"Fire?"

"Yes, it's hospital policy."

"My son...burned..."

"Yes, that's what this is."

"Oh, now I get it. You killed an innocent person and then you destroyed everything to get rid of the evidence, you filthy sons of bitches. I'll kill you with my own hands, you hear me!" She started up from the stool, clenching her fists tightly. "No, it's impossible," she cried, biting her lip and forgetting her grief for a moment, "I want my son back! Who told you to burn my son?" The man in the smock took a few steps backward. "You can't, you can't beat my son to death and then get rid of—"

"Calm down please. Whether one lives or dies is for God to decide. It's all written down in the Bible."

"I don't have a god, now give me back my son."

"It will do you no good to offend the will of God. Nor will it help your son—"

"Hurry up and give me back my son, can't you do that?"

"In commemoration of your son's eternal life the reverend missionary has asked me to..." The man in the smock extended to her a paper envelope, a little condolence gift from the missionary.

"The missionary—" She slapped it away. "A fine lot of missionaries they are, the bastards, the murderous God-selling sons of bitches." Sugil's mother snatched the box of remains from the orderly's hand and clutched it to her breast. At the same time the envelope containing the missionary's money fluttered to the ground. She snatched it up with her free hand like a kite swooping down on a chick, then kicked open the door and hurtled out.

6

One of her feet struck the jagged edge of a rock and began to spout blood, but she took no notice of it. Blood had clotted on her lower lip, swollen from where she had bitten it. In her mind she saw the protruding bald head, the eyes like lamps...Like a tornado she flung open the third heavy door of the missionary's brick house to find her three enemies around the dinner table. As if fixing on a target she looked around at their faces, which grew and shrank before her eyes as if shown on a moving screen. The old jackal's spade-shaped eagle's nose hung villainously over his upper lip, while the vixen's teats jutted out like the stomach of a snake that has just swallowed a demon, and the slippery wolf cub gleamed with poison like the head of a venomous snake that has just shed its skin. Their six sunken eyes seemed to Sugil's mother like open graves constantly waiting for corpses. Like demons before the king of the underworld this pack of wolves quaked at the sight of Sugil's mother, with her tangled hair, bloodshot eyes, blood-soaked feet and torn skirt.

"Oh...oh my God..." The vixen was the first to begin praying.

"Give me back my son!"

"Oh...God our Father!"

"You sons of bitches, I told you to give me back my son!" Sugil's mother bit so hard into her blood-caked lips that red blood came spurting out. Flinging the envelope at the old jackal with the one hand, she tried to grab hold of the wolf cub's skull with the other.

Standing up, the vixen cried out again in a trembling voice, "Hey, God is up there. My dear, your son has gone to heaven."

"Heaven? *You* sons of bitches can go to heaven for all I care, I have no use for it." Sugil's mother thrust out her hand again. "Hurry up and hand me back my son, 'cos if you don't I'll take yours!"

"My dear, this is no way to act. The devil has gotten hold of you."

"The devil? You want to see a devil, just draw some water and look at your reflection. Your son is still important to you, you murderous bastards, but you beat my son to death...you say he'll get better in the hospital, then say I can't come because he has a contagious disease, then you secretly kill him...burn him till nothing's left. Hurry up and hand him over, you sons of bitches, hand him over! You can't get away with this, you can't!" She reached out again for the wolf cub. The vixen stepped in the way, signalling to her son with her eyes to run off. Shielded by his fat mother's stomach he scurried into a room at the back. After a while one could hear the sound of a telephone being dialed.

"Give me back my boy!" Sugil's mother put her head down and lunged forward in an effort to get past, but the vixen, taking a few steps backward, blocked her way.

"God will not forgive you for this."

Just then the old jackal stood straight up. "Out, devil!" he shouted at the top of his voice.

"Devil? You son of a bitch, you kill someone for taking a ball you've thrown away. *You* bastards get out! Who gave you the right to come to another country and kill innocent people? This is our Korean land, Korean land...do you think all Koreans have died?"

"I told you to get out."

"Give me back my son, you thieving bastards, give me back my son."

"Go and look for him at the hospital."

"You bastards want to play hide-and-seek like a bunch of goblins, I see. But I won't let you. Your son did the killing, so give him to me, I won't let him get away with it, I won't."

"You godless barbarian—," said the vixen, shielding her husband and striding forward.

"I told you to hand over the bastard that killed my son, now hurry up!" Ramming into the vixen's belly with her head, Sugil's mother again tried to force her way past.

"Kill that demon!" The old jackal yelled out urgently, "The gun, Simon, the gun!"

Shortly the wolf cub came out with a long hunting rifle, which he thrust at Sugil's mother's breast. "I'll shoot!" he cried.

"Go ahead, try and shoot me. If you want to kill me too, go ahead and try." She advanced, puffing out her chest. Flinching like a frightened rabbit, the wolf cub stepped backwards. The old jackal wrested the rifle from him and jabbed her in the chest with the muzzle. She staggered one or two steps back, then steadied herself. Puffing out her chest again, she wrested the rifle away with all her strength. The old jackal, his body bent over the rifle, was pulled forth a few steps before finally letting go. With all her strength Sugil's mother took the gun by the barrel and smashed it over the edge of the huge stove, breaking it in half. The pair jumped back while their little bastard retreated once more into the back room. The telephone gave out a loud ring as it was cranked.

"Yes...Hurry, hurry...yes." The words could be vaguely made out. "He's left already? Yes, yes...yes...she has a gun now and she's—"

"You sons of bitches, you try to kill me with a gun and then—well, you're not going to get away with it. I won't die until I've cut out your livers and eaten them. You think I won't eat the liver of that bastard son of yours, the one who killed my son?" Grinding her teeth, Sugil's mother ran into the back room, where the son of a bitch and his wife blocked her way. A shoving match ensued. Just then the sound of shouting could be heard. In the next instant Sugil's mother was grabbed firmly on the back of her neck as if attacked by a kite, then kneed so hard in the base of her spine that she felt a stabbing pain in her joints. It was the cop.

"You bitch, can't you leave well enough alone?" He said, kicking her repeatedly in the shins with his boot.

"So there's more of you, huh?" Sugil's mother spat out the blood that had filled her mouth. "So you're all in this together eh, well that's fine, let's just see who lives and who dies." At this the policeman too staggered back.

"Bitch!" He struck her in the face with his massive hand. Red lights flashed before her eyes.

"Give me back my son! You son of a bitch. Does being a policeman mean taking the side of these sons of bitches?" But finally she was tied up fast in rope. Only then did the wolf cub come back into the room. "Why do you tie me up instead of that murderous bastard?" She cried.

"Can't you just shut up, you bitch?" The cop turned to the missionary pair. "I'm sorry, Reverend. If I'd known earlier, none of this would have happened."

"That's all right; you've done your job well. God has found out, and now He is punishing her, is He not?"

"Well then, I will deal firmly...I'll take this gun along as evidence."

"As an American I have one request: should she repent her crime, I hope you will be so kind as to forgive her. Please make her a good person. All kind people are the brothers and sisters of the American people. This is God's will."

"Who said I wanted your forgiveness? You've tricked an ignorant person, used your gun to boss me around, tried to kill me—all those tricks, but you won't get away with it, you won't!"

"Stop babbling, you bitch, and carry this gun." The policeman shouted.

"Why should I carry it? I have something else to carry." Bending over despite her bonds she picked up the box of her son's remains. It was bitterly mortifying to be taken away before exacting vengeance on her enemies.

"But just you wait," she said, "Not all Koreans have died." As she walked, it seemed the darkening street would never end. The birds were flying back and forth across the low sky in search of their nests.

Note: The following is the conclusion of the version of Jackals *contained in Han's* Selected Works *(1960). While not going as far as Sŏ Manil and Yun Kihong's 1955 dramatization of the novella, which ends with a concerted attack on the missionary's house, it does imply more solidarity on the part of the villagers.—B.M.*

"Just you wait," she said, "Not all Koreans have died." She was dragged outside past the villagers, who had gathered behind the fence as if awaiting a sign. Kyedŭk's mother had found one of Sugil's mother's rubber shoes by the cowshed, and now bent down to slip it on her friend's bloodied foot.

"Out of the way," shouted the Japanese cop, "what are you all standing around for?"

But far from dispersing, the neighbors quietly began to follow the two. Sugil's mother stumbled along the darkening twilit street. Suddenly she was reminded of the song she had heard the children singing in the mountains the day before:

> The knot in the heart—
> How will it be untied?

Of course she did not remember these lines word for word, but their meaning had been planted unmistakeably in her brain. The Yankees and Japs had incessantly brought the blackest gloom down upon on the Korean people, but in the heart of every Korean raged eternal flames...Even now the beautiful rhythm of those lines resounded in her ears. Suddenly she looked up. The birds were flying back and forth across the low sky in search of their nests.

Chronology

1900	On 3 August in Hamhŭng, Han Sŏrya is born Han Pyŏngdo to a county magistrate and his wife.
1919	Han graduates from middle school.
1921-24	Han studies at Nippon University in Tokyo.
1925	Han emigrates to Manchuria. KAPF is formed in August in his absence.
1926	Han participates in published serial debates with KAPF's ideological opponents.
1927	Han returns to Seoul and formally joins KAPF.
1929	*Transition Period* and *Wrestling Match*, Han's most highly regarded short stories, are published.
1934	Han is among the KAPF members arrested by police.
1935	KAPF is dissolved. Han is convicted of subversive activity, but released several months later, after having spent over a year in jail.
1936	Han's first novel *Dusk* is serialized in the newspaper *Chosŏn ilbo*.
1940	Han's autobiographical novel *Pagoda* appears in the pro-Japanese newspaper *Maeil sinbo*. He joins pro-Japanese writers' organizations.

1943	Han is jailed (according to at least one account) for spreading news garnered from Syngman Rhee's Hawaii-based radio broadcasts.
1944	Han is released from jail and returns to Hamhŭng.
1945	Korea is liberated on 15 August. Han arrives in Pyongyang in November.
1946	Han meets Kim Il Sung in February and assumes the post of party director of cultural affairs. The NKFLA is formed. Han edits the group's organ *Munhwa chŏnsŏn*. He is elected to the NKWP's CC in August. *Path of Blood, Mining Settlement, The Hat*
1948	In January Han replaces Yi Kiyŏng as NKFLA chairman. The DPRK is inaugurated in September.
1949	*Growing Village, Brother and Sister*
1950	The Korean War breaks out on 25 June.
1951	In March, during the KPA's occupation of Seoul, the North and South Korean writers' organizations are united; Han becomes chairman of the KFLA. *Jackals*
1953	The Korean War truce is signed in July. Yim Hwa is convicted of espionage in August. The KFLA is dissolved during the First Korean Writers' Congress in September. Han becomes chairman of the WU. *History*
1955	Kim Il Sung purges WU vice-chairman Yi T'aejun and his Soviet-Korean backers. In his *Chuch'e* speech in December he declares his support for Han. *Man'gyŏngdae, Taedong River* (trilogy)
1956	Han becomes Minister of Education while retaining the chairmanship of the WU.

1957   Han oversees an anti-revisionist campaign and begins enlisting writers directly from the proletariat.

1958   Han (by most accounts) is awarded the People's Prize for *History*, and the title People's Artist for general service to the state. The Ch'ŏllima campaign is launched on the literary sector.

1960   Han's sixtieth birthday is the cause of effusive tributes in literary publications.
            Love, Emulate the Leader

1961   The KFLA is reestablished in March with Han as chairman.

1962   During a September meeting of KFLA cadres Han is attacked for parochialism, bourgeois decadence and other transgressions. In October he is stripped of his offices and expelled from the party.

1963   Han is exiled to a village in Chagang province.

1969   Han reappears for the last time on the roster of the KWP's CC.

Reference List

Abbreviations:

HCMS *Hyŏndae Chosŏn munhak sŏnjip.* Pyongyang, 1958-1960.
HSYS *Han Sŏrya sŏnjip.* Pyongyang, 1960-1962.
HSYT *Han Sŏrya tanp'yŏn sŏnjip.* Edited by Kim Woegon. In 3 volumes.
      Seoul, 1989.
STP   Han Sŏrya. *Suryŏngŭl ttara paeuja.* Pyongyang, 1960.

HAN SŎRYA

Non-Fiction

"A. P'ajeyebŭe taehan hoesang: kŭŭi sŏgŏrŭl ch'umo hamyŏnsŏ." In *HSYS*, 14:129-150.

"Chakka chŭk tokcha." In *HCMS*, 9:107-110.

"Changjinho kihaeng." In *HCMS*, 9:132-143.

"Chihasirŭi sugi: ŏrisŏgŭn chaŭi tokpaekhan t'omak." In *HCMS*, 9:111-113.

"Ch'insŏn." In *HSYS*, 14:190-198.

"Chŏnhu Chosŏn munhagŭi hyŏn sangt'aewa chŏnmang: Che 2 ch'a Chosŏn chakka taehoeesŏ han Han Sŏrya wiwŏnjangŭi pogo." In *Che 2 ch'a Chosŏn chakka taehoe: Munhŏnjip,* 5-61. Pyongyang, 1956.

"Chosŏn chakka tongmaeng chungang wiwŏnhoe 5 kaenyŏn chŏnmang kyehoege kwanhayŏ: tongmaeng che 12 ch'a hwaktae sangmu wiwŏnhoeesŏ han Han Sŏrya wiwŏnjangŭi pogo." *Munhak sinmun,* 15 May 1958.

"Geroicheskie budni Korei." *Ogonek,* April 1953, 5-6.

"Haebang chŏnhu." In *HSYS*, 14:182-189.

"In'gan Kim Ilsŏng changgun." In *STP*, 5-81.

"Kamgakkwa sasangŭi t'ongil: chŏnhyŏngjŏk hwan'gyŏnggwa chŏnhyŏngjŏk sŏnggyŏk." In *HCMS*, 9:82-84.

"Kim Ilsŏng changgun insanggi." In *STP*, 153-167.

"Kim Ilsŏng changgun'gwa minjok munhwaŭi paltchŏn." In *HSYS*, 14:23-33.

"Kim Ilsŏng changgun'gwa munhak yesul." In *HSYS*, 14:13-22.

"Kim Ilsŏng susangŭi kyosirŭl pattŭlgo." *Chosŏn munhak*, January 1961, 4-8.

"Kohyange torawasŏ." In *HCMS*, 8:153-159.

"Kongsanjuŭi kyoyanggwa uri munhagŭi tangmyŏn kwaŏp." *Chosŏn munhak*, May 1959, 4-25.

"Kongsanjuŭi munhak kŏnsŏrŭl wihayŏ." *Chosŏn munhak*, March 1959, 4-14.

"Kukche munhwaŭi kyoryue taehayŏ." In *HSYS*, 14:70-81.

"Musan munyegaŭi ipchangesŏ Kim Hwasan'gunŭi hŏgu munyeronŭi kwannyŏmjŏk tangwironŭl pakham." In 9 parts. *Tonga ilbo*, 15-27 April 1927.

"Munye undongŭi silch'ŏnjŏk kŭn'gŏ." In *HCMS*, 8:79-102.

"Naŭi in'gan suŏp, chakka suŏp." In *HSYS*, 14:85-128.

"Ŏmŏni." In *HCMS*, 9:124-131.

"Pabo k'ongk'ŭl: Amerik'anijŭmŭi masulsŏng, angmasŏnge taehayŏ." In *HSYS*, 14:264-305.

"Paltchŏn tosange orŭn chŏnhuŭi Chosŏn munhak." *Chosŏn munhak*, January 1955, 112-125.

"P'ŭro yesurŭi sŏnŏn." *Tonga ilbo*, 6 November 1926.

"P'ŭroret'aria chakkaŭi ipchangesŏ: Kim Hwasanŭi munyeron —kwannyŏmnonjŏk tangwironŭl pandae hayŏ." In *HCMS*, 8:63-78.

"P'yŏngyang sidang kwanha munhak yesul sŏnjŏn ch'ulp'an pumun yŏlsŏngja hoeŭiesŏ han Han Sŏrya tongjiŭi pogo." *Rodong sinmun*, 15 February 1956.

"Radostnoe chuvstvo. Ob uspekhakh sotsialisticheskogo stroitel'stva v KNDR. Stat'ia iz Pkhen'iana." *Inostrannaia literatura*, January 1959, 164-166.

"Reninŭi hoesanggi." In *HSYS*, 14:242-263.

"Saenghwal kamjŏngŭi chaehyŏn chŏndal: 1932 nyŏn mundan chŏnmang." In *HCMS*, 9:92-99.

"Saenghwarŭi kyohun: Sahoejuŭi noryŏk t'ujaeng sogŭro." In *HSYS*, 14:330-341.

"Sasilgwa kongsang: naŭi ch'angjak suŏp." In *HCMS*, 9:153-158.

"10 nyŏn." *Chosŏn munhak*, August 1955, 76-83.

"Ssŭttallinŭn uriwa hamkke sara itta." In *HSYS*, 14:199-211.

"Suryŏngŭl ch'ŏŭm poeptŏn nal." In *STP*, 170-182.

"Suryŏngŭl ttara paeuja." In *STP*, 194-216.

"Uri munhagŭi saeroun ch'angjakchŏk angyangŭl wihayŏ: Chosŏn chakka tongmaeng chungang wiwŏnhoe che 2 ch'a chŏnwŏn hoeŭiesŏ han Han Sŏrya wiwŏnjangŭi pogo." *Chosŏn munhak*, December 1957, 3-22.

"Uri sŭsŭng Kim Ilsŏng changgun." In *STP*, 184-191.

"Yŏngung Kim Ilsŏng changgun." In *STP*, 83-152.

Fiction

Adongdan. Pyongyang, 1959.

Charanŭn maŭl. In *HSYS*, 8:242-293.

Chi. In *Kokumin bungaku/Kungmin munhak* 1 (1 1942): 167-190.

Chinch'ang (Inyŏng). In *KHSYC*, 155-179.

Ch'ohyang (Maŭmŭi hyangch'on). Pyongyang, 1958.

Chŏnbyŏl. In *HSYS*, 8:396-419.

Ch'ŏngch'un'gi. Vol. 2 of *Han Sŏrya sŏnjip*. Edited by Kim Ch'ŏl. Seoul, 1989.

Der Freund (Ŏlgul). Translated by Hermann Gleistein from the Russian translation of D. Usatov. In *Korea erzählt: Ein Einblick in die koreanische Literatur*, edited by J. Herzfeldt, 84-92. Berlin, GDR, 1954.

Haebangt'ap. Tokyo, 1954.

Hapsuksoŭi pam. In *HSYT*, 1:100-109.

Hwangch'oryŏng. In *HSYS*, 8:492-549.

Hwanghon. Vol. 1 of *Han Sŏrya sŏnjip*. Edited by Kim Ch'ŏl. Seoul, 1989.

Hyŏllo. In *HSYS*, 8:3-31.

Kaesŏn. In *HSYS*, 8:110-136.

Kŭmgangsan. In *Munhak sinmun*, 14 August 1962.

Kŭnal pam. In *Chosŏn mundan* 4 (1 1925): 87-92.

Kwadogi. In *KHSYC*, 7-23.

Man'gyŏngdae. In *HSYS*, 9:362-491.

Moja: Ŏttŏn Ssobet'ŭ chŏnsaŭi sugi. In *HSYS*, 8:32-64.

Nammae. In *HSYS*, 8:156-241.

Ŏlgul. In *HSYS*, 8:137-155.

Perelom (Kwadogi). Translated into Russian by O Pyŏnjo. In *Khan Ser ia: Sbornik rasskazov*, 5-25. Pyongyang, 1957.

P'yŏnji. In *8.15 haebang 15 chunyŏn kinyŏm sosŏlchip*, 5-16. Pyongyang, 1960.

Reninŭi ch'osang. In *HSYS*, 8:597-640.

Ryŏksa. In *HSYS*, 9:1-360.

Samilp'o. In *Munhak sinmun*, 14 August 1962.

Sarang. Vol. 12 of *HSYS*.

Sŏlbongsan. Vol. 12 of *Tonggwangminjok munhak chŏnjip*. Edited by Im Hŏnyŏng. Seoul, 1989.

Sŏngjang. Pyongyang, 1961.

Sulchip. In *KHSYC*, 141-154.

Sŭngnyangi. Tokyo, 1954.

Sŭngnyangi. Dramatized by Sŏ Manil and Yun Kihong. *Chosŏn munhak*, January 1955, 6-67.

Sŭngnyangi. In *HSYS*, 8:420-491.

Taedonggang. Vol. 10 of *HSYS*.

T'an'gaengch'on: chihaesŏ ssaunŭn saramdŭl. In *HSYS*, 8:65-109.

T'ap. Vol. 5 of *Sŭlgi sosŏlsŏn*. Seoul, 1987.

Tonggyŏng. In *Chosŏn mundan* 8 (5 1925):46-54.

Ttangk'ŭ 214ho. In *HSYS*, 8:550-596.

Volki (Sŭngnyangi). Translated by Elena Berman. In *Khan Ser ia: Sbornik rasskazov*, 143-160. Pyongyang, 1957.

"Yŏlp'ung: Changp'yŏn sosŏl *Yŏlp'ung* ŭi ilbu." *Chosŏn munhak*, September 1958, 86-105.

OTHER KOREAN LANGUAGE SOURCES

Published in North Korea

AN HAMGWANG. "Changp'yŏn *Sŏngjang* ŭi myŏkkaji hyŏngsangjŏk t'ŭksŏng." *Munhak sinmun*, 15 May 1962.

————. "Haebangjŏn chinbojŏk munhak." *Chosŏn munhak*, August 1955, 174-181.

————. "Han Sŏryaŭi chakkajŏk haengjŏnggwa ch'angjojŏk kaesŏng." *Chosŏn munhak*, December 1960, 107-126.

CH'AE ŬI. "Ho P'ungŭi purŭjo yusimnonjok sasangŭl pip'anham." *Chosŏn munhak*, November 1955, 142-162.

"Chakka tongmaengesŏ." *Chosŏn munhak*, September 1955, 199-201.

CHANG HYŎNGJUN. "Uri tangŭi munye rosŏnŭl ch'ŏnmyŏng han Kim Ilsŏng wŏnsuŭi kangnyŏngjŏk kyosi." *Chosŏn munhak*, May 1961, 4-12.

"Changp'yŏn sosŏl *Hwanghon* e taehan kamsanghoe." *Munhak sinmun*, 3 April 1958.

"Che 2 ch'a Asea, Ap'ŭrik'a chakka taehoee ch'amga hettŏn uri nara chakka taep'yodan kwiguk." *Munhak sinmun*, 2 March 1962.

Che 2 ch'a Chosŏn chakka taehoe: Munhŏnjip. Pyongyang, 1956.

CH'OE SŎHAE. *Hongyŏm*. In *Ch'oe Sŏhae sŏnjip*, 1:166-193. Pyongyang, 1963.

"Chogugŭi p'yŏnghwajŏk t'ongirŭi chujee taehan hyŏbŭihoe." *Chosŏn munhak*, September 1956, 183-185.

"Ch'ŏllimaŭi kisangŭro." *Chosŏn munhak*, November 1958, 3-7.

Chŏlmŭn taeo: Kŭlloja chakp'umjip. Pyongyang, 1960.

CH'ŎN SEBONG. *Sŏkkaeurŭi saepom*. Pyongyang, 1955.

"Chosŏn chakka tongmaeng che 3 ch'a chungang wiwŏnhoeesŏ: pogo yoji." *Chosŏn munhak*, August 1956, 175-186.

"Chosŏn chakka tongmaeng chungang wiwŏnhoe che 26 ch'a sangmu wiwŏnhoeesŏ." *Chosŏn munhak*, June 1956, 209.

Chosŏn chungang yŏn'gam. Pyongyang, 1948-1959.

"Chosŏn munhak yesul ch'ongdongmaeng: Kyuyak." *Chosŏn munhak*, March 1961, 150-152.

Chosŏn munhaksa. Pyongyang, 1964.

Chosŏn munhak t'ongsa. In 2 vols. Pyongyang, 1959.

Chosŏn munhwaŏ sajŏn. Pyongyang, 1973.

"Chosŏn rodongdang che 3 ch'a chŏndang taehoerŭl nop'ŭn chŏngch'ijŏk yŏrŭiwa ch'angjakchŏk sŏnggwaro majihalte taehan chakkadŭrŭi kwaŏbŭl chesi." *Chosŏn munhak*, February 1956, 214-221.

"Chosŏn rodongdang che 3 ch'a taehoe kyŏlchŏngŭl pattŭlgo munhak ch'angjo saŏbŭl kanghwahalte taehayŏ t'oŭi: Chosŏn chakka tongmaeng che 2 ch'a chungang wiwŏnhoeesŏ: Pogo yoji." *Chosŏn munhak*, August 1956, 175-186.

HAN CHUNGMO. *Han Sŏryaŭi ch'angjak yŏn'gu.* Pyongyang, 1959.

HAN HYO. "Tosikchuŭirŭl pandaehayŏ." In *Che 2 ch'a Chosŏn chakka taehoe: Munhŏnjip,* 174-184. Pyongyang, 1956.

————. "Uri munhagŭi 10 nyŏn". In 3 parts. *Chosŏn munhak,* June 1955, 138-172; July 1955, 123-146; August 1955, 149-173.

HONG SUNCH'ŎL. "Kŭllojadŭrŭi kyegŭpchŏk kyoyanggwa munhak p'yŏngnon." *Chosŏn munhak,* April 1955, 170-179.

————. "Saehae insa." *Rodong sinmun,* 1 January 1956.

HWANG KŎN. *Pul t'anŭn sŏm.* In *Mokch'ukki,* 182-206. Pyongyang, 1959.

————. *T'anmaek.* In *Mokch'ukki,* 5-82. Pyongyang, 1959.

KANG HYOSUN. "Urido ch'ŏllimarŭl t'aja." *Chosŏn munhak,* December 1958, 3-7.

"K'AP'Ŭ ch'anggŏn 30 chunyŏn kinyŏmŭi pam." *Chosŏn munhak,* September 1955, 201-205.

KI SŎKPOK. "Uri munhak p'yŏngnone issŏsŏŭi myŏkkaji munjee taehayŏ." In 2 parts. *Rodong sinmun,* 28 February 1952, 1 March 1952.

KIM IL SUNG (KIM ILSŎNG). "Ch'ŏllima sidaee sangŭnghan munhwa yesurŭl ch'angjohaja: Chakka, yesurindŭlgwaŭi tamhwa, 1960 nyŏn 11 wŏl 27 il." In *Uri hyŏngmyŏngesŏŭi munhak yesurŭi immu,* 16-33. Pyongyang, 1965.

————. "Chŏnch'e chakka yesulgadŭrege: 1951 nyŏn 6 wŏl 30 il chunggyŏn chakkadŭlgwaŭi chŏpkyŏn sŏksangesŏŭi tamhwa." In *Kim Ilsŏng sŏnjip,* 3:238-251. Pyongyang, 1954.

————. "Hyŏngmyŏngjŏk munhak yesurŭl ch'angjak halte taehayŏ: munhak yesul pumun ilggundŭl ap'esŏ han yŏnsŏl, 1964 nyŏn 11 wŏl 7 il." In *Uri hyŏngmyŏngesŏŭi munhak yesurŭi immu,* 34-49. Pyongyang, 1965.

————. "Munhwaindŭrŭn munhwa chŏnsŏnŭi t'usaro toeoya handa: Pukchosŏn kakto inmin wiwŏnhoe, chŏngdang, sahoe tanch'e sŏnjŏnwŏn, munhwain, yesurin taehoeesŏ chinsurhan yŏnsŏl, 1946 nyŏn 5 wŏl 24 il." In *Kim Ilsŏng sŏnjip,* 2nd edition, 1:96-101. Pyongyang, 1963.

————. "Munhwawa yesurŭn inminŭl wihan kŏsŭro toeŏya handa: 1946 nyŏn 5 wŏl 24 il Pukchosŏn kakto inmin wiwŏnhoe, chŏngdang, sahoe tanch'e, sŏnjŏnwŏn, munhwain, yesurin taehoeesŏ chinsurhan yŏnsŏl." In *Kim Ilsŏng sŏnjip*, 1:96-104. Pyongyang, 1955.

—————. "Sasang saŏbesŏ kyojojuŭiwa hyŏngsikchuŭirŭl t'oech'i hago chuch'erŭl hwangnip halte taehayŏ: tang sŏnjŏn sŏndong ilggundŭl ap'esŏ han yŏnsŏl, 1955 nyŏn 12 wŏl 28 il." In *Kim Ilsŏng sŏnjip*, 4:325-354. Pyongyang, 1960.

—————. "Uri munhak yesurŭi myŏkkaji munjee taehayŏ." In *Uri hyŏngmyŏngesŏŭi munhak yesurŭi immu*, 1-10. Pyongyang, 1965.

KIM SARYANG. "Urinŭn irŏk'e igyŏtta: Taejŏn kongnyakchŏn." In *Kim Saryang sŏnjip*, 341-369. Pyongyang, 1955.

Kkot' p'anŭn ch'ŏnyŏ: changpy'ŏn sosŏl. Pyongyang, 1977.

Kkot' p'anŭn ch'ŏnyŏ: purhuŭi kojŏn myŏngjak 'Kkot' p'anŭn ch'ŏnyŏ' rŭl kaksaekhan hyŏngmyŏng kagŭk. Pyongyang, 1973.

KUO MOJO (kor. KWAK MARYAK). "Ho P'ungŭi pansahoejuŭijŏk kangnyŏng." *Chosŏn munhak*, July 1955, 172-181.

"Munhak yesul ch'ongdongmaengi kŏdŭn pit'nanŭn sŏnggwa." *Munhak sinmun*, 2 March 1962.

"Munyech'ong chungang wiwŏnhoe che 10 ch'a hwaktae chiphaeng wiwŏnhoe chinhaeng." *Munhak sinmun*, 23 February 1962.

"Munyech'ong kakto wiwŏnhoe chidojŏk kinŭngŭl chegohaja: Munyech'ong che 15 ch'a hwaktae chiphaeng wiwŏnhoeesŏ." *Munhak sinmun*, 3 August 1962.

ŎM HOSŎK. "Han Sŏryaŭi munhakkwa *Hwanghon*." *Chosŏn munhak*, November 1955, 142-162.

—————. "Uri munhage issŏsŏŭi chayŏnjuŭiwa hyŏngsikchuŭi chanjaewaŭi t'ujaeng." *Rodong sinmun*, 17 January 1952.

PAEK PONG. *Minjogŭi t'aeyang Kim Ilsŏng changgun.* Pyongyang, 1968.

PAK CH'ANGNAK. "Changp'yŏn sosŏl *Chŏngch'un'gi* e taehayŏ." *Munhak sinmun*, 10 July 1958.

PAK CHONGWŎN; RYU MAN. *Chosŏn munhak kaegwan.* In 2 vols. Pyongyang, 1986.

PAK SŎKCHŎNG. "Hong Sunch'ŏrŭi chakp'ume taehayŏ." *Munhak sinmun,* 27 February 1958.

"4 ch'a tang taehoega chesihan munhak yesurŭi kangnyŏngjŏk kwaŏp." *Chosŏn munhak,* October 1961, 4-15.

"Sin'gan sogae: Han Sŏrya chak *Hwanghon* kaegan." *Chosŏn munhak,* April 1955, 200-201.

"*Sŏlbongsan* tokcha moim." *Munhak sinmun,* 15 February 1959.

SONG YŎNG. *Kippŭn nal chŏnyŏk.* In *HCMS,* 5:90-91.

————. *Ŭlmiltae.* In *HCMS,* 10:90-91.

Sujŏngjuŭirŭl pandaehayŏ. Pyongyang, 1964.

"Tokchadŭrŭi p'yŏnjie taehayŏ." *Chosŏn munhak,* March 1958, 143-144.

"Tongmaeng che 17 ch'a hwaktae sangmu wiwŏnhoe." *Chosŏn munhak,* June 1955, 205-209.

"Tongmaeng kakkŭp kigwandŭrŭi sŏn'gŏwa kak pusŏ sŏngwŏndŭrŭi immyŏng." *Chosŏn munhak,* November 1956, 202-204.

"Tongmaeng kigu kanghwawa chojikchŏk taech'aegŭl wihan kyŏlchŏng." *Chosŏn munhak,* February 1956, 218-219.

YI CH'UNJIN. *Anna.* In *Kojiŭi yŏngungdŭl: Yi Ch'unjin tanp'yŏnjip,* 5-39. Pyongyang, 1960.

YI HYOUN; KYE PUK. *'Kohyang' gwa 'Hwanghon' e taehayŏ.* Pyongyang, 1958.

YI KIYŎNG. "Ch'angjak pangbŏp munjee kwanhayŏ." In *HCMS,* 8:257-267.

————. "Han Sŏryawa na." *Chosŏn munhak,* August 1960, 169-172.

————. *Kaebyŏk.* In *Kaesŏn,* 16-38. Pyongyang, 1956.

————. *Ttang.* 3rd edition. Pyongyang, 1960.

————. *Ttang.* Revised edition. Pyongyang, 1973.

YI PUNGMYŎNG. *Rodongŭi ilga.* In *Kaesŏn,* 56-86. Pyongyang, 1956.

YIM HWA (IM HWA). *Kijie toragamyŏn.* In *Rodong sinmun,* 7 February 1952.

YU HANGNIM. *Sŏngsire taehan iyagi.* Pyongyang, 1958.

YU KIHONG. "Tosikchuŭiwa munanjuŭinŭn ssangdungida." In *Che 2 ch'a Chosŏn chakka taehoe: Munhŏnjip*, 292-296. Pyongyang, 1956.

YUN SEP'YŎNG. "Choguk t'ongirŭi chujewa changp'yŏn sosŏl *Sarang* ŭi segye." *Chosŏn munhak*, January 1961, 91-106.

————. "Han Sŏryawa kŭŭi munhak." *Chosŏn munhak*, August 1960, 173-182.

————. "Uri naraesŏ changp'yŏn sosŏrŭi kusŏngsang t'ŭksŏnggwa chegidoenŭn munje." *Chosŏn munhak*, January 1962, 98-114.

————. "Widaehan hyŏnsil saenghwarŭi hwap'okkwa kongsanjuŭijaŭi chŏnhyŏng." *Chosŏn munhak*, August 1961, 110-123.

Published in South Korea

AN MAK. "Chosŏn p'ŭrollet'aria yesul undong yaksa." In *K'AP'Ŭ pip'yŏng charyo ch'ongsŏ 1: K'AP'Ŭ sidaee taehan hoegowa munhaksa*, edited by Im Kyuch'an and Han Kiyong, 113-133. Seoul, 1989.

CHO CHŎNGMAN. "Ssosial rearijŭm munhagŭi pyŏnyong." *Pukhan* 126 (9 1972): 208-217.

CHO MYŎNGHŬI. *Naktonggang.* In *Nakdonggang: Cho Myŏnghŭi sŏnjip*, edited by Im Hŏnyŏng, 148-160. Seoul, 1988.

CHO TONGIL. *Han'guk munhak sasangsa siron.* Seoul, 1978.

————. *Han'guk munhak t'ongsa.* 2nd edition. Seoul, 1989.

CHŎN YŎNGT'AE. "Iyagi pulgamjŭnge kŏllin chakkadŭl." *Tongsŏ munhak* 170 (9 1988): 68-72.

HAN CHAEDŎK. *Kim Ilsŏnggwa pukkoeŭi silsang.* Seoul, 1969.

————. *Kim Ilsŏngŭl kobal handa.* Seoul, 1965.

HONG KISAM. *Pukhan munye iron.* Seoul, 1981.

HYŎN SU. *Chŏkch'i yungnyŏn Pukhanŭi mundan.* Seoul, 1952.

IM CHONGGUK. *Ch'inil munhangnon.* Seoul, 1966.

IM HŎNYŎNG. "Ch'iyŏrhan nongmin undongŭi chŭngŏn." In Han Sŏrya, *Sŏlbongsan*, 406-412. Seoul, 1989.

KIM CH'ŎL, ET AL. "Pukhanmunhwa paro ilkkiŭi ipmun." *Munye chungang* 12 (3 1989): 246-277.

KIM SONG. "Mundanŭi chwauik taegyŏlgwa 'Paengmin munhak': 1945 nyŏn." *Pukhan* 164 (8 1985): 56-61.

KIM SŬNGHWAN. "Haebang kongganŭi Pukhan munhak: munhwajŏk minju kiji kŏnsŏllonŭl chungsimŭro." *Han'guk hakpo* 17 (Summer 1991): 201-224.

KIM TONGNI, ed. *Han'guk munhak taesajŏn*. Seoul, 1973.

KIM UJŎNG. *Han'guk hyŏndae sosŏlsa*. Seoul, 1968.

KIM YUNSIK. "Haebang kongganŭi nambuk munhak chojik pigyo: Pukchosŏn munhak yesul ch'ongdongmaenggwa Chosŏn munhakka tongmaeng." *Yesulgwa pip'yŏng* 18 (12 1989): 128-144.

————. "Haebanghu nambukhanŭi munhwa undong." In *Haebang kongganŭi munhak undonggwa munhagŭi hyŏnsirinsik*, edited by Kim Yunsik, 9-31. Seoul, 1989.

————. "Han Sŏryaron: 'Kwadogi' esŏ 'Sŏlbongsan' kkaji." In two parts. *Tongsŏ munhak* 194 (9 1990): 162-189; 195 (10 1990): 196-215.

————. "Han Sŏryaron: Kwihyang mot'ip'ŭwa chŏnhyangŭi yulli kamgak." *Hyŏndae munhak* 416 (8 1989): 354-375.

————. *Han'guk hyŏndae hyŏnsilchuŭi sosŏl yŏn'gu*. Seoul, 1990.

————. "Inyŏmŭi hyŏngsikkwa kyŏnghŏmŭi hyŏngsik: Han Sŏrya, Yi Kiyŏngŭi ch'angjak pangbŏmnon pip'an." *Yesulgwa pip'yŏng* 23 (3 1991): 81-106.

————. "Pukhan munhagŭi segaji chikchŏpsŏng: Han Sŏryaŭi *Hyŏllo Moja Sŭngnyangi* punsŏk." *Yesulgwa pip'yŏng* 21 (9 1990): 179-204.

KU SANG. "Sijip *Ŭnghyang* p'irhwa sakkŏn chŏnmalgi." In *Ku Sang munhak sŏnjip*, 396-408. Seoul, 1975.

KWŎN YŎNGMIN. *Wŏlbuk munin yŏn'gu*. Seoul, 1989.

MUN PYŎNGMUN. *Chaebŏl: Nalgaerŭl tarara*. Seoul, 1992.

NA PYŎNGCH'ŎL. "Pujŏngjŏk hyŏnsilset'ewa kŭngjŏngjŏk chuin'gongŭi tonggyŏng." In *Ch'ongch'un'gi*, vol. 2 of *Han Sŏrya sŏnjip*, 401-419. Seoul, 1989.

No CH'ŎNMYŎNG. *Hwangmach'a*. In *Mogajiga kirŏsŏ sŭlp'ŭn sasŭmŭn: No Ch'ŏnmyŏng siwa saengae*, edited by Sin Kyŏngnim, 15. Seoul, 1984.

O MANBAEK. "Ch'unwŏn adŭri palkhinŭn 'Yi Kwangsu irok'e chugŏtta'." *Chubu saenghwal*, U.S. edition, 319 (10 1991):176-181.

O YŎNGJIN. *Hanaŭi chŭngŏn: Chakkaŭi sugi*. Seoul, 1952.

PAEK CH'ŎL. *Munhak chasŏjŏn*. Seoul, 1975.

―――. *Sinmunhak sajosa*. 4th edition. Seoul, 1980.

"Sijip *Ŭnghyang* e kwanhan kyŏlchŏngsŏ: Pukchosŏn munhak yesul ch'ongdongmaeng chungangsangimwiwŏnhoeŭi kyŏlchŏngsŏ." In *Han'guk hyŏndae hyŏnsilchuŭi pip'yŏngsŏnjip: Wŏnbo*. edited by Kim Yunsik, 398-401. Seoul, 1989.

SONG HOSUK. "Tanp'yŏn sosŏrŭl chungsimŭro pon Han Sŏryaŭi munhak segye." In *KHSYC*, 399-408.

YI CH'ŎLCHU. *Pugŭi yesurin*. Seoul, 1966.

YI HANGGU. "Pukhanŭi chakka taeyŏlsogesŏ." *Pukhan* 118 (1 1974): 240-253.

YI KIBONG. *Pugŭi munhakkwa yesurin*. Seoul, 1986.

YI KWANGSU. "Munsawa suyang." *Ch'angjo* 8 (1 1921): 9-18. Reprinted by Kim Kŭnju. Seoul, 1980.

YI SONGWŎN. "Han'guk munhagŭi Maksim Gorŭk'i suyong." *Kugŏ kungmunhak* 88 (12 1982): 165-184.

YI YUSIK. "Yŏkkarae nŭrigi sigŭn kollanhada." *Tongsŏ munhak* 170 (9 1988): 89-93.

YIM HWA (IM HWA). *Munhagŭi nolli*. Seoul, 1940.

YUN KIBONG. *Naega pon pungnyŏk' ttang*. Seoul, 1973.

YUN YŎT'AK. "Haebang chŏnggugŭi munhak undonggwa chojige taehan yŏn'gu: chwap'a mundanŭl chungsimŭro." In *Haebang kongganŭi munhak undonggwa munhagŭi hyŏnsirinsik*, edited by Kim Yunsik, 47-73. Seoul, 1989.

SOURCES IN OTHER LANGUAGES

ACHEBE, CHINUA. *Things Fall Apart*. London, 1958.

ADAMI, NORBERT. *Die russische Koreaforschung: Bibliographie 1682-1976*. Wiesbaden, 1978.

ARENDT, HANNAH. *The Origins of Totalitarianism*. Revised edition. San Diego, 1973.

AVTORKHANOV, A. *Zagadki smerti Stalina*. Frankfurt am Main, 1976.

BAIK BONG (PAEK PONG). *Kim Il Sung: Biography*. Beirut, 1973.

BAKHTIN, M.M. "Discourse in the Novel." In *The Dialogic Imagination: Four Essays by M.M. Bakhtin*, edited by M. Holmquist, translated by Caryl Emerson and Michael Holquist, 259-422. Austin, Texas, 1981.

——. "Epic and Novel: Toward a Methodology for the Study of the Novel." In *The Dialogic Imagination: Four Essays by M.M. Bakhtin*, edited by M. Holmquist, translated by Caryl Emerson and Michael Holquist, 3-40. Austin, Texas, 1981.

BARBUSSE, HENRI. *Stalin—Eine Neue Welt*. Paris, 1935.

BERNHARD, HANS-JOACHIM. *Die Romane Heinrich Bölls*. Berlin, GDR, 1970.

BODEN, DIETER. *Die Deutschen in der russischen und in der sowjetischen Literatur: Traum und Alptraum*. Munich and Vienna, 1982.

BORTOLI, G. *The Death of Stalin*. London, 1975.

BRAUN, MAXIMILIAN. *Der Kampf um die Wirklichkeit in der russischen Literatur*. Göttingen, 1958.

BROWN, EDWARD J. *The Proletarian Episode in Russian Literature 1928-1932*. New York, 1971.

CHEE, CHANGBOH. "Korea Artiste Proletarienne Federation: A Case of Literature as A Political Movement." In *Korea Under Japanese Colonial Rule*, edited by Andrew C. Nahm, 231-248. Ann Arbor, 1973.

CLARK, KATERINA. "Little Heroes and Big Deeds: Literature Responds to the First Five-Year Plan." In *Cultural Revolution in Russia 1928-1931*, edited by Sheila Fitzpatrick, 189-206. Bloomington and London, 1978.

——. *The Soviet Novel: History as Ritual*. Chicago and London, 1981.

————. "Utopian Anthropology as a Context for Stalinist Literature." In *Stalinism: Essays in Historical Interpretation*, edited by R.C. Tucker, 180-198. New York, 1977.

CUMINGS, BRUCE. *The Origins of the Korean War: Liberation and the Emergence of Separate Regimes 1945-1947*. Princeton, 1981.

————. *The Origins of the Korean War: The Roaring of the Cataract, 1947-1950*. Princeton, 1990.

DAWSON, RAYMOND. *Confucius*. New York, 1981.

DING LING (TING LING). *The Sun Shines Over the Sanggan River*. Translated by Yang Xianyi and Gladys Yang. Beijing, 1984.

DOWER, JOHN. *War Without Mercy: Race and Power in the Pacific War*. New York, 1986.

ECKERT, CARTER J.; LEE KI-BAIK; LEW YOUNG ICK; ROBINSON, MICHAEL; WAGNER, EDWARD W. *Korea Old and New: A History*. Seoul, 1990.

FAIRBANK, JOHN; REISCHAUER, EDWIN. *East Asia: The Great Tradition*. Boston, 1960.

FITZPATRICK, SHEILA. "Culture and Politics Under Stalin: A Reappraisal." *Slavic Review* 35 (12 1976): 211-231.

GARRARD, CAROL AND JOHN. *Inside the Soviet Writers' Union*. New York, 1990.

GASIOROWSKA, XENIA. *Women in Soviet Fiction: 1917-1964*. Madison, Wisc., 1968.

GOLDMAN, MERLE. *Literary Dissent in Communist China*. Cambridge, Mass., 1967.

GROYS, BORIS. *Gesamtkunstwerk Stalin*. Munich and Vienna. 1988.

GÜNTHER, HANS. *Die Verstaatlichung der Literatur: Entstehung und Funktionsweise des sozialistisch-realistischen Kanons in der sowjetischen Literatur der dreißiger Jahre*. Stuttgart, 1984.

GUSEV, VIKTOR. *Stalin v Kremle*. In *Pesnia o Staline: Izbrannie stikhi sovetskikh poetov*. Moscow, 1950.

HALLIDAY, JON; CUMINGS, BRUCE. *Korea: The Unknown War*. London, 1988.

HERZFELDT, J., ed. *Korea erzählt: Ein Einblick in die koreanische Literatur.* Berlin, GDR, 1954.

HOHENDAHL, PETER UWE; HERMINGHOUSE, PATRICIA. *Literatur und Literaturtheorie in der DDR.* Frankfurt am Main, 1976.

HSIA, C.T. *A History of Modern Chinese Fiction.* New Haven and London, 1961.

————. "Residual Femininity: Women in Chinese Communist Fiction." In *Chinese Communist Literature.* edited by C. Birch, 158-179. New York, 1963.

HSIA, TSI-AN. *The Gate of Darkness: Studies on the Leftist Literary Movement in China.* Seattle, 1968.

IM HŎN-YŎNG (IM HŎNYŎNG). "The Meaning of the City in Korean Literature." *Korea Journal* 27 (May 1987): 24-35.

Iosif Vissarionovich Stalin: Kratkaia biografiia. Moscow, 1945.

IVANOVA, V.I. "Sovetskaia literatura v Koree (1945-1955)." *Problemy Dal'nego vostoka* 3 (11 1974): 187-193.

————. "Sovetskaia voenno-patrioticheskaia literatura v Koree 40-50-kh godov." In *Literatura stran zarubezhnogo vostoka i sovetskaia literatura: Sbornik statei,* 124-138. Moscow, 1977.

JACOBS, NORMAN. *The Korean Road to Modernization and Development.* Urbana and Chicago, 1985.

JUNG, C.G. *Symbols of Transformation.* Vol. 5 of *The Collected Works of C.G. Jung.* Translated by R.F.C. Hull. Princeton, 1956.

KASACK, WOLFGANG. *Dictionary of Russian Literature Since 1917.* Translated by Maria Carlson and Jane T. Hedges. New York, 1988.

KERNIG, C.J., ed. *Sowjetsystem und demokratische Gesellschaft: Eine vergleichende Enzyklopädie.* Freiburg, 1972.

KIM DONGUK (KIM TONGUK). *History of Korean Literature (Chosen bungakushi).* Translated by Leon Hurvitz. Tokyo, 1980.

KWON, YOUNGMIN (KWŎN YŎNGMIN). "Literature and Art in North Korea: Theory and Policy." *Korea Journal* 31 (Summer 1991): 56-70.

The Leader of People: Collection of Works at the National Art Exhibition in Celebration of the 70th Birthday of Great Leader President Kim Il Sung. Pyongyang, 1984.

LEE, CHONG-SIK. *The Politics of Korean Nationalism.* Berkeley, 1963.

LEE, PETER H. *Korean Literature: Topics and Themes.* Tucson, 1956.

――――. *Modern Korean Literature: An Anthology.* Honolulu, 1990.

LENIN, V.I. *Chto delat'? Nabolevshee voprosy nashego dvizheniia* (Moscow, 1968).

LEVENSON, JOSEPH. *Confucian China and Its Modern Fate: A Trilogy.* Berkeley, 1968.

LI CHI. "Communist War Stories." In *Chinese Communist Literature*, edited by C. Birch, 139-157. New York, 1963.

LONDON, JACK. "How the Hermit Kingdom Behaves in Time of War." In *Jack London Reports: War Correspondence, Sports Articles, and Miscellaneous Writings*, edited by King Hendricks and Irving Shepard, 73-77. New York, 1970.

MANN, MICHAEL, ed. *The International Encylopaedia of Sociology* (New York, 1984).

MATSUMOTO SEICHO. *Kita no shijin.* Tokyo, 1974.

MESERVE, WALTER AND RUTH. *Modern Literature from China.* New York, 1964.

MYERS, BRIAN. "Mother Russia: Soviet Characters in North Korean Fiction." *Korean Studies* 16 (1992): 82-93.

――――. "Personenkult und Poesie: Die Panegyriken der Stalin-Zeit." Master's thesis, Ruhr-Universität Bochum, 1989.

MYERS, JAMES T. "The Political Dynamics of the Cult of Mao Tse-Tung." In *China: A System-functional Reader*, edited by Yung Wei, 78-101. Columbus, 1972.

OSTROVSKII, NIKOLAI. *Kak zakalialas' stal'.* Moscow, 1979.

PICHT, HELGA. *Asien: Wege zu Marx und Lenin.* Berlin, GDR, 1984.

PIHL, MARSHALL R. "Engineers of the Human Soul: North Korean Literature Today." *Korean Studies* 1 (1977): 63-110.

RENTNER, RETA. "Koreanische Literatur: Literaturhistorischer Abriß." In *Lexikon ostasiatischer Literaturen*, edited by Jürgen Berndt, 81-93. Leipzig, 1985.

ROBINSON, MICHAEL. *Cultural Nationalism in Colonial Korea, 1920-1925.* Seattle and London, 1989.

SCALAPINO, ROBERT; CHONG-SIK LEE. *Communism in Korea.* In 2 vols. Berkeley, 1972.

SCALAPINO, ROBERT. "The Foreign Policy of North Korea." In *North Korea Today*, edited by Robert Scalapino, 30-50. New York, 1973.

SCHAPIRO, LEONARD. *The Communist Party of the Soviet Union.* New York, 1960.

―――. *Totalitarianism.* London, 1972.

SHEFNER, V. *Pereklichka.* In *Zvezda*, April 1950, 4.

SHIH, C.W. "Co-operatives and Communes in Chinese Communist Fiction." In *Chinese Communist Fiction*, edited by C. Birch, 195-211. New York, 1963.

SHOLOKHOV, MIKHAIL. *Podniataia tselina.* Vols. 6 and 7 of *Sobranie sochinenii.* Moscow, 1966/1967.

SLONIM, MARC. *Soviet Russian Literature: Writers and Problems, 1917-1977.* New York, 1977.

STRITTMATTER, ERWIN. *Ole Bienkopp.* Berlin, GDR, 1963.

SUH, DAE-SOOK. *Kim Il Sung: The North Korean Leader.* New York, 1988.

―――. *Korean Communism, 1945-1980.* Honolulu, 1981.

―――. *The Korean Communist Movement, 1914-1948.* Princeton, 1967.

SUN TZU. *The Art of War.* Translated and with an introduction by Samuel B. Griffith. Oxford, 1963.

Third Congress of the Workers' Party of Korea, April 23-29, 1956: Documents and Materials. Pyongyang, 1956.

USATOV, D.M. "Obraz rabochego v rannem tvorchestve Khan Ser ia." In *Koreiskaia literatura.* Moscow, 1959.

VICKERY, WALTER. "Zhdanovism (1946-53)." In *Literature and Revolution in Soviet Russia, 1917-62*, edited by Max Hayward and Leopold Labedz, 99-125. London, 1963.

WELLEK, RENE; WARREN, AUSTIN. *Theory of Literature*. 3rd edition. New York, 1956.

ZABOROWSKI, HANS-JÜRGEN. "Die klassische Erzählliteratur Koreas." In *Ostasiatische Literaturen*, edited by Günther Debon, 237-252. Wiesbaden, 1984.

CORNELL EAST ASIA SERIES

For ordering information, please contact the Cornell East Asia Series, East Asia Program, Cornell University, 140 Uris Hall, Ithaca, NY 14853-7601, USA; phone (607) 255-6222, fax (607) 255-1388.

2-94/.2M cloth/.5M paper/BB

CPSIA information can be obtained
at www.ICGtesting.com
Printed in the USA
LVHW091923290120
645204LV00012B/30